EX LIBRIS
Yvonne Markowitz

The Aigina Treasure

Aegean Bronze Age jewellery and a mystery revisited

The Aigina Treasure

Aegean Bronze Age jewellery and a mystery revisited

Edited by J. Lesley Fitton with a technical report by Nigel Meeks

With essays by Dyfri Williams, Florens Felten, Stefan Hiller, Robert Laffineur, Dominique Collon, Joan Aruz, Robert Schiestl, Yvonne J. Markowitz and Peter Lacovara and J. Lesley Fitton

THE BRITISH MUSEUM PRESS

This book is dedicated to Reynold Higgins

© 2009 The Trustees of the British Museum

Published in 2009 by the British Museum Press
A division of the British Museum Company Ltd
38 Russell Square, London WC1B 3QQ

www.britishmuseum.org

A catalogue record for this book is available from the British Library

ISBN 978-0-7141-2262-5

Designed by Ros Holder

Printed in Spain by Grafos, SA, Barcelona

The papers used in this book are natural, renewable and recyclable products and the manufacturing processes are expected to conform to the environmental regulations of the country of origin.

Frontispiece: The Aigina Treasure in its display case in the Arthur I. Fleischman Gallery of the Greek Bronze Age in the British Museum.

Contents

Contributors		6
Preface		7
1	**Aigina: an introduction** Dyfri Williams	9
2	**The Story of the Aigina Treasure** Dyfri Williams	11
3	**The Aigina Treasure: Catalogue and Technical Report** J. Lesley Fitton, Nigel Meeks and Louise Joyner	17
4	**Aigina–Kolonna in the Early and Middle Bronze Age** Florens Felten	32
5	**Ornaments from the warrior grave and the Aigina Treasure** Stefan Hiller	36
6	**The Aigina Treasure: the Mycenaean connection** Robert Laffineur	40
7	**The Aigina Treasure: Near Eastern connections** Dominique Collon	43
8	**The Aegean or the Near East: another look at the 'Master of Animals' pendant in the Aigina Treasure** Joan Aruz	46
9	**Three pendants: Tell el-Dabʿa, Aigina and a new silver pendant from the Petrie Museum** Robert Schiestl	51
10	**Egypt and the Aigina Treasure** Yvonne J. Markowitz and Peter Lacovara	59
11	**Links in a chain: Aigina, Dahshur and Tod** J.L. Fitton	61
Plates		67
Bibliography		116
Index		124

Contributors

Joan Aruz
The Metropolitan Museum of Art
Department of Ancient Near East
1000 Fifth Avenue
New York 10028-0198
USA
joan.aruz@metmuseum.org

Dominique Collon
c/o The British Museum
Department of the Middle East
Great Russell Street
London WC1B 3DG
United Kingdom

Florens Felten
Institüt für Klassische Archäologie des Universität Salzburg
Universität Salzburg
Residenzplatz 1/2
A-5010 Salzburg
Austria
florens.felten@sbg.ac.at

J. Lesley Fitton
The British Museum
Greek and Roman Department
Great Russell Street
London WC1B 3DG
United Kingdom
jfitton@thebritishmuseum.ac.uk

Stefan Hiller
Institüt für Klassische Archäologie des Universität Salzburg
Universität Salzburg
Residenzplatz 1/2
A-5010 Salzburg
Austria
stefan.hiller@sbg.ac.at

Louise Joyner
c/o The British Museum
Department of Conservation and Scientific Research
Great Russell Street
London WC1B 3DG
United Kingdom

Peter Lacovara
Michael C. Carlos Museum
Emory University
Atlanta
GA 30322
USA
placovara@emory.edu

Robert Laffineur
University of Liège
Quai Roosevelt 1b
B-4000 Liège
Belgium
R.Laffineur@ulg.ac.be

Yvonne J. Markowitz
Museum of Fine Arts
465 Huntington Avenue
Boston
MA 02115-5597
USA

Nigel Meeks
The British Museum
Department of Conservation and Scientific Research
Great Russell Street
London WC1B 3DG
United Kingdom
nmeeks@thebritishmuseum.ac.uk

Robert Schiestl
Seminar für Ägyptologie
Freie Universität Berlin
Altensteinstr. 33
14195 Berlin
Germany
schiestl@zedat.fu-berlin.de

Dyfri Williams
The British Museum
Greek and Roman Department
Great Russell Street
London WC1B 3DG
United Kingdom
dwilliams@thebritishmuseum.ac.uk

Preface

Reynold Higgins memorably described the Aigina Treasure as a 'rich, beautiful and very perplexing collection'. It was his work on the treasure in the British Museum in the second half of the twentieth century that set the scene for this new evaluation at the beginning of the twenty-first century, and we have echoed the title of his 1979 booklet *The Aigina Treasure: an Archaeological Mystery* in homage to his fundamental studies.

By the year 2000 much new information had come to light, not least about the archaeology of Aigina itself, and so an international group of scholars met in London to reconsider the treasure, its nature and its history. They approached the material with open minds and from a variety of different perspectives. Their thoughts are presented in the essays in this volume, in which differences remain but some common themes emerge. There can be no ultimate certainty about a group of material that lost its archaeological context more than a century ago. Nonetheless, it now seems probable that the treasure came to light in one or more of the Middle Helladic tombs that must have been in the Bronze Age cemetery of Kolonna on Aigina. Whether some or all of the pieces were indeed made on the island by local craftsmen remains a moot point. The extensive and detailed technical analysis carried out in the British Museum finds similarities between many of the pieces that suggest a workshop link, but the stylistic affinities of the group are undoubtedly widespread, as the essays indicate.

We offer this volume, then, in the hope that scholars will find the story has moved on, and will use the information included here in the formulation of future hypotheses. At the same time, a wider readership will find much to intrigue. Archaeology has long eschewed treasure hunting, and no amount of ingenuity can replace the lost context for this treasure. But the recognition of an overlooked 'treasure-map', complete with an X to mark the spot (Fig. 10), perhaps has a certain romance, as well as making a real contribution to the archaeological understanding of this rich and remarkable assemblage.

Thanks are expressed to Jack Ogden, Ingo Pini and Margaret Sax for useful discussions of aspects of the treasure, and Dudley Hubbard, Trevor Springett and Tony Milton for various object photographs and digital images. We are also grateful to Kim Overend and the Museum Assistants in the Greek and Roman Department for their painstaking handling of this fragile material as it was taken from display for study and later replaced. We thank all the contributors to this volume, and in particular Dyfri Williams, who supported this research from the outset as well as making a major contribution to it.

J. Lesley Fitton

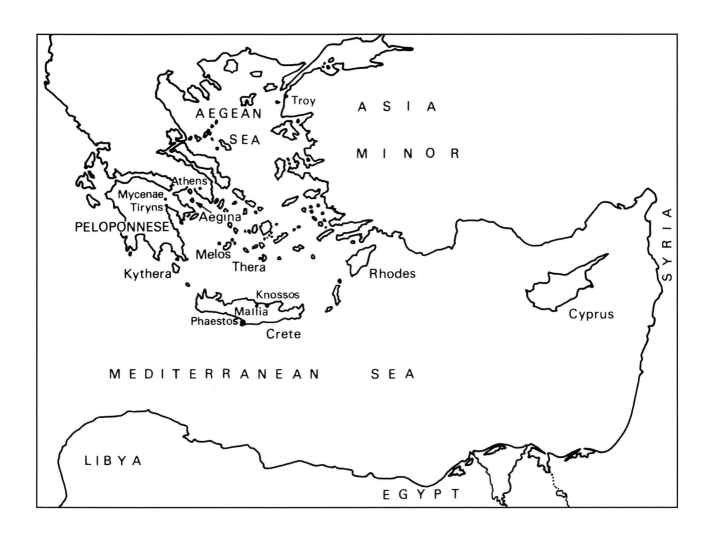

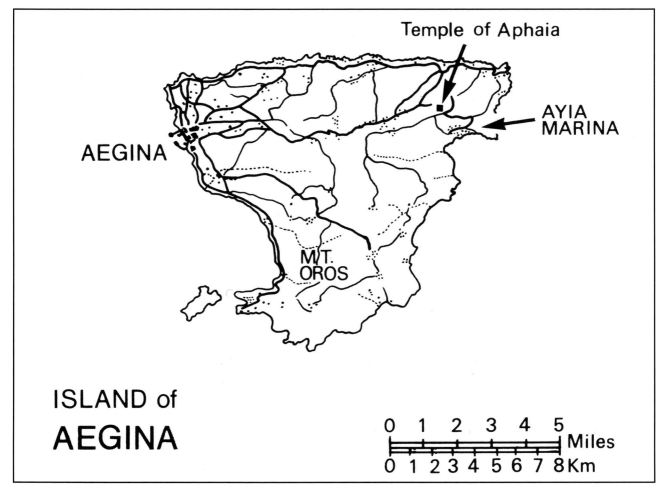

1
Aigina: an introduction

Dyfri Williams

The Aigina Treasure is a fabulous group of Greek Bronze Age gold jewellery and other objects that is believed to come from the island of Aigina. The group was acquired for the British Museum in 1891 and is displayed there in a special showcase in the Arthur I. Fleischman Gallery of the Greek Bronze Age (Gallery 12).

The island of Aigina (Fig. 1) lies roughly in the centre of the Saronic Gulf, midway between Attica to the north-east and the Argolid to the south-west. It is roughly triangular in shape with an area of some 84 square kilometres. The north-west corner is dominated by the modern city of Aigina, the main port with a small rising plain behind it. In 1828 it was briefly the capital of the new state of Greece, under Kapodistrias, and it boasts the first museum of Greece. This is also where the main ancient city with its distinctive double harbour lay. Today the site of the ancient city on the northern promontory is called Kolonna, after the one remaining column of the Classical temple of Apollo (Fig. 2), although in the early nineteenth century there were still two columns standing.

In the Classical period the island's symbol on its famous and far-travelled silver coinage was the sea-turtle (*careta careta*; Fig. 3). This choice has sometimes puzzled historians. Comparisons, for example, between the island's roughly triangular shape cresting the waves and the rugged back of the turtle are not completely convincing. But there is another possibility, for the bay on the north side of Kolonna is one of the very few sandy beaches in the area and it is even today often to be found carpeted with seaweed, hence its local name, Xeflouda (this is even a family name in this part of the island). Nesting turtles require both these things, sandy beach and seaweed – the former to dig holes to lay their eggs in, the latter for their tiny offspring to feed on after they have scuttled across the dangerously open sand as fast as they can. The sight of hundreds of baby turtles crossing the beach beside the city walls may well have suggested to the islanders their badge – the turtles taking to the water like Aiginetan ships.

In general the north coast of Aigina is not very hospitable, being rocky and open to the northerly gales. The north-east corner, however, is dominated now by the Classical temple of Aphaia, the sculptures from which are in Munich, and the ever-expanding tourist town of Aghia Marina with its sheltered bay and unfinished Junta-period hotel slowly melting into the landscape. The whole of the southern end of the island is overshadowed by the pointed form of Mount Oros, which is visible even from Kolonna. On the top of the peak are the remains of buildings ranging from the Late Bronze Age to the Hellenistic period – the modern chapel on the top sits upon the remains of a small Classical temple; farther down the slope is a group of Hellenistic buildings associated with the sanctuary of Zeus Hellanios.

The first Aiginetans that we meet are two ladies, one of marble and one of shell, that were probably carved early in the fifth millennium BC, in the Late Neolithic period. The marble one, now in the National Museum in Athens, was found in the north-east part of the island, to the south of the temple of Aphaia, in the area of the village of Alones. The shell example, now in the Antikensammlung in Munich, came from the same part of the island, but apparently from near the north coast (Figs 4 and 5). Both show a standing woman with exaggerated hips, bottom and thighs. Their significance lies in the nexus of rituals and beliefs that they suggest, even if we cannot be sure of their exact use and meaning. From Kolonna itself comes pottery of the Final Neolithic period (4500–3200 BC), together with the remains of stone structures that indicate that Aigina was already a very sophisticated society, probably reliant on overseas trade – perhaps of a fairly piratical nature, if the series of terracotta figurines wearing conical helmets can be considered indicative of the culture.

It is, indeed, at Kolonna that the early history of Aigina unfolds and where the story of the treasure is set. Generations of archaeologists have uncovered there a sequence of defensive walls and other structures. From the Early Bronze Age come a number of monumental, sometimes two-storeyed houses, one of which has been called the 'White House' since it was originally stuccoed. They suggest that already some sort of a wealthy aristocracy had developed. Towards the end of the Early Bronze Age these great houses were abandoned and a completely new and deliberate settlement plan was developed (Aigina V) that enclosed within a fortification wall a whole complex of grouped buildings and streets. It also seems that an exciting new treasure, found in 2000, consisting of gold and silver jewellery, as well as pieces of rock crystal and carnelian, may be associated with this phase of Aigina's history – it testifies vividly to the prosperity and outward-looking nature of the island at this period.

Aigina V came to a violent end, as did other contemporary settlements in Greece. The new towns of the very end of the Early Bronze Age (VI) and the Middle Bronze Age (VII–X), with their expanding populations, were increasingly heavily fortified, leading to the development of an upper and lower town. It is with this period that a stone-lined shaft grave, containing a gold diadem similar to those from the Aigina Treasure, may be associated. It was found in 1981 in front of the city wall of the lower town and contained the trappings of wealth and overseas interests, including a bronze sword with a gold and ivory hilt, a knife with gold animal-head fittings, the remains of a boar's tusk helmet, and pottery imported from both the Cyclades and Crete. This tomb was specially revered for a number of generations.

It is at this period that several scholars, including Gabriel Welter and, more recently, Stefan Hiller, have also argued for a small Minoan community on Aigina. This attractive idea is based on the presence of a Minoan potter's wheel, locally produced Minoanizing pottery, Minoan stone *kernoi* and a Minoan ritual stone hammer. The presence of such a community has been plausibly connected with the Minoan elements in the British Museum's Aigina Treasure.

After 1650 BC, the beginning of the Late Bronze Age, the city site at Kolonna again expanded beyond the limits of its old walls to sprawl over the whole promontory and beyond. The cemetery was moved to the east on Windmill Ridge, where burials from the early Mycenaean period onwards have been found in considerable numbers.

Elsewhere on the island, the sanctuary of Aphaia provides modest evidence of a Middle Bronze Age cult from about 1600 BC. The finds include fragments of Middle Helladic matt-painted pottery and a fragment of what is either an imported Minoan vase or a local imitation, as well as two Early to Middle Bronze Age seal stones that are probably Minoan. On the basis of these finds, along with later Iron Age offerings that name the goddess Aphaia, and later literary sources that describe her as a Cretan goddess connected with Artemis, we might imagine that Cretan immigrants or long-term visitors – perhaps from the western end of Crete – brought with them the worship of the goddess Aphaia. Any Cretans must have been quickly absorbed into the population for there are no later peculiarly Cretan offerings at Aphaia's sanctuary.

During the Late Bronze Age the cult of Aphaia rapidly grew in local popularity. We find large quantities of pottery, some local, some imported, engraved seal stones, fragments of glass jewellery and a staggering seven hundred terracotta votive figurines of women and animals – an unparalleled total. One of the most remarkable Bronze Age finds is a fragmentary large wheel-made idol, perhaps one of the first cult images of Aphaia (*c.* 40 cm high).

The spread of settlements across the whole of the island in the Late Bronze Age can be ascertained from the cemeteries discovered on the south-west coast and those in the centre of the island at Lazarides and Kilindra. High on Mount Oros itself a settlement was established in the Late Bronze Age. There was also a cult there, as a fine terracotta figure reveals. It is possible that the Oros settlement served as a refugee site when, around 1100 BC, Aigina suffered severe depopulation and poverty as the Mycenaean world began to collapse.

In conclusion, it is clear that Aigina had from very early on attained considerable wealth and importance, no doubt based on commercial activities connected with the sea. To earlier scholars the Aigina Treasure seemed a rare and isolated phenomenon that led some to postulate it had actually been found elsewhere. Now we can see more clearly, thanks to the new Early Bronze Age treasure and the rich Middle Bronze Age shaft grave, that the Aigina Treasure is not an isolated phenomenon but an integral and valuable part of our understanding of the wealth and sophistication of the island of Aigina in the Bronze Age.

2
The Story of the Aigina Treasure

Dyfri Williams

The late Reynold Higgins wrestled with the problem of the history of the Aigina Treasure over a number of years. His book on it, *The Aegina Treasure: an Archaeological Mystery*, published in 1979, is presented as a detective story and so tends to obscure the considerable scholarship that lies behind it.[1] More than 110 years after the key events, we must presume that, although there is some new evidence to place before the archaeological sleuth, far too much will always remain little more than unsupported speculation. The reason for briefly re-examining the story is to assess what information is now available about the likely find-spot of the treasure, since this is of great importance to its archaeological interpretation.

The treasure was offered to the British Museum in July 1891. The keeper, A.S. Murray, wrote a hurried report to the trustees on 10 July, the day before they were due to meet. He described it as 'a magnificent collection of gold ornaments, lately found together in a tomb in Aegina'. They were offered through Cresswell Bros, sponge merchants of 2 Red Lion Square, London, for £6,000. Murray went on to say that he had 'endeavoured to get this price reduced but the actual owner of the objects states that his expenditure in connection with the excavation and the personal risks he has run entitle him to a liberal price'. Murray's report thus indicates that Frederick R. Cresswell (Fig. 7), the senior brother of the London-based firm, was acting on someone else's behalf, but there is no mention in the documents in the British Museum of the identity of the real owner.

The treasure was eventually purchased in May 1892 for £4,000 and was very quickly published by Arthur Evans in 1893.[2] Evans reported the find-spot as the island of Aigina, but could offer no details, and went on to date the group to around 800 BC, for he thought that on Aigina Mycenaean traditions lingered long after the collapse of that civilization.

There was clearly some local fuss over the discovery and export of the treasure, and in 1894 the Greek archaeologist Valerios Staïs began excavating in the area around the temple of Apollo.[3] He commented that he had 'heard from many people on Aigina that the seller or finder of the objects frequently purchased whatever was brought to him whether from clandestine excavations or from chance finds'. He also argued that it was unlikely that all the pieces came from one and the same tomb, since he considered some to be Mycenaean and others rather later. Rumours no doubt continued to circulate until by 1904 they had begun to focus on the idea that the treasure had been found in a tomb in George Brown's vineyard on the ridge to the north of the town, dominated by windmills. In October 1904, A.D. Keramopoullos began excavations in that area.[4] The first published mention of George Brown's involvement in the affair appears in Keramopoullos's article on his excavations. These excavations uncovered four Late Helladic IIIB tombs, three intact and one rifled, the latter of which Keramopoullos took to be the one that had held the jewellery, though he found no trace of it.[5]

Further corroboration that George Brown was the unnamed owner was provided in 1914 when a letter from a Miss Margaret Sinclair arrived at the British Museum.[6] I quote it in full:

> In the summer of 1891 Mr George Brown, of Egina, Greece, brought to England, and sold to the British Museum, treasures found in an old tomb of a priestess of the Temple of Venus; sold for £4,000. I believe treasures consisting of gold rings, bracelets, pieces of cornelian, jade, and glass beads. At that time I was English governess in their family, coming to England with them and returning with them. Mrs Brown gave to me two pieces of cornelian with carved fingers on it, also a pottery vase – height 6 inches, having an eye painted on each side (a very ancient form). A lot of pottery was found in the tomb, but not brought to England. I have a small lamp and bowl in which they put food for the dead in those days. As the things are genuine I wonder if I could sell them, to you or anyone else; as I am now very poor, and rather infirm to come to town unnecessarily, so I presume to write, to enclose stamped envelope for reply, if you could kindly do so, giving any advice I should be glad.

The Museum declined to buy the vases and the lamp, but offered £4 10s for the jewellery. It is comforting to note, however, that Miss Sinclair succeeded in raising the price to £5. Her letter of acceptance gives a list of her items from the treasure: 'Two cornelian beads carved – Four green beads, three of them topped with gold – Three red glass beads, one piece of arched gold – All out of the tomb of the Priestess of Venus – 3000 BC.'[7]

Other scholars went on to make comments on the treasure and the story of its discovery. J.P. Harland, who visited Aigina in 1920–1, wrote as follows:

> The very place where the Treasure was discovered has been pointed out to me by an old inhabitant of Aigina, and the device resorted to by the finder in order to conceal his digging has also been explained to me. If this evidence is trustworthy, then the gold ornaments came from one or possibly two graves. And since this spot is in the midst of the 'Mykenaian' or Late Helladic cemetery, it seems to me that the grave and the 'Gold Treasure' should be dated in the Late Helladic period…[8]

Gabriel Welter, who excavated much of the Kolonna site and lived on Aigina, wrote in 1938 that the treasure was found roughly buried in a hole in the corner of a rifled Late Mycenaean chamber tomb on the southern slopes of Windmill Hill, a tomb robber's cache.[9] He went on to suggest that one could not be certain that the cache itself came from an Aiginetan tomb.

This was essentially the evidence carefully collected and considered by Reynold Higgins in his two articles of 1957.[10] He argued that the jewellery was Minoan, formed a homogenous deposit and should be dated to approximately 1700–1500 BC. He therefore maintained that it could not be from one of the Late Helladic tombs excavated by Keramopoullos, and built on Welter's question as to the original find-spot by suggesting that the jewellery might have come from the Chrysolakkos cemetery north of Mallia on Crete, which had been robbed between 1880 and 1885.[11]

On 11 April 1959, however, Reynold Higgins was introduced to a George Brown on Aigina.[12] He was forty-eight years old and said that his father, also George Brown, found the treasure and sold it to the British Museum. Although this had all happened before he was born, he remembered in his youth seeing three or four chamber tombs in the side of Windmill Hill, one of which he was told had contained the treasure. He also said that his father, who was in his early twenties at the time, had found the tomb by accident when planting vines. He mentioned that the treasure included a gold doll and ended by admitting that his father had to face numerous tribunals as a result of disposing of the treasure. This testimony did little to change the position that Higgins had already developed, and he decided to look no further.

In 1976, however, one Michel G. Emmanuel unexpectedly arrived at the British Museum and asked to see some of the Aigina Treasure that was temporarily off display.[13] Emmanuel explained to Higgins that his grandfather, Michel D. Emmanuel, had been employed by Cresswell Bros on Aigina at the time of the discovery of the treasure. Emmanuel went home to the United States and then sent Higgins a letter setting out what his family could remember collectively of the affair (he consulted his father and three of his aunts). Many new details were added to the story and, to complicate matters, another George Brown was added to the sequence. He was a senior figure who was the agent and manager of the Cresswell firm on Aigina and it was for him that the young Michel Emmanuel went to work as an assistant in 1879 at the age of twenty-two. Emmanuel reported that George Brown (I) had discovered the treasure around 1880 while cultivating a parcel of land that he owned. There were several pieces of jewellery and a gold doll (but Emmanuel's father and aunts never saw the material). Emmanuel's family thought that the find had then been reburied by George Brown in his cellar. Following his death in 1887, Mrs Brown in due course decided to return to England and persuaded Michel Emmanuel to help her smuggle the 'gold doll' off Aigina. Mrs Brown died at sea, and Emmanuel was reported for helping in the smuggling and subsequently arrested and convicted. Nevertheless, he had powerful friends, including 'the British Ambassador', who was a good friend of the Brown family, and he was pardoned. The young George Brown also went back to England in 1891 and, according to Emmanuel, was effectively relieved of his duties as head of the Cresswell agency on Aigina. Emmanuel went on working for the Cresswells until 1905, when he emigrated to the United States. The modern Emmanuels presumed that the young George Brown then took with him the rest of the Aigina Treasure and sold it to the British Museum.

Reynold Higgins made a further trip to Aigina the following year with Michel Emmanuel and through him met some local figures whose stories tended to confirm the general story as outlined, although they could only really reflect general gossip rather than reliable information.

A paper given by E. Semantoni-Bournia at a congress on Poros in Greece in 1998 has, however, reopened many aspects of the story by adding some more important new pieces of information and some corrections, derived from research carried out by the present George Brown (IV), the son of Thomas Brown, who was a younger brother of the George Brown interviewed by Reynold Higgins, and supported by family documents.[14] The main thrust of the argument developed by Brown (IV) is that George Brown II was too young to have been involved, and if he was involved he was probably duped by the older Emmanuel – a very different picture from that given by Brown's uncle to Reynold Higgins in 1959.

As a result, it is important to go back over the whole story and weave all the available new information in with the old, while trying to understand both events and motives in this tale of Browns, Cresswells and Emmanuels. The Browns and Cresswells were not only in the same business, but were related by marriage.[15] Edward Brown, one of the elder brothers of George Brown (I), married a Cresswell, and was uncle to the Frederick Cresswell and his two brothers in the London business, Ernest and Alfred. Edward worked in the Bahamas office and even became a member of the Bahamas Legislative Council. It was this connection that probably took George Brown (I) into the same business. In 1865 Brown had married Eliza Mattocks, a farmer's daughter from his own county of Suffolk. She stayed in Paris, where the Cresswells had an office and where she gave birth to three children, the firstborn being given the family name of George, while her husband travelled around the Mediterranean buying sponges for the Cresswells. After a while he settled in Greece, first at Kranidi on the Argive peninsula and then later, perhaps as early as 1878 and certainly by 1881, on Aigina, where the whole family joined him.[16] By 1886 George Brown (I) had established for Cresswell Bros a sponge factory with warehouses on the harbour front of Aigina, now the site of the Hotel Brown.[17] In August 1887, aged only fifty, George Brown (I) died on a sponge-purchasing expedition to Kalymnos.

Michel Emmanuel apparently began his career with the firm in 1879 at the age of twenty-two, perhaps at the moment when George Brown (I) began to set up operations on Aigina. He was thus some ten years older than George Brown (II), who had been born in October 1867. It would seem natural to imagine that he looked after the business immediately after the unexpected death of George Brown (I). The young George Brown (II), who was a cousin of the Cresswell brothers, had, however, developed a very special relationship with the Greeks. This is made clear by Ernest Cresswell, who commented in a magazine article in 1900[18] that the young George Brown was 'the only Englishman who has been through an entire season of sponge diving with the Greeks themselves. The reason for his being accorded the privilege, however, is not far to seek. He has always lived amongst them, and is regarded as a blood-brother.' A photograph of the members of the Aigina office (Fig. 6), supplied by the Emmanuels in 1976, clearly records a visit to Aigina by Frederick Cresswell not many years after the death of George Brown senior. It shows Cresswell seated in the centre with the young George Brown on his right hand and Michel Emmanuel at his left. Behind stand three of the Greek employees, identified by the Emmanuel family as Leousis, Yanoulis and Loukakis.[19] It is interesting to note the body language of this portrait: Emmanuel seems rather isolated from the others. It would seem likely, therefore, that by this time the young George Brown was in charge of the office.

It is from about 1889 that we find Cresswell Bros selling antiquities to the British Museum. Although this might tempt one to suggest that this 'side-line' was prompted by the influence of either George Brown (II) or Michel Emmanuel in the Aigina office, this is very unlikely, since the early letters of Frederick Cresswell only ever refer to 'our Greek friend' and imply that this friend came from the island of Chalki.[20] Furthermore, the link between sponge-fishing and the trade in antiquities was a very common and perhaps inevitable one. Ernest Cresswell commented in his book on sponges: 'Our divers have made some queer finds: for instance, we have in our possession some remarkable amphorae, which date as far back as 200 BC. They are the envy of lovers of antiquity, and needless to add are also extremely valuable.'[21] In addition to the pieces sold to the British Museum, the Cresswells put some antiquities on loan in the South Africa Museum at Cape Town, which they seem to have sold around 1902.[22] This material included items from Aigina, Rhodes, Chalki, Symi and Egypt. At this period there was also material coming on to the market from other sponge merchants. For example, a pair of Roman gold vessels was found off Cape Krio (Knidos) in the early 1890s, one of which came to the British Museum through the dealers Rollin and Feuardent.[23]

The story told by the Emmanuels has the treasure found by the first George Brown around 1880, in other words at just the time that the Aigina office was being set up. George Brown (III), however, told Higgins in 1959 that the treasure was found by his father (George Brown II). The comment made by Staïs in 1894 that the finder or seller 'frequently purchased whatever was brought to him whether from clandestine excavations or from chance finds' could refer to anybody. The fact that antiquities from Aigina only passed through the Cresswells to the British Museum and elsewhere after 1890 might be thought to militate against the finder being George Brown senior, but this need not be so if he was simply collecting and the selling began only after his death. Nevertheless, George Brown (III) also told Higgins that 'his father had discovered the Treasure by accident in a chamber tomb with a sloping dromos, having broken through the top of the tomb when planting vines'.[24] This seems to echo a rumour that clearly led Keramopoullos to excavate on the slopes of Windmill Hill in 1904. His comment that 'he remembered in his youth [born 1911] seeing three or four chamber tombs in the side of the hill, one of which he was told contained the Treasure' clearly fits with the outcome of Keramopoullos's excavations, but probably represents a story being further elaborated at the time of or after the First World War.

The reports of Harland and Welter do nothing more than continue this tradition. Even the posthumous Greek edition of Welter's book on Aigina, written around 1950, only adds more details about the converted windmill.[25] Further discussions with locals in 1977, when Higgins talked to Mrs Stella Xefiouda, a relative of the Petritis family who had purchased the property from the Browns, only added that George Brown (II) never finished his work on the hexagonal windmill before he sold it to the Petritis family.[26]

The research of George Brown (IV), however, has now revealed not only that the date of purchase of the Windmill Hill property by Brown (II) was 13 March 1890, but also that Brown actually purchased it from Michel Emmanuel, who had himself bought it only eleven days earlier on 2 March from a Georgios Markellos (who had inherited it from his father). A further oddity of this transaction is that Brown effectively paid less for the property than Emmanuel did, for an extra three and a half *stremmata* at Limpones (near the old prison in the south-east of the town) were included in the resale. This hurried business deal is a puzzle that may or may not be of particular significance, and we shall have to return to it.

We now also have a sequence of letters from Cresswell Bros to George Brown (II) that tell us something of his travels in 1890–91 in search of sponges. On 3 June 1890 Cresswell Bros wrote to him on Lampedusa with various instructions about how and what he was to purchase. The ending of the letter, 'trusting that you have arrived safely', clearly indicates that this is the beginning of an expedition. On 24 January 1891 they wrote to him again on Lampedusa. George Brown (IV) and Dr Semantoni-Bournia argue as a result that Brown must have been absent from Aigina at least between mid-May 1890 and mid-February 1891. It seems most unlikely, however, that the young George Brown stayed on Lampedusa for eight to nine months and did not go home at least for Christmas. Furthermore, the letter of 24 January begins with mention of a letter sent by Brown to the London office, which is perhaps best interpreted as a note to say that he was off to Lampedusa again, while the body of the letter contains the usual specific request for types and quantities of sponges that were sent at the beginning of an expedition. A further letter from Cresswell Bros is addressed to George Brown on Aigina on 13 April 1891, noting receipt of Brown's letters of 8 and 15 March, the latter enclosing an invoice. From these we might guess that Brown wrote on 8 March at the end of his trip to Lampedusa and again with a final invoice on his arrival on Aigina on 15 March.

On 3 June Cresswell Bros sent a brief letter of instructions to George Brown (II) on Aigina. We cannot be certain whether this letter reached Brown before he, his mother and all his siblings set off for England. This journey was clearly not a simple one and it is not possible now to follow it with certainty until they boarded the SS *Bokhara*, a three-masted P&O steamer, at Brindisi during the night of 20/21 June.[27] To reach Brindisi they probably made their way via Patras, taking one or more boats, so that the Emmanuels' story of their grandfather rowing out with two other men at night to deliver the treasure secretly may well reflect the truth, however incompletely understood. Eliza Brown, however, was not to complete her journey home, for she died of pneumonia on 27 June as the SS *Bokhara* sailed north across the Bay of Biscay, some hours out of Gibraltar, and was buried at sea.[28] While on board the *Bokhara*, Eliza Brown dictated her will. It was witnessed by the ship's doctor (Arthur Nicholson) and the ship's priest (J. Caulfield) and left everything to her son, George Brown (II).[29] The SS *Bokhara* reached Plymouth on 30 June, when Dr Nicholson registered the death.

Bereft of his mother, the twenty-three-year-old George Brown was faced with two problems: his siblings and the treasure. He seems to have taken the children on to Suffolk, leaving them with his grandparents, where Alexander was to die in 1896. As for the treasure, he must have taken that straight to his uncle, Frederick Cresswell.

Fred Cresswell, already known to the British Museum as a result of the successful sale of a silver cup and bronze hydria from Chalki,[30] wasted no time in contacting the Museum and opening negotiations on behalf of the young Brown (after his mother's death, the unnamed 'actual owner') with the keeper, A.S. Murray, at the price of £6,000. By 7 August, however, the price had been dropped to £4,000 and Murray had already secured a promise of £2,000 towards this from the chancellor of the Exchequer. In September Murray requested that the trustees pay £1,000 immediately for a selection of the objects (the 'Master of Animals' pendant, the curved pectoral with heads, and the beads) and this interim arrangement was agreed, the sum being paid in October to Cresswell, who said he was off on a trip to the east – this trip may have taken him to Aigina, where he passed on funds to George Brown (II).[31]

We probably should imagine George Brown (II) returning to Aigina in August, family matters settled and the price for the treasure agreed, to find that both Michel Emmanuel, who had clearly helped in the smuggling, and he himself were in trouble.[32] The legal proceedings seem to have been lengthy and Emmanuel was eventually convicted of smuggling, while Brown had to face 'numerous tribunals as a result of disposing of the Treasure'.[33] It was perhaps the fear of such troubles that forced Brown to close the deal quickly with the British Museum. Furthermore, the fact that Arthur Evans lectured at the British School in Athens on the treasure in 1892 may have further exacerbated matters.[34] In any case, by May 1892 the British Museum had completed the payment of the whole £4,000, although we do not, of course, know how this sum was divided up (the stakeholders probably being Brown, Cresswell and Emmanuel).

We know little about young George Brown's movements in the years after the initial sale negotiations, but Fred Cresswell was again offering a group of material from Aigina to Murray in May 1892 (Fig. 8). It included Mycenaean, Corinthian and Athenian (black- and red-figured) pottery, archaic gold jewellery, Mycenaean bronze implements and a piece of sculpture.[35] Cresswell was pressing the British Museum for a resolution of this deal in June 1893.[36] By July of that year all was settled, and four of the vases went to the Ashmolean Museum for £6.[37] This is most probably another group of material, perhaps brought out by young Brown on a trip to London in 1892 or even by Fred Cresswell himself after his visit to Aigina in late 1891. Although some have chosen to connect the Late Helladic IIIA2–C pieces in this sale with the tomb in which the Aigina Treasure was said to have been found, there is no supporting evidence at all. It is much better to see them as having come from the area of Windmill Hill in general, and their sale beginning to focus rumour on the Brown property there. The other pieces are of a wide range of dates, archaic, Classical and later, and must have come from different cemeteries all around the port of Aigina.[38]

On 13 August 1893 George Brown became engaged to Avra Drakopoulou, the daughter of the British consul at Athens. This information comes from an important letter that she wrote to George Brown on 13–14 August 1895. This charming love letter, though now missing its envelope, was clearly written to George while he was far away. Not only does she complain of a separation which seems to have already been of some duration and is given no clear end, but in it she describes a show she was taken to that was so bad that it ended in a near riot. Her final comment was: 'I wished myself at the Antipodes (to be sure I did, for I would find you there).' This wish fits in with the information contained in Ernest Cresswell's book, in which he notes that around 1895 a special two-year concession was granted to Cresswell Bros in British Honduras, and an expedition of Greek divers and sponge fishermen was formed and led there by George Brown.[39] This all clearly shows that George Brown remained a very highly valued member of Cresswell Bros.

Avra Drakopoulou's letter also contains a tantalizingly oblique mention of the treasure: 'Mrs. Lounghi was telling me a funny story. Some time ago a tourist was visiting Aegina and was conducted by a guide who gave him information about everything in the island.' The following section is in Greek:

> They arrived in a house which had its ground-floor warehouses closed. 'What are these?' asked the tourist. 'These, Efendi, belong to an English millionaire who found a large ancient treasure and ran off to America. With all the riches he has now, he does not need these any more', answered the guide. Oh! Georgie! How funny the world is. What an incongruous pell-mell where each one sees his way through as he likes, where we stare at each other like stupid goldfish in a bowl, forming our own conclusions and know no more about our neighbours than the man in the moon.

In the light of the expedition to Honduras, we can now understand why the warehouses were closed down – no sponges were coming in that needed processing and packing. The Englishman must have been George Brown, who was indeed in the Americas. Avra is clearly laughing at the idea that George has left for ever, because she knows better. One could also argue that she might have been making fun of the idea that George Brown (II) had found the treasure, for she knew it had not been him. Her father, however, must have known something of the affair too, for he came to the rescue of Michel Emmanuel. Emmanuel was arrested and convicted of aiding in the smuggling of the treasure, but Drakopoulou intervened and managed to have him pardoned.[40] Emmanuel, as a result, remained in post on Aigina until 1905, when he left for the United States with 'financial reverses, caused in part by his legal problems', as the Emmanuel family admitted in their letter to Reynold Higgins.[41] We might imagine that Keramopoullos's excavations begun on Windmill Hill in 1904 reawakened the pressure on Emmanuel (and perhaps on Brown), but there may well be nothing particularly sinister about his departure, for it coincided with the move of another sponge merchant, John Cocoris, to Florida Bay to introduce Greek methods there.[42]

It is clear that Michel Emmanuel felt a real gratitude to the Drakopoulou family, for the Emmanuel family's letter to Higgins refers to an aunt Avra Emmanuel, who was able to identify all the Greek employees standing in the back of the photograph given by Emmanuel to Higgins.[43] This means that she must have been born out there and offers the likelihood that Emmanuel named his own daughter after the British consul's daughter in acknowledgement of his help.

In all of this, however, we cannot see with any clarity what impact legal proceedings had on George Brown (II); we only have his son's testimony that he had to face 'numerous tribunals'. It may well be that Drakopoulou naturally protected Brown too, while his exceptionally good relations with the Greek community also secured him a certain immunity, since it is always easier to blame a foreigner than a compatriot. Whatever the pressure was on George Brown, the one thing that did not last was his engagement to Avra Drakopoulou, for he eventually married an Aiginetan girl called Olga Skrivanou.

This reassessment of the available evidence for the period, however, has not really revealed when the treasure was found, nor who it was that discovered it, nor even where it was found. There is too much rumour and not enough fact. We can only try to evolve a scenario that fits what information and rumour we do have. It seems most probable that it was George Brown (I) who discovered the treasure, as the Emmanuels remembered, perhaps 'about 1880', and that he kept it hidden until his death. Then in 1891, four years after his death, his widow, as its owner, took it with her to London. On her death the treasure passed to her son. This would explain why George Brown (II) was never convicted of anything: he did not discover the treasure and he did not smuggle it out of Greece, although he presumably received the proceeds of its sale (or at least a share of this). Emmanuel did aid in the smuggling and was therefore punished.

Such a scenario, however, omits the whole of the Windmill Hill story. Although Windmill Hill (Fig. 9) was most probably the find-spot of some of the acquisitions made by the British Museum and the Ashmolean Museum in 1892, material assembled by George Brown (I), nothing as early as the treasure is otherwise thought to have been found there. Furthermore, it should be realized that the Windmill Hill episode seems to be a late addition to the story, perhaps first being promulgated only shortly before 1904. If the scenario set out above is correct, then this addition was particularly dangerous for George Brown (II), since it drew attention to a property that he owned, thus pointing the finger at him as the finder, rather than his father. The fact that all of this happened immediately prior to Emmanuel's departure is perhaps significant. Could Emmanuel have tried to use Brown's ownership of the Windmill Hill property against him by spreading the rumour of the treasure's having been found there? When this did not work, he quit his job and the island. Was it, then, the spiteful act of a disappointed man, who had worked for the Cresswells for years, only to see the younger and more popular Brown succeed where he could not? Is some memory of this scenario buried in the reported opinions of the descendants of two of young Brown's close friends, Mr Lounghis and Mr Vatides, namely that 'G. Brown, due to his youth, inexperience and grief for his mother's death, was mainly a victim of circumstances but was also framed'?[44]

The Emmanuel family story thus contains a good deal of truth, especially at the beginning, but becomes rather muddled and unconvincing when the tellers reach the period after Mrs Brown's death, as their sources became more evasive and Brown had to be 'painted black' in order to disguise Emmanuel's treachery. The testimony given in 1956 by George Brown (III) is thus reduced to the somewhat boastful bluster of a man who was too young to have ever actually known the true story, but remembered elements of the story put about in 1904.[45]

In all our sifting of the evidence, however, there remains one detail in the British Museum that Reynold Higgins must have once known to which he did not give any weight as he began his investigations and which he never returned to consider later. This takes the form of a signed note by A.H. Smith in the Greek and Roman Department register. It reads: 'Nov. 12 1913. Mr Cresswell showed me the spot which I have marked [with a circle] on the plan of the Port of Aegina, Cockerell's Aegina & Bassae (Dept copy) p.1, S.E. of temple site, at the port [Fig. 10].' Since this was before Miss Sinclair's letter, one might guess that the visit was prompted by Cresswell's wish to inform the new keeper of all the confidential elements of the story, in part perhaps so that Miss Sinclair's approach would not fall on deaf ears.[46] One can quite see why Higgins would not have thought it of relevance because the spot marked was not on Windmill Hill, where all his attention was focusing. If, however, he had gone back to it following the discovery by Hans Walter and his Austrian team of the burial of a Middle Bronze Age warrior, he would have quickly realized its significance.

This warrior's tomb was discovered in 1981 immediately to the east of the later temple of Apollo, close to the south gate of the lower town.[47] Here they found an unrobbed shaft grave dating to about 1700 BC. The grave goods included – in addition to Middle Minoan II, matt-painted Middle Helladic and Middle Cycladic pottery – a bronze sword with a gold and ivory hilt, two bronze daggers, a knife with gold animal-head fittings, a bronze spear-head, two arrow-heads of obsidian, many boars' tusks from a boar's tusk helmet, and a gold sheet diadem. Soon after this tomb's publication, Reynold Higgins wrote a brief article rightly comparing the new Kolonna diadem with tapering ends and simple dot-repoussé decoration to the two plain diadems from the Aigina Treasure.[48] Hans Walter has connected the warrior with the ruler of his Town IX.[49] The context of this shaft grave is discussed further in this volume by Stefan Hiller.

The warrior's shaft grave is the first major Middle Bronze Age tomb to have been found and surely points to the area of the Middle Bronze Age cemetery, as opposed to the Late Bronze Age cemetery on the ridge to the north-east of the town on Windmill Hill. It is, therefore, just the area to be looking for the tomb or tombs that once held the Aigina Treasure. The accuracy of Cresswell's spot cannot perhaps be completely relied upon, but he was a frequent visitor to Aigina and will have had the full story from George Brown himself (whether I or II). The find-spot for the Aigina Treasure would seem to be farther out of Welter's 'Vorstadt' than the warrior's shaft grave, but on roughly the same line. Perhaps the warrior grave was the exceptional interment, connected as Welter speculates with the warrior's prowess in defence of the city. The regular Middle Bronze Age cemetery was outside the city but in the same general area. It has always been slightly puzzling that no Early or Middle Bronze Age cemetery has ever been found and Smith's spot seems to provide the answer: it was in the low-lying area near the old Karantina port. It seems likely that much of this early cemetery area was destroyed when structures such as the Hellenistic and Roman theatre and the nineteenth-century Lazzaretto were built.

Turning back to the British Museum's Aigina Treasure, there is perhaps one more question to ask: can we determine how many burials or assemblages it represents? First, we might separate off the gold cup, normally associated with male burials, not females, the plain massive open-ended bracelet, and the five plain and heavy gold rings – these three pieces display the same encrustation, not found on the other pieces, perhaps suggesting that they were found together. The two pairs of large earrings probably indicate two female burials, but this does not explain some of the fragments, especially the lone owl which in its workmanship recalls the less sharply finished pair of earrings. Was there a third pair of earrings and thus a third female burial? Secondly, the six necklaces could be divided between three female tombs easily enough: to each tomb one of the three necklaces just of gold and one of the three necklaces that employ semi-precious stones. The diadems may come from male or female burials. The shroud ornaments – the fifty-four rosette and spiral discs and the thin gold strips – may have decorated the shroud of the male or they could have been divided between the women. Finally, the two-headed pectoral may have belonged to the male, as a symbol of royal power, following Egyptian precedents, but there is even less firm ground here than there has been for any of the elements of the mystery of the treasure itself.

Notes

1. Higgins 1979. I am very grateful to Elizabeth Goring for providing the images that were used in Higgins's book.
2. Evans 1892–3, 195–226.
3. Staïs 1895, 252–3.
4. Keramopoullos 1910, 178–208.
5. Keramopoullos 1910, 183.
6. British Museum, Department of Greece and Rome Archive, letter of 17 July 1914, quoted in Higgins 1979, 16–18.
7. Letter of 21 July 1914. The objects were registered as GR 1914.7-25.1–10. The piece of 'arched gold' was an element of the necklace with double curves – what Higgins called palm leaves.
8. Harland 1925, 24.
9. Welter 1938a, 55; see also Welter 1938b, 512.
10. Higgins 1957a, 42–57; Higgins 1957b, 27–41.
11. Demargne 1945, 42–57.
12. Higgins 1979. George Alex Brown, born 1911 Aigina; died there in 1977.
13. Higgins 1979, 45–7.
14. Semantoni-Bournia 2003. I am very grateful to Dr Semantoni-Bournia for sending me the text of her paper in advance of publication. I myself met and discussed matters with Mr Brown on Aigina in August 2002; he very kindly gave me copies of his documents and his interpretation of them, written up in January 1997, and a copy of his family tree.
15. The family connections are made clear in Cresswell 1921, 2nd edn 1930, 40, 48 and 120. They are not mentioned in Semantoni-Bournia 2003.
16. A business letter was written by him from Aigina in May 1878; the family was clearly already settled on the island by 1881, for their fifth child died on the island in November 1881; their sixth child was born in December of the same year; their seventh and last child was born there in 1884.
17. The building and warehouses were eventually purchased by the Brown family from Cresswell Bros in the late 1950s. The Browns converted it into a hotel, adding an extra storey on top; it has recently been renovated by George Brown (IV).
18. *Strand Magazine* 1900; see Cresswell 1921, 120.
19. They were identified by Avra Emmanuel, one of Michel Emmanuel's aunts: letter of Michel G. Emmanuel to Reynold Higgins (not quoted in Higgins 1979).
20. For example, letter to Murray, 17 October 1889.
21. Cresswell 1921, 121; there are illustrations of such amphorae and other finds on pp. 4 and 14.
22. A partial list was given to the Greek and Roman Department of the British Museum in March 1914.
23. GR 1894,0615.1: BM Cat Jewellery 3168. The companion piece was sold at Christie's, 23 June 1965, 'a highly important Roman gold vase'; it is now in the J. Paul Getty Museum (2001.6).
24. Reported by Higgins, 10 July 1959.
25. Welter 1962, 46–7; quoted by Higgins 1979, 49.
26. Higgins 1979, 50. George Brown (IV) informs me that Mrs Xeflouda and Mrs Papaleonardou were cousins of the Emmanuels.
27. The SS *Bokhara* was built in 1873 and regularly ran between London and Bombay, passing through the Suez Canal and calling at Brindisi and Malta in the Mediterranean. For a copy of its log, see P&O Nautical Reports 40/23, National Maritime Museum, London; for its passenger lists, see Kew PRO BT 26/17 – 'Brown and family: 1 married woman, 1 male over 12 years old [George], 2 females over 12 [Eliza and Sarah], 2 males under 12 [Alexander and Alfred]'. The *Bokhara* sank in October 1892 en route from Shanghai to Hong Kong. I am especially grateful to Alan Scollan for researching the SS *Bokhara* and other documentary matters for me.
28. She died at 40.49 N, 9.35 W, according to the Marine Register of Deaths 1891.
29. The Greek record of the will was discovered by George Brown (IV). It was witnessed by two officials of the ship as a matter of course; George Brown (II) could not be a witness because he was the sole beneficiary. The date and the fact of the burial at sea are from the family tomb on Aigina.
30. GR 1889,1112.1–7.
31. Letter of 8 October 1891. It is, of course, possible that Brown stayed in London throughout this period and actually returned to Aigina in Cresswell's company. The photograph of him with the rest of the Aigina office could even have been taken at this moment.
32. The Emmanuels' account is clearly rather muddled here.
33. Higgins 1979, 45.
34. A letter of 5 June 1892 from Arthur Evans mentions this lecture; a letter from Fred Cresswell of 13 January 1894 comments on Evans's article in the *Journal of Hellenic Studies* (Evans 1892–3) and notes that it is 'certainly very interesting but I do hope it will not cause any more bother on the other side'.
35. Walters 1897, 63–77, and Walters 1898, 281–301. The pottery is as follows: Mycenaean, GR 1893,0712.6 (BM Cat Vases A 1092) and 12.9 (BM Cat Vases A 1091); Corinthian, GR 1893,0712.10; Athenian, GR 1893,0712.11 (bf amphora), 12.12 (bf cup) and 12.13 (rf bell-krater; BM Cat Vases E 508); two Hellenistic *stamnoi*, GR 1893,0712.7 and 12.8. The other material consists of the following: fragment of a terracotta epinetron, GR 1893,0712.5 (BM Cat Terracottas 150); Archaic gold jewellery, GR 1893,0712.1 and 12.2 (BM Cat Jewellery 1217 and 1218); two Late Helladic bronze knives or scrapers, GR 1893,0712.14 (BM Cat Bronzes 47); marble head, GR 1893,0712.3 (BM Cat Sculpture 1811); marble pyxis with modern decoration, GR 1893,0712.4.
36. Letter of 15 June 1893.
37. Letter of 13 July 1893 from Cresswell accepting £6 for Oxford vases; letter of 15 July 1893 from Evans accepting price. The Oxford vases are AE 299–302.
38. The British Museum also purchased in 1893 from the dealer E. Triantaphyllos a group of terracottas that were said to come from Aigina: GR 1893,0111.2–10; BM Cat Terracottas 2021, 2023–30. No connection with Cresswell Bros is discoverable from the British Museum documentation.
39. Cresswell 1921, 48.
40. Drakopoulou must be the 'British Ambassador to Greece' mentioned in Emmanuel's letter; Higgins 1979, 46.
41. Letter of 7 July 1976, quoted in Higgins 1979, 46–7.
42. Cresswell 1921.
43. This is in Emmanuel's letter, but it was not included in the account in Higgins 1979.
44. I am grateful to George Brown (IV) for this information.
45. Mr George Brown (IV) has suggested that his uncle, George Brown (III), was known not to be of very sound mind.
46. It was in March 1914 that the Department was given a list of other Cresswell pieces sold off at auction in London around 1902.
47. Walter 1981, 183–4.
48. Higgins 1987, 182 with pl. 5a–b.
49. Walter 1983, 131–3.

3 The Aigina Treasure: Catalogue and Technical Report

J. Lesley Fitton, Nigel Meeks and Louise Joyner

The Aigina Treasure is presented here in a complete catalogue that incorporates the results of an extensive technological and analytical examination. This addressed particularly those aspects that might throw light on the origins and history of the treasure. Since the time of its emergence in the nineteenth century it has always been considered as a group but, with scant information about the circumstances of the treasure's discovery, the significance of the grouping has not been clear. Technological examination was therefore undertaken with a very basic set of questions in mind. These included consideration of which gold alloy compositions were used and how the gold was worked, as well as which gemstones were used and how they were worked. The examination addressed the question of whether all the items in the treasure were genuinely ancient, and whether any ancient or modern repairs or restorations had been made. It also considered whether and in what way the treasure could be seen as a group, by looking for internal connections within the individual pieces of jewellery based on their raw materials, their workmanship and their state of preservation.

Methods of examination and analysis

The scientific work was carried out using complementary methods for observation, analysis and micro-photography. The objects were all examined by optical binocular microscopy to give an overview of the construction and materials of the jewellery before detailed examination and analysis by other methods. The gemstone beads and blue ring inlays were identified using standard gemmological techniques, laser Raman microscopy and x-ray diffraction (XRD) analysis. The beads were photographed in transmitted light with dark-field illumination to show the true colours of the gemstones and any internal physical characteristics. This also allowed the method of drilling the holes in the beads to be studied.

Scanning electron microscopy (SEM) with x-ray microanalysis (EDX) was used for detailed observation and gold analysis. With its wide range of magnification and depth of focus, the SEM was used for observation and photomicrography of gold-working techniques, bead drilling and filing and for quantitative analysis. Gold analysis was made on representative components of the majority of objects on tiny cleaned surfaces of gold to avoid errors due to surface enrichment: that is, the loss of copper – and possibly some silver – at the surface, which often occurs with ancient gold.

The results of these examinations for each of the items in the treasure form part of their catalogue entries, while general observations and conclusions from the scientific analysis are included at the end of the catalogue section.

Catalogue of the Aigina Treasure

1

The 'Master of Animals' pendant
GR 1892,0520.8; BM Cat Jewellery 762; Fig. 11

A gold pendant with a male figure with outstretched hands touching the necks of two large birds, perhaps geese, which face away from him. He stands among lotus flowers on a horizontal ground-line, possibly a stylized boat. Pairs of ridged, curving elements with bud-like ends flank the figure and enclose the birds. Five hanging discs decorate the lower edge of the pendant.

The figure stands with his upper body facing the front and his legs in profile to the right. He wears a tall headdress with vertical elements, perhaps feathers. A striated band across the top of this forms a loop for suspension. His face is somewhat triangular, with the features quite carefully delineated. Two large discs may be earrings or hair curls. He wears a belted kilt-like garment with a long tassel down the front, and striations at his ankles may indicate boots. His upper torso is bare, and he has bracelets around his upper arms and around his wrists.

The back of the pendant is flat.

Technical notes
The pendant is made of two pierced sheets of gold. The back sheet is flat while the front sheet has the relief designs of the figures embossed in the repoussé technique. The outer edges of the back sheet and the edges around the pierced areas are all turned up around the correspondingly shaped front sheet, and this mechanically locates and to some extent holds the two sheets together. At the same time the two sheets are partly soldered together; for example on the top of the crown, the bud-like terminals, the heads of the geese and in some places on the outer overlapped seam around the pendant. This part-soldering is found elsewhere in the treasure, notably on the main bodies of the two pairs of earrings and among the suspended birds, and thus indicates a close workshop connection.

The ornamental headdress of the male figure has a horizontal tube at the top, from which the pendant could have been suspended. The suspension cord, chain or wire is missing. The pendant has chased details on the front of the male figure, the geese, the lotus flowers and the curving bud-like elements. For example, the effect of the goose-wing feathers is created by a straight-edged tool (Fig. 14) and is very similar to the straight-line chevron decoration on the four earring main hoops (763–766).

There are five gold discs suspended from the pendant, three from where the male figure stands and one from each of the outer curved elements. The discs have an integral wire that loops through a pierced suspension hole in the pendant and is secured by twisting the wire back on itself (Fig. 15). This is similar to the four earrings in the treasure, but different from the pectoral ornament with profile heads in which similar discs hang from neatly soldered loops on the pendant, rather than from pierced holes. The discs are made in the same way as those on the other items in the treasure, and are hammered gold sheet with integral hammered suspension wire. The only difference is that these discs have simple dot-punched decoration around their edges (Fig. 12), similar to that on the sheet diadem. The discs are slightly variable in size, four being between 11.5 mm and 11.7 mm diameter, while the fifth, on the left, is noticeably larger at 13.0 mm diameter. This larger disc is different from the others. It has a clean cut on the base of the neck where the original wire is now missing. The disc has been pierced through and a piece of ancient wire has been twisted round to suspend it from the curving element (Fig. 16) (like discs 2 and 8 of the pectoral ornament, Fig. 41). It is possible that the wire is the original wire that broke, and that the fractured end on the disc was filed smooth before piercing and resuspending. However, in addition, the circumferential pierced-dot decoration appears to dip below the pierced hole as if it were added after the hole was made (Fig. 13). On all the other discs the dotted decoration follows the circumference without dipping. This disc appears to be an ancient repair.

The central disc (no. 3 in Fig. 12) has broken across the neck region and has been inaccurately soldered back together. This repair is probably recent. Yet another disc shows stress corrosion cracks in the same neck region. Stress corrosion cracking is also seen on all of the discs where the original gold surfaces of the domed, dot decoration was stretched during punching and was left in a stressed condition without further annealing (Fig. 17). Clearly all these discs have been left in the work-hardened condition, and have the same weaknesses as the discs on the pectoral with profile heads.

2

Pair of gold ornaments, probably earrings
GR 1892,0520.11 and 20.12; BM Cat Jewellery 763 and 765; Fig. 18

Within a hoop in the form of a double-headed snake is a symmetrical arrangement of two dogs face to face and, beneath their fore paws, a pair of back-to-back monkeys. The dogs have slender bodies and elongated muzzles, and have been described as greyhounds. Their tails are formed from wire, and wire decorates their ears. Their left fore paws rest on the monkeys' heads; their right fore paws are raised to rest on a carnelian bead. Fine wire around their necks represents their collars, while two chains decorated with grooved cylindrical carnelian beads are like leashes. These are attached to the inside of the hoop.

The monkeys, also with slender bodies, are in a seated position, their hands raised to their faces. Their heads are rather shapeless, though a large eye is indicated. A curving element springs from their feet to support the dogs' hind paws.

The birds suspended from the hoop can probably be identified as owls. They are suspended from the tail, and thus hang upside down. They have outspread wings with a beaded upper edge. Their faces are frontal with two big eyes.

Fourteen pendants are suspended from the hoop, seven in the form of plain discs on chains, seven in the form of owls on chains decorated with a carnelian bead. One of the owls is missing on earring 763, and two on earring 765.

The ornaments are hollow and reversible, being essentially identical on each side.

3

Pair of gold ornaments, probably earrings
GR 1892,0520.13 and 20.10; BM Cat Jewellery 764 and 766; Fig. 19

These ornaments are identical in form to the above, but have differences in detail as follows:

The owls are slightly smaller and have less carefully delineated faces and wings. The upper edges of the wings are not beaded. The leads of the dogs are decorated with a small spherical carnelian bead.

Overall the surface details on the dogs and monkeys are less precise. The general impression is of slightly less high-quality workmanship on this pair of ornaments, which is rather less elaborate than the other pair.

Technical notes on the two pairs of earrings
The four earrings are identifiable as two distinct pairs from the quality of the goldsmith's workmanship (763 and 765, detail Fig. 20, and 764 and 766, detail Fig. 21). There are similarities that link the two pairs together and thus to one workshop, but there is also evidence for two goldsmiths at work.

Each earring is a complex assemblage of sheet gold, chain and carnelian beads. The hoop or main ring of each comprises embossed, symmetrical front and back halves of gold sheet part-soldered together. Within each main ring the symmetrically embossed relief design of two dogs joined to two monkeys is formed from front and back halves. The symmetry and sizes of the main rings and the animal motifs of the four earrings have been compared stereoscopically. Their similarity indicates the use of one mould to produce all eight sides of the main rings and another to produce all eight sides of the animal motifs. In this way the complex symmetrical shapes fit together exactly. The symmetrical halves were assembled back to back. They were part-soldered together at a few points around the perimeter and wired together with gold at other places where attachments are fitted (Figs 22 and 23). The details on the animal heads and the chevron decoration around the main rings were added by punching and chasing (Figs 24 and 22).

On each earring the main embossed gold ring, 65 mm in diameter, joins in a double serpent head at the top. There do not appear to be any suspension points from the serpents' heads, either existing or missing, that would have allowed the 'better' earrings (763 and 765) to be suspended from the ear. The other pair (764 and 766) has cuts in the rings between the serpents. This might have provided a means of suspension, though in fact the earrings could have been cut at any time. In any case, the design and placement of the suspension chains around the main ring is such that they would fall inelegantly in front of or behind the ring if they were worn suspended from the ear. They may never have been worn and there is no evidence of wear from use. Indeed they are most effectively displayed flat with radiating chains. This may suggest they were made specifically for funerary use.

Each earring has fourteen chains radiating from the main ring (Figs 20 and 21). The chain links are of uneven strip-twist wire (Fig. 31). At the end of the chains owls and discs are alternately suspended (Figs 20 and 21). The chains are suspended from holes pierced in the edges of the rings (Figs 32 and 24). Each owl has a small spherical carnelian bead on the wire connecting it to the chain, and at the other end is a well-polished elongated carnelian bead where the chain joins the ring (Figs 25 and 26, detail Fig. 27). Similarly, each gold disc has a small carnelian bead on the disc wire (Figs 25 and 26). Two of the earrings (nos 763 and 765) have a chain with the associated beads and owls missing. Earring 763 also has a repair, connecting one owl directly to the elongated carnelian bead, because the chain is missing. Earring 764 has one broken disc with about one third missing. Earring 766 is complete.

The carnelian beads in these earrings are translucent with an orange-red colour and are of high quality. Some show an uneven distribution of dark red-brown patches, and a few show fine-scale dark red-brown banding (Fig. 27). They were all but one identified gemmologically as carnelian, a translucent red-orange chalcedony, which is a microcrystalline variety of quartz. The carnelian beads in all four earrings appear to be remarkably similar, suggesting that all came from the same source. However, one small round bead in earring 764, on the wire forming the dog's lead, appears to be of finely fractured quartz with an orange-red colour concentrated in the fractures (Fig. 28). This may indicate that a colourless variety of quartz was heated to fracture the structure, and then artificially dyed, producing what is known as crackled quartz. Alternatively it is possible that the quartz may be naturally fractured, with iron oxides concentrated in the fractures giving the orange-red appearance. All the beads appear to have been drilled through from two directions (Fig. 29).

Distinguishing features defining the two pairs of earrings
The overall design of the four earrings and the basic construction of the main components are almost identical. The use of a single mould to make the main elements of all four clearly indicates the products of a single workshop. Yet they also have detailed features that are shared only between the earrings that form each pair, which suggests the work of two individual goldsmiths on these particular components, before the final assembly of the earrings.

There are four distinguishing features that separate the goldwork of the earrings into two distinct pairs: a) the owls of each pair are distinct in form and detail; b) the details punched on to the heads of the dogs and monkeys at the centre and the serpents' heads on the main ring differ; c) different pairs of carnelian beads are used for the dogs' leads; and d) there is a difference in the composition of the gold between the pairs.

The details of the owl and animal figures are essentially finishing processes that make one pair of earrings (763 and 765) of superior quality. For example, in these two earrings the small owls have a more intricate design on the wing feathers, the heads and eyes (Fig. 25) compared to the owls of the other pair (764 and 766) (Fig. 26). Nonetheless the physical form of the owls is basically the same between the pairs, with images of the birds on both front and back. All are made of two pre-formed halves soldered together to form hollow birds. The owl halves are only part-soldered together, in the same manner as the main rings, rather than fully soldered round the perimeter join. The two types of owl were not mixed between the four earrings, showing that a deliberate choice was made during assembly to select only the same type of owl for the appropriate pairs. Similarly the amount of detail punched on to the animal figures of the earrings corresponds to that of the owls.

The workmanship of the owls allows important comparisons to be made with other pieces of goldwork in the treasure. The overall design and characteristics of both types of owl can be seen in other pieces. An example is the lion's head ornament (746), which has chains suspending high-quality duck-like birds with details similar to the best owls, while the chain pendant (752) has the more simple type of bird corresponding to the other pair of earrings. The similarities of style and form suggest production in the same workshop as the earrings, but the differences in the finished detail again suggest two goldsmiths at work.

The composition of the earrings also distinguishes the two pairs: the main rings of nos 763 and 765 – the better-quality ones – have about half the silver content of the other pair (see Table 1, p. 31).

Another distinguishing feature of the earring pairs is the use of two types of carnelian bead that are wire-mounted between the canine necks and the main rings, forming the dogs' leads. The simpler pair of earrings has round beads (Fig. 33; one is missing as the wire is broken), while the more elaborate pair has cylindrical beads (Fig. 34). These are carved both longitudinally and circumferentially with grooved decoration (Figs 39 and 40), while the round beads are plain. Again, the deliberate choice of incorporating these particular decorative beads into the better-quality earrings was made during assembly.

These decoratively carved beads lead to an intriguing association between this pair of gold and carnelian earrings and the carnelian and amethyst necklace of the treasure (see cat. no. 25 below). The necklace also has three almost identical carved cylindrical carnelian beads (Fig. 30). This can only mean that the necklace was made or assembled in the same workshop as the earrings. Thus we have a direct association between objects of different materials, and an indication that we are dealing with a jewellery workshop and not simply a gold workshop.

All the other components of the earrings are of very similar construction between the two pairs. For example, the discs at the ends of the chains are hammered into sheet from one end of a gold rod, the remainder of which was hammered into wire to suspend the discs from the earring (Fig. 37). They are all of the same size and are very similar to other pendant discs in the treasure, for example on the pectoral ornament with profile heads and the 'Master of Animals' pendant.

4
Two half owls, perhaps originally joined to form a single owl
GR 1892,0520.111 and 20.112; uncatalogued; Figs 35 and 36

These two elements probably originally formed the front and back of a single owl. In style and technique they are very like the owls of the less elaborate pair of earrings, but none of these seems to be missing. These owl halves presumably therefore originally came from another piece of jewellery that has not survived.

Technical notes
These two owl halves must be considered separately from the other pieces of jewellery. The suggestion that they may be the front and back of a single owl that has come apart is supported by the fact that the owls on the other items are only soldered together in a few places, and are susceptible to separation. It seems most likely that these are of the same type. They are both of very similar design and manufacture to bird ornaments in the treasure as a whole and most like those on the less detailed earrings (764 and 766). However, this single owl is not one of those missing from earrings 763 and 765, which have owls of the more detailed type. The owl halves have suspension holes in their tail feathers and presumably were once suspended from another object that is now missing, probably hanging freely from a chain in the manner of all the other birds. The owls are of pale gold colour and have severe stress corrosion cracking at various places on the surface (Fig. 38). Analysis (Table 1, p. 31) confirms a high silver content ($c.$ 33% Ag), which is an alloy susceptible to this form of corrosion attack (Dugmore and Des Forges 1979, Rapson and Groenewald 1978, Ogden 1983).

5
Gold necklace or pectoral ornament with twin profile heads
GR 1892,0520.7; BM Cat Jewellery 761; Fig. 41

A curved element with raised edges terminates in two profile heads facing outwards and has ten discs suspended from its lower edge. Suspension loops above the heads show that the ornament was originally attached to cords or chains, and was presumably worn round the neck or on the chest.

The heads have straight profiles, large oval eyes and two backward-sweeping locks of hair terminating in large curls. The eyes and eyebrows are now empty spaces, but were probably originally inlaid.

The back is flat.

Technical notes
This object is of very high-quality workmanship (Fig. 41). The curved body of the pectoral is made from two sheets of gold, front and back, soldered together fully and very accurately around the rim, making a thin, strong construction. Around the edge of the top sheet is an hemispherical ridge that was chased from

behind before the front and back were soldered together. This not only makes a decorative border but also provides additional strength to the composite sheet. The low relief design of the heads is only on the front sheet, and was also worked initially by repoussé from behind (Fig. 42). Details of the noses and mouths and the long hair with curls were chased in from the front, and the tool marks are clearly visible in the chased lines (Fig. 44). The eyes and eyebrows were cut out of the front sheet before it was soldered to the back, leaving the hollow cavity of the head behind (Fig. 43). Higgins (1979) remarks that 'the eyes and eyebrows were originally inlaid with a blue substance, probably lapis lazuli'. However, there is now no trace of any inlay. It is not clear whether he based his comment on observation of some traces now lost or simply on general probability.

Suspension loops of gold wire are soldered to the top of each head (Fig. 41), presumably for attachment of a now-missing cord or chain by which the pectoral was suspended to be worn. There is only slight evidence of wear on one loop (proper right), which suggests that the pendant has not had much use. Similarly, there are eight soldered suspension loops arranged uniformly along the bottom of the curved pectoral, with an additional loop on the chin of each of the two heads. Suspended from each loop is a sheet-gold disc with its hammered suspension wire (Fig. 45). Very little wear or damage is seen on the suspension loops and pectoral, though some of the discs have suffered damage and breakage to their suspension wires. Numbering the discs 1–10 from the proper left head, the following observations were made:

- All discs are of the same construction, from hammered sheet with an integral hammered suspension wire, and are of very similar size, 11–11.5 mm diameter. They all appear to be ancient.
- Discs 4–7 seem to be in original condition.
- Disc 9 seems to be in original condition but the neck is twisted through 90 degrees, causing slight cracking.
- The wires of discs 2–9 pass through the suspension loops of the pectoral and are neatly coiled back onto themselves to form a mechanical fix; the ends of the wires are not soldered (Fig. 45).
- Discs 1 and 10 have a different method of suspension. They are fixed with short pieces of apparently ancient wire, bent rather untidily through both the pectoral loops and the loops in the neatly coiled wires of the discs (Fig. 46). This seems unnecessary, as neither the loops nor the well-coiled suspension wires are damaged or repaired. There is no obvious reason why these could not originally have been fixed like the others.
- On discs 2 and 8 the wires have broken at the discs. A hole has been pierced in each disc through which ancient strip-twist wire has been passed and coiled back on itself to link the discs mechanically back onto the suspension loops on the pectoral (Fig. 47). These are probably ancient repairs. Disc 8 certainly has the original broken ancient wire. Disc 2 also has strip-twist wire, but probably not the original piece broken from the disc.
- Disc 3 has a broken disc wire with a modern solder repair that has been painted gold. Higgins (1979) shows the disc separated from the wire, before repair.

Thus, three discs have suspension wires that have broken at the base of the neck where it widens into the flat sheet: clearly the weakest point. There is little wear from use on the suspension loops and disc wires, so it perhaps seems odd that several of the disc wires have been broken, and two have apparently been repaired in antiquity, while the pectoral itself is undamaged. However the same type of damage can be seen on the discs of the 'Master of Animals' pendant (see cat. no. 1 above). It is probably the result of a combination of stress corrosion cracking and the discs being susceptible to twisting at this weak point.

The disc and wire construction is similar to that of the discs on the four large earrings (which are some 18 mm in diameter) and those of the 'Master of Animals' pendant (some 12 mm in diameter) but the method of suspension of the discs on the pectoral shows a completely different approach. While the earrings and the pendant have discs suspended from holes pierced through the actual sheet object, the pectoral has dedicated soldered suspension loops. This indicates a different workshop practice for the manufacture of the pectoral, as does the quality of edge soldering, discussed above. This either suggests that we are seeing evidence for the work of a different goldsmith within the same workshop, or that the pectoral is not directly related in manufacture to the other pieces in the treasure.

6
Elaborate gold ornament with a lion's head
GR 1892,0520.9; BM Cat Jewellery 746; Fig. 48

This ornament, of unknown function, seems to be missing some central element. As preserved, it consists of a lion's head encircled by an elaborate collar decorated with filigree gold wire. From this a gold pin descends to a hollow basket; between the collar and the basket some perishable element has probably been lost.

Four chains hang from the collar, two ending in birds with stubby wings suspended from their tails and two in egg-shaped beads. Three longer chains hang from the basket, and three larger birds with pronouncedly bent wings hang from these, also head downwards.

The lion's head has almond-shaped eyes with arching eyebrows, a carefully delineated muzzle and a ridged nose. The ears are triangular and pricked upwards.

The birds are hollow and reversible, like the owls on the earrings from the treasure, but are of a rather different type, with broader wings, smaller eyes and pronounced beaks. They probably represent a duck-like bird: the larger ones particularly resemble ducks.

Technical notes on the lion's head ornament
The ornament is an assembly of several gold components: the lion's head, from which hang four chains, two terminating in ovoid gold beads and two with gold duck-like birds with short wings (Fig. 50). A wire spindle passes through the top of the lion's head and supports the ovoid/hemispherical lower component or basket. The spindle is simply looped round itself at each end to hold the components in place. The space between the head and base gives the impression that material is missing that could have formed the lion's body. Three chains with larger duck-like birds hang from the lower piece (Fig. 49). The chain links are the same as on all the other pieces in the treasure: block-/strip-twist wire with soldered links and of slightly variable wire thickness (Fig. 60).

The lion's head is of a single hammered sheet, possibly formed into a mould, with details of the eyes, mouth and mane chased on (Fig. 58). Other features are soldered on, for example the backward sloping ears and the block-twisted, filigree wire neck decoration (Fig. 59). This is the only piece in the treasure with filigree wire decoration. Below the ears are round holes encircled and reinforced by block-twisted wire, soldered in place (Fig. 59). The holes may be for suspension of the pendant. Although they appear to have been rounded by rotating a tool through them after the encircling wire was soldered, there is little further evidence of suspension wear at these points, nor does the whole object appear to be particularly worn.

Two of the four chains suspended from the head have a small bird that appears to be of similar form to the three larger ducks on the lower component, but with stubby swept-back wings (Fig. 51). They are made in two halves soldered together with suspension holes pierced through their tails, and fixed to the chains by twisted wire. Each of the other two chains from the lion's head has a suspended oval egg- or seed-shaped bead. Again, these beads are made from two halves fully soldered together, each with a soldered wire loop at the broader end – very similar to those of the gold bead necklace (see cat. no. 23 below), providing another association between objects. The first link in each chain passes neatly through the bead's suspension loop and the chains are 'knitted' from the seed-shaped beads (Fig. 56).

The lower half of the pendant is the ovoid basket of sheet gold (Fig. 52) with chased chevron type decoration (Fig. 54) similar to the mane on the back of the lion's head (Fig. 59). Some chevron tool marks end abruptly, leaving the shape of the tool in the gold. It was apparently hemispherical in section, with the end cut squarely (Fig. 55). The rim of this lower component is neatly folded outwards and gently hammered onto itself, making a thin, stronger lip. Two wire loops are soldered to the underside of the piece from which two chains hang, terminating in ducks. The third chain and duck are suspended from a loop on the end of the central spindle.

The three larger ducks are made of back and front embossed sheets with their edges turned up and partly soldered together, like the birds on other pieces. The cranked, slender wing shape and the feathers are very lifelike (Fig. 49 and detail Fig. 62), while the heads have pronounced eyes and pointed beaks (Fig. 62). It is as though these birds were viewed from above, in contrast to the owls, which have round, flat faces as if viewed from the front underside. The birds are of similar high-quality workmanship to the owls on the quality earring pair (763 and 765). They have suspension holes in their tails and are mechanically connected to the last link in the chains by twisted wires (Fig. 57).

7
Gold and carnelian ornament with twin owls on chains, an element from a more elaborate piece of jewellery
GR 1892,0520.101; BM Cat Jewellery 752; Fig. 53

Two gold chains are suspended from a gold-capped carnelian bead. From each chain a bird, probably an owl, hangs by its tail.

Technical notes
This piece was almost certainly part of a larger piece of jewellery now missing from the treasure. It consists of a single oval carnelian bead with gold cup mounts at each end and fixed by a suspension wire twisted at the ends (Fig. 53), similar to that used on the jasper bead necklace (see cat. no. 24 below). The carnelian bead is of translucent orange-red colour with some dark red-brown patches, and is similar to those used in the large earrings, indicating a similar source. The chains are both 'knitted' from the suspension loop in the manner of the lion ornament (Fig. 61). The suspension wire passes through the long axis of the bead from which two chains are suspended, and each terminates in a small owl. The design and assembly of this simple piece is similar to various other pieces in the treasure, which suggests similar workshop origins. In this case the two owls are the smallest in the treasure, with very stubby wings and with few detailed features (Fig. 53). They have the same generic style as the other less detailed birds and may well be the work of the same goldsmith. Again they are made from two halves, part-soldered together. The chains are interesting as they exemplify the variability of the link wires seen on all of the chains in the treasure. Fig. 61 shows the range of link sizes and wire thicknesses as well as the spiral grooves from strip twisting. Large blobs of solder are found on the link joins (Fig. 61).

8
Fifty-four gold plaques, probably dress ornaments
GR 1892,0520.18–71; BM Cat Jewellery 692–745; Fig. 63

The gold plaques consist of a convex central boss surrounded by a border of eight running spirals. The central boss is decorated with an eight-petal rosette indicated by dotted lines, and has a raised edge with hatched lines. The spirals are decorated with grooved lines.

Each disc is pierced in four places at the outer edge of the spirals.

Technical notes
There are fifty-four convex sheet gold plaques, decorated with an impressed dot pattern and spiral edge decoration, and are pierced probably for attachment to a garment (Fig. 63). They appear to be almost identical; the differences are only due to the individual variations in hand-craftsmanship. Five discs were chosen as representative for study (cat. nos 707, 716, 726, 739, 740).

It is probable that the basic dome and spiral form of all the plaques was made by embossing the gold sheets into a single open mould. The plaque decoration was finished by chasing details from the front and by punching dots along scored guidelines that are seen on the surface of the domes (Fig. 64). Each plaque has eight interconnecting spirals that stand proud of the edges, and these have straight, oblique chased or punched lines of decoration that are very similar to those on the four large earrings and the 'Master of Animals' pendant. Each plaque has four pierced holes, one on every other spiral. Some are pierced from the front and others from the back. The pierced holes have the same unsophisticated crudeness (Fig. 65) as those that pierce the bodywork of the earrings and 'Master of Animals' pendant. The front surfaces of the plaques are quite highly polished while the backs are matt. It appears that the fronts have been polished relatively recently while the backs represent a more ancient surface. The interconnecting spiral design is similar to that on the gold cup and on one diadem (as punched dots).

9
A plain gold diadem, the ends twisted into loops for fastening
GR 1892,0520.77; BM Cat Jewellery 683; Fig. 66

This plain band of thin sheet gold is not very strong. It was probably worn as a diadem, perhaps decorating a headdress or hairstyle, but may have been specifically for funerary use.

10
A plain gold diadem, the ends twisted into loops for fastening
GR 1892,0520.787; BM Cat Jewellery 684; Fig. 66

This plain band of thin sheet gold is as the above, but shorter and broader.

11
A gold diadem with spiral decoration; the ends have punched holes for fastening
GR 1892,0520.73–76; BM Cat Jewellery 691; Fig. 66

This band of thin sheet gold is decorated with two rows of punched dots in the form of running spirals. It was probably worn as a diadem, like the two examples above.

12
Eleven fragments of thin gold bands
GR 1892,0520.79–99; BM Cat Jewellery 685–90; Fig. 66

The fragmentary gold bands were perhaps worn around the head as diadems or attached to clothing. As restored they form one long, thin band and eleven fragments of about the same width.

Technical notes on the three diadems and the fragmentary gold bands
These items are from gold sheet of about 0.1 mm thickness. Two plain diadems have wire ends that have been looped round and twisted several times back around their shafts (Fig. 67). As the ends could not clip together in use they must have been held in place or attached with a cord tied through the loops. The wire ends are integral with the sheet and have not been soldered on. Therefore the diadem was made by starting with a thick gold rod, the ends would have first been hammered into thinner wire (c. 0.8 mm diameter), then the main rod was hammered flat between the wire ends to a thickness of 0.1 mm (the same construction as the discs suspended from the 'Master of Animals' pendant, earring pairs and pectoral). This would have produced a thin but uneven width in the sheet, which was then cut and trimmed to the final shape of the diadems, being parallel in the middle and curving towards the end wires. There is evidence of a few overlapped folds in the sheet during manufacture.

One diadem has spiral-dot repoussé decoration, and the gold sheet is broadest in the middle and tapers gently towards the ends. One end has nine small punched holes for fixing with a thin cord or thread. The other end has broken away and is missing, but it is assumed that this would also have been pierced. The decoration consists of four rows of punched dots; a single row parallel with each cut side of the diadem and within these are two spiral rows of dots in mirror image (detail Fig. 68 front and Fig. 69 back). The decoration is a series of punched dots from the use of a single round pointed punch, used from one side of the gold (Fig. 68). The decoration has been very carefully carried out with the two mirror-image rows in exact registration. The spiral pattern gently tapers with the tapering gold.

The present condition of the gold of the four items is quite brittle, as seen from stress corrosion cracks in some regions, and one piece has been strengthened with thin cloth or paper backing during conservation. The gold pieces are very flexible due to their thinness. Although the diadems are now flat, they appear to have evidence of kinks or folds from earlier times.

One fragment from the eleven gold bands was examined, and this was 12 mm wide and 0.1 mm thick, and had some osmium/iridium/ruthenium inclusions (Table 1, p. 31). One double inclusion was sufficiently large to appear on both sides of the sheet (Fig. 70). These inclusions are very hard, but their shiny, flat surfaces are evidence of hammering against a hard surface (probably a metal anvil) during the gold sheet preparation.

13
Gold bracelet
GR 1892,0520.2; BM Cat Jewellery 767; Fig. 71

The bracelet is in the form of a simple flat strap of gold. It is open, and the ends overlap slightly. It is undecorated.

Technical notes
The plain gold bracelet is made from thick, worked gold strip forming a slightly oval loop with open ends that overlap 12 mm and are offset by a few millimetres. The bracelet loop is 66 × 58 mm in diameter, it is 13 mm wide and tapers a little towards the ends. The gold is thickened along the edges by hammering – 1.3 mm compared with 0.9 mm at the centre, which gives the bracelet a concave cross-section. Such mechanical working of the gold gives strength and stiffness to the bracelet so that it is springy, rather than soft and bendable, when slipped over the hand and onto the wrist. Some pink-coloured deposits of mineralized material are found on some areas of the gold, as is quite common on ancient gold surfaces.

14
A set of forty-three double-arc-shaped gold beads
GR 1892,0520.16; BM Cat Jewellery 759a; Fig. 72 (top)

The beads are double-sided and hollow. The shape has been thought to resemble palm leaves. The stringing is speculative, and done for museum display. As strung, the beads form a dense band, but because they are double-sided it would equally be possible to string them with each alternate bead reversed, creating a looser and more open pattern.

15
A set of fifty-two double-arc-shaped gold beads
GR 1892,0520.17 and GR 1914,0725.1; BM Cat Jewellery 758a; Fig. 72 (middle)

These beads are slightly larger than the set of forty-three, but like them they are double-sided and hollow. The arcs of this group are wider and flatter. The same comments on stringing apply.

Technical notes on both sets of double-arc beads
These two necklaces are made of double-arc-shaped gold beads, one with forty-three beads and the other with fifty-two, slightly larger beads with flatter arcs. While the individual beads on each necklace are essentially of identical shape and size, the beads of the two necklaces differ (Fig. 73). The hollow beads have central axial holes so they can be strung together. The beads are of 'W' shape and, as strung, hang closely together forming flexible interlocking chains. For this reason, such stringing is perhaps more satisfactory than the alternative outlined above. Each bead is made of two similar halves which were probably formed by impressing gold sheet into a mould (or punching with a stamp) and were then soldered together. Punched decoration has been added around the bead edges (Figs 75 and 76). The bead manufacture has similarities to the various hollow sheet birds on other pieces of jewellery, although the soldering on these beads is more thorough.

16
Eleven beads in the form of a right hand holding a woman's breast, three of carnelian, three of lapis lazuli and five of gold
GR 1892,0520.106; BM Cat Jewellery 756.a; Fig. 79 (also Fig. 101, top)

This necklace is made up of eleven beads of identical design, though of three different materials. The stringing, with gold beads alternately between the carnelian and lapis lazuli beads, was done for museum display.

Technical notes
The gold beads are hollow and each made from four components: a flat backing sheet, the embossed front sheet with the hand and breast design, a round granule for the nipple and an internal tube for the suspension string. The components are all soldered in place, the tube passing right through each bead against the backing sheet, within the bead, and soldered at each end to the side of the deeply embossed bead. The tubes pass through the wrist of the hands down the longer axis of the beads. The tube construction is an interesting detail on these beads (Fig. 80) and is not seen on any of the other gold beads of the treasure.

The gemstone beads are carved from carnelian and lapis lazuli, and are drilled through from the wrist, parallel with the flat backs (Figs 83 and 80), for suspension in the same manner as the gold beads. The carnelian beads are of translucent orange-red colour (Fig. 83). Two have dark red-brown spots and fine-scale banding like those of the earring. These are only visible on the back of the beads (Fig. 83) suggesting they were carved to avoid these markings showing on the front (Fig. 84). On one bead the drill hole has been started off-axis, abandoned and realigned. This has left a characteristic central peg in the hole, indicating that a hollow drill was used (Fig. 82). This is of similar size to the faulty drill holes in the carnelian bead necklace and the green jasper bead necklace (see cat. no. 24 below), which again suggests a possible workshop link.

The carved lapis lazuli beads are composed of blue and white grains with a granular texture (Figs 79 and 80), typical of natural lapis lazuli rock (Fig. 81). The blue grains are lazurite and the white are, in this case, diopside (rather than calcite). The presence of significant diopside in the blue beads is similar to lapis lazuli reported as coming from Afghanistan (Badakshan) (Plesters 1993). Some beads have brown grains, apparently of degraded pyrite. Pyrite occurs in some lapis lazuli, and is a diagnostic constituent. Some of the lapis lazuli beads have cracks with adhesive, which are traces of restoration.

One of the most important facts to emerge from the observation of this necklace is that the identical design and size of the beads of the three materials – gold, carnelian and lapis lazuli – means that these beads were most probably associated at their manufacturing stage. Again this is strong evidence of a multidisciplinary jewellery workshop producing both gold and carved, polished beadwork, of original design. This is important for the interpretation of the association of various other composite pieces of the treasure during manufacture. The use of lapis lazuli in a multidisciplinary workshop could arguably be the one link between the lapis lazuli rings (see below) and the majority of the jewellery of the treasure.

17
Gold finger ring, the outer surface inlaid with lapis lazuli
GR 1892,0520.6; BM Cat Finger Rings 693; Fig. 86)

The cloisons holding the lapis lazuli on this ring form a meander pattern in gold.

Technical notes
This gold ring is of toroidal shape but with a complex scroll or meander pattern of oblique, square-walled cells or cloisons with inlaid pieces of blue lapis lazuli. The cloisons are made of strips of gold soldered into a complex arrangement of sheet components forming the ring (Figs 94 and 95). A gold strip forms the inner ring backing the complex layered and walled cellular construction. This strip is soldered to another of similar thickness, which has vertical outer walls of gold strip soldered to make the basic cellular form of the ring. Within this are circumferential, parallel walls of gold. On the bottom of the channel formed by these walls is another flat strip of gold that forms the base for the cloison pattern, which is made of gold strips soldered into place. This method of construction gives solidity and strength to the ring, which is built up from gold strips that are relatively thin and of uniform thickness.

Small segments of lapis lazuli have been cut to the appropriate shapes to fit into the gold cloison pattern, mainly small rectangular blocks (Fig. 94) and others with angular corners that fit the oblique cells (Fig. 95). However, some look more like broken pieces, rather than being cut accurately to shape. The lapis lazuli is held in place by the burnished (rubbed) top surfaces of the cloison walls that have deformed and spread a little over the edges of the lapis lazuli pieces. Some of the lapis lazuli has been lost and there is no evidence of restoration to replace it.

18
Gold finger ring inlaid with lapis lazuli, the bezel shaped like a reef knot
GR 1892,0520.3; BM Cat Finger Rings 691; Fig. 85 left

The hoop of this ring is formed from two parallel grooves inlaid with lapis lazuli, which open out to form two loops. These are interlaced to create a bezel in the form of a reef knot, also inlaid with lapis lazuli.

Technical notes
This reef-knot ring has been fashioned from shaped pieces of sheet and strip gold, soldered to form an interlinked figure of eight or reef knot, inlaid with blocks of lapis lazuli (Figs 85, 88 and 89). The two loops that form the interlinked design were each made separately from a sheet base with side walls and a central wall soldered to form a double row of cloisons for the lapis lazuli. The two loops were then fitted together, the ends bent to form the finger loop and the two components soldered together.

The lapis lazuli segments are composed of the natural rock containing blue lazurite grains and white diopside (Fig. 90), similar to the mixed-bead necklace lapis lazuli beads. Some inlay has a powdery texture, probably due to weathering, and there are some brown grains of degraded pyrite. Lapis lazuli segments in the form of small oblongs were cut to the appropriate curved shape and inserted into the cloisons and held in place by burnishing or rubbing the top of the gold walls so that the gold spreads a little over the lapis lazuli. These segments are accurately cut to shape and are relatively long with appropriate curvature, and the surface of the lapis lazuli has been polished relatively smooth (Fig. 91). About half of the lapis lazuli segments are missing, and there is no evidence for replacement of lapis lazuli with a substitute, but there are traces of adhesive indicating some restorative stabilization of loose pieces.

19
Gold finger ring inlaid with lapis lazuli, the bezel in the shape of a double axe or shield
GR 1892,0520.4; BM Cat Finger Rings 690; Fig. 85 right

This gold ring has a solid gold hoop and an oval bezel set at right angles to the hoop. The bezel has a semicircular indentation on each side, and thus resembles a figure-of-eight shield or – if like most Minoan rings it should be 'read' horizontally – it becomes a fairly rounded version of a Minoan double axe. It is inlaid with lapis lazuli in gold cloisons.

Technical notes
The hoop of the ring is flat on the inside and rounded on the outside (Fig. 85 right). The inner side of the hoop has an additional thin strip of gold sheet soldered to it. This seems to serve no obvious function apart from making it slightly thicker. The ends of the hoop are covered by a sheet of gold that forms the back of the flat, oval bezel. From the front, the ends of the hoop are seen to be soldered onto this sheet, and the rounded ends also form part of the design, being outlined by a cloison wall. Gold strip is soldered onto the bezel sheet, forming the cloison walls for the lapis lazuli inlays.

The ring has eight fields of flat lapis lazuli inlaid in segments into the symmetrical shield or axe pattern. The lapis segments have been shaped to fit the curved cloison patterns and are secured by burnishing the top of the gold cloison walls which have spread a little to overlap the inlaid pieces (Figs 92 and 93). Some of the lapis is completely missing, while in other areas only the top surface of the lapis is lost, which reveals the bright blue mineral surface below. Where the original lapis remains at the surface, it is somewhat darker in colour. There is no evidence of restoration.

20
Gold finger ring with an inlay of fluted lapis lazuli
GR 1892,0520.5; BM Cat Finger Rings 692; Fig. 87

A round gold ring shaped with a groove around the outer surface to enclose an inlay of lapis lazuli, fluted diagonally.

Technical notes
The ring is of toroidal shape and made from a single piece of gold sheet with the edges turned out to form a deep groove, much like a rimmed wheel, into which lapis lazuli was inlaid (Fig. 87).

The lapis lazuli was cut in an interesting way. Not only does it fit circumferentially into the curved rim, but it stands proud of the gold surface and is hemispherical in cross-section (Figs 96 and 98 detail). Segments of lapis lazuli were inserted within the gold torus walls which have been burnished and gently punched with indentations to hold the inlay in place physically (Fig. 98). The lapis lazuli has been decorated with a diagonal fluted pattern carved over the curved surface giving it the appearance of a 'scooter tyre' (Figs 87, 96, 98). The lapis lazuli is shaped from pieces of original rock, and not a composite of crushed and consolidated grains.

Some of the inlay is missing. There is also an area of repair on the lapis lazuli. This contains a modern wax-impregnated mixture of dark-blue material with tiny white grains of gypsum, intended to simulate the blue and white colour of the natural rock. However, the natural lapis lazuli in the ring is a bright, medium blue while the simulated material is dull and much darker.

21
Small gold finger ring
GR 1892,0520.100; BM Cat Finger Rings 888; Fig. 85 upper

The bezel and part of the hoop of a ring in very thin gold. The bezel is a convex oval decorated with chased cross-hatched lines. The hoop has a groove down the middle.

Technical notes
This small gold ring is made of thin sheet gold with a cross-hatched pattern chased into the convex bezel (Fig. 85). This is similar in some ways to the chased cross-hatched decoration of the wing detail of the 'Master of Animals' pendant, but the link is tenuous. It has been suggested that the gold sheet is too thin to form a self-supporting ring, and that it may have been a covering that was wrapped over a core material, of which there is no trace remaining. Without a supporting core the ring would be impractical to wear as it would have no strength. The ring has been repaired, rather crudely, with lead solder and modern glue.

22
Five plain gold hoops with open ends
GR 1892,0520.72; BM Cat Jewellery 751; Fig. 99

These plain gold rings could have served a number of decorative purposes. They may have been worn as earrings, either singly or linked together, though in either case the odd number means they cannot be seen as pairs.

Technical notes
The gold rings have open ends that have allowed them to be linked together, as they are now found, but it would have been easy to separate them in antiquity if required. The rings are made of thick gold wire with round cross-sections (*c*. 9 mm diameter) thinning a little towards the ends (Fig. 100). The rings are a little ovoid and of slightly different diameters (*c*. max. 30.2 x 28 mm). There is evidence of faceting along some of the wires which is typical of hammering the gold to shape (Fig. 100). One ring has overlapping folds from hammering. This ring also has several small, grey-coloured osmium/iridium/ruthenium (platinum group elements – PGE) inclusions of various compositions. Some pink-coloured deposits of mineralized material are found on some rings, as with the bracelet above.

23
A necklace of gold beads
GR 1892,0520.14; BM Cat Jewellery 753.a; Fig. 72 lower.

The beads were brought together and strung for museum display. They are as follows:

- 26 gold collared beads decorated with circular depressions
- 6 small spherical and biconical beads
- 25 elongated oval pendants with pointed ends suspended from short chains

Technical notes
Each of the twenty-six identical hollow gold beads is 9 mm long and has a symmetrical geometric pattern of eight circular depressions. The twenty-five plain seed-shaped or ovoid beads are also hollow, and identical. Each is 12 mm long. These beads are suspended from short chains between the main beads (Fig. 74). On each end of the suspension cord are three small rounded gold beads (Fig. 72). The arrangement of the strung beads is a reasoned guess as the original suspension material was missing.

The geometrical beads are made of identical halves, well soldered together along their longitudinal axes. The regularity of the halves indicates they were made by working gold sheet into a mould to produce identical halves that fit accurately together. The bead shape is quite complex and well executed (Fig. 77). The suspended hollow seed-shaped beads are similarly made from identical moulded halves soldered longitudinally, and each seed has a wire suspension loop soldered at one end. These beads are similar to those of the lion ornament, but not of exactly the same shape. The chains for these seeds are of strip-twist wire construction, and are similar to all the other chains in the treasure, having slightly irregular wire thickness and with some prominent solder blobs on the links. The seed loops are connected to the last link in each chain by pieces of wire twisted round and back onto themselves, but not soldered (Fig. 78). This is the reverse of the method used for the similar seeds on the lion ornament, in which the suspension loop of the seed neatly forms the first link in the chain. The chains for the necklace must have been made separately from the seeds, otherwise they could have been 'knitted' on. This gives an insight into workshop practice: some chains seem to have been made separately for general use, to be incorporated into whichever piece of jewellery required them, while others seem to have been made specifically for a component from which the chain is 'knitted', as seen in the lion's head ornament (above).

24
A necklace of gold and green jasper beads
GR 1892,0520.107–8 and GR 1914,0725.2–5; BM Cat Jewellery 754.a); Fig. 101 lower

Beads of two different types were brought together and strung for museum display. They are as follows:

- 80 hollow gold melon-shaped beads, 7 of them collared
- 15 green jasper pendants with gold caps, shaped as acorns. The upper part of the green jasper beads is shaped to accommodate the cap. The ends of the gold wire running through each bead protrude slightly, increasing the resemblance to acorns.

Technical notes
The necklace is strung with the acorn beads suspended between pairs of melon-shaped beads (Fig. 102). The green jasper acorn beads are arranged symmetrically according to size, the largest beads being in the middle of the necklace and the smallest at the ends. The beads are dark green and opaque with a sub-vitreous lustre (Fig. 102). Under magnification they show a slightly mottled appearance, some with minute brown patches. Analysis confirms they are of green jasper, a quartz-rich gemstone with traces of iron (less common than the red-brown type; Frondel 1962).

The melon-shaped beads were made from moulded sheet halves soldered together longitudinally, in the same manner as the gold bead necklace, but not as neatly (Fig. 104). Seven of the gold beads are of slightly different design and smaller than the majority, and are located at the ends of the necklace (Fig. 101, lower).

Each green jasper bead sits in a gold cap and resembles an acorn. The beads are carved with a waist and drilled with a central hole for the hammered wire fixing-pin to pass through. Each gold fixing-pin has one end flattened into an oblong section and made into a suspension loop after passing centrally through the pierced gold caps, to which they are soldered. The green jasper beads sit neatly in the gold caps, and are fixed with a pig-tail twist of the pin end (Figs 102 and 105 detail) (some tails have broken off and the beads have been stuck with modern glue). One of the beads has an offset, incomplete drill hole that was clearly a mistake. It was abandoned, leaving a central core, which shows that a tubular drill was used. Misaligned drill holes of similar size are seen on the carnelian bead necklace and the mixed bead necklace (see below). This may indicate a manufacturing cross-link between objects, although this fault might generally be common in bead manufacture.

25
A necklace of carnelian and amethyst beads
GR 1892,0520.15 and GR 1914,0725.8–10; BM Cat Jewellery 760; Fig. 101 centre

The beads were assembled and strung for museum display. They are as follows:

- 165 spherical or slightly biconical carnelian beads
- 1 oval carnelian bead
- 15 carnelian elongated barrel-shaped beads
- 3 carnelian cylindrical beads with engraved lines
- 3 large amethyst spacer beads, of flattened oval and grooved shape, each pierced three times.

Technical notes
The necklace is strung as three rows of highly polished carnelian beads, mainly round (165), and some of longer double conical or lozenge shape (15) (Fig. 101). The carnelian beads are of translucent orange-red colour with a vitreous lustre. Some show distributions of small dark red-brown spots or thin banding (Fig. 103). They are similar in colour and texture to the carnelian beads of the earrings, suggesting a similar source. The banded beads are, like those of the earrings, mostly made with the banding at right angles to the perforations, showing careful orientation of the original raw material during shaping and drilling, which may suggest a similar origin. Three amethyst spacer beads hold the three strings of carnelian beads apart (Fig. 106).

On this necklace there are three cylindrical carved carnelian beads that have the same decorative pattern of filed grooves as those of the dog leads on one pair of large earrings (763 and 765; Fig. 30). These are the most important tangible workshop link between this necklace and the large earrings, indicating that the loose beads in the treasure and those incorporated into the earrings had a common workshop origin.

Some of the beads show evidence of the method of drilling their suspension holes. One in particular shows the original drill hole was started off-axis and drilled only part-way into the bead. The drilling was abandoned, leaving a central peg as evidence for the use of a hollow drill (Fig. 107). The drill core is 0.8 mm in diameter and the drill hole 1.5 mm diameter. This type of mistake is also seen on the green jasper bead necklace and the mixed bead necklace. Although the method of hollow drilling is reported for other material (Gwinnett and Gorelick 1993), the presence of mistakes on some beads in these necklaces may link the necklaces to a single workshop, or at least the same source of beads if these were bought in rather than made on site.

Three elaborate amethyst spacer beads hold the three strings of carnelian beads apart. These broad amethyst beads are each carved to represent the shape of three adjacent, touching beads and are each drilled from both ends to create three suspension holes. The amethyst beads show colour zoning of purple to colourless. They are transparent and lustrous with needle-like orange and black inclusions.

26
A flanged disc bead of rock crystal
GR 1892,0520.109; BM Cat Jewellery 757; Figs 101 centre and 108

The bead is spool shaped and pierced across the diameter. It may have been used to take a cord for the suspension of a pendant.

Technical notes
This is a single disc-shaped, colourless, transparent bead with a frosted appearance (11 mm diameter, 5 mm thick). It is gently domed on each side. It is of quartz (rock crystal) and has some chipping on the edges, resulting in conchoidal fracture surfaces. The bead has a circumferential groove and a hole drilled diametrically (Fig. 109). These two features would have allowed both suspension from and attachment to other components within a piece of jewellery. The hole has been drilled from opposite sides and meets in the middle of the bead. The bead has no obvious parallels with any other bead in any of the pieces of jewellery in the Aigina Treasure, nor does it appear to have been attached to any of the other pieces.

27
Gold cup
GR 1892,0520.1; BM Cat Jewellery 768; Figs 110 and 111

A gold cup with a fairly deep offset concave rim, decorated with an embossed sixteen-petalled rosette in the centre of the interior, surrounded by four running spirals around the body of the cup. These also appear in relief in the interior: the repoussé technique means that both the rosette and the spirals are in intaglio from the outside. On the exterior a ring around the rosette forms a base for the cup. Three holes at one side show where a single handle was attached. This was probably a vertical strap handle, also of gold and attached by rivets.

Technical notes
The gold cup was formed from a gold disc by raising (hammering) and has a concave rim (Fig. 110). It has an embossed, spiral design on the curved sides and a circular, rosette design on the base (Fig. 111). The designs were all chased onto the gold. There is no reinforcing base ring: the ring on which the cup stands is simply formed by the outer edge of the chased rosette design standing proud. There are three rivet holes, two on the rim and one below on the curved side where a handle, now missing, was probably fixed.

Manufacturing techniques and materials

Goldwork

The Aigina goldwork is made from a variety of components of flat and embossed sheet, hollow sheet beads, wire and chain. All are made by mechanical means, essentially hammering gold to sheet, embossing sheet into concave moulds for producing repeat components (or using a convex stamp), and adding decorative texture and details by chasing or punching (Higgins 1961, Ogden 1982, Untracht 1982). The components are joined together by soldering, fixing mechanically with twisted wire or suspending from chains. The chains of the treasure are all of classic, single loop-in-loop style with each single link looping through the next (Higgins 1961, fig. 4, Untracht 1982). This is consistent throughout the Aigina Treasure; there are no multiple loop-in-loop chains. Most of the gold collection does not appear to have much wear on chain links and other susceptible places, as some other ancient jewellery does, suggesting the treasure was not a collection of items worn over an individual's lifetime.

Wire

Three types of wire are used in the earrings and jewellery: hammered, block twist and strip twist, though there is some overlap between the methods of making these wires (Oddy 1977). Hammering gold to a square section rod, twisting and then rolling produces block-twist wire with its characteristic solid core and two spiral grooves (Fig. 112). Also present is wire made from twisted, oblong section rod, which produces essentially solid cores but with quite broad twisted grooves (Fig. 113), which are half-way to being strip-twist wire. True strip-twist wire is also present, made from thin gold strips (cut from sheet) twisted and rolled, thus making the typically hollow wire, but of variable thickness – particularly seen in chain links (Figs 31, 60, 61). All chain links are made from short pieces of strip-twist wire bent into a ring and the butt ends soldered. Some of the chain links have excessively large blobs of solder (Figs 61 and 114). The early date of the treasure is perhaps a factor in the variations seen in the wire diameters, link sizes and soldering quality compared to that of later Classical jewellery where we generally find finer strip-twist wire that is much more regular in thickness, and where blobs of solder on links are less common (Williams and Ogden 1994). Thus the general variability of the treasure wire, without the regularity found in later goldwork, is indicative of an early date, and generally supports the contemporaneity of the group.

Gold soldering

Much of the soldering between the back and front sheetwork on the earrings, the owls, the 'Master of Animals' pendant and the ducks on the lion's head ornament has been done by only part-soldering the components together in places, and not forming a complete soldered seal around the edges (Figs 23, 36). By comparison, the pectoral with profile heads has soldering carefully executed around the entire peripheral seam between the front and back sheets, and the suspension loops for the discs are all carefully soldered in position (Figs 41, 42). Similarly, all the hollow gold beads have fully soldered seams (Figs 77, 104). There seems to have been a deliberate choice made by the goldsmith only to part-solder the hollow components of the earrings and birds, and so on, and also to avoid soldering suspension loops on the earrings for all the pendant chains. Instead, the main earring loops have been pierced for suspension points: a less elegant, but simple, solution (Figs 23, 32). However, the lion's head ornament does have soldered suspension loops for its pendant chains (Fig. 48). Thus there is a mixture of techniques between objects. Analyses were made of various soldered joins. They contained only gold, silver and copper, although the compositions were similar to adjacent unsoldered areas due to interdiffusion during the soldering process (see below).

Stress corrosion cracking of goldwork

Stress corrosion cracking is seen on a number of gold items, for example the necks and punched decoration on the gold discs of the 'Master of Animals' pendant, and the two separate owls (Figs 17 and 38). This form of corrosion manifests itself as tiny cracks in the gold. The cracks are very angular, owing to the separation of metal grains along grain boundaries. The occurrence of stress corrosion cracking results from four factors: the residual worked stress in the gold, the corrosive environment, the composition of the gold alloy, and time. Analysis of the objects with stress corrosion cracking shows that the gold is relatively silver rich (21–32% Ag). This is known to make the alloys susceptible to the phenomenon (Dugmore and Des Forges 1979, Rapson and Groenewald 1978, Ogden 1983). The corrosive environment is of interest, and possibly the close proximity of the sea is the primary cause, as salt-laden air is chemically aggressive to silver. This adds an argument in favour of the location of the alleged find-spot of the treasure near to the coast, but does not prove it.

Analysis of the gold

Samples were taken from tiny scraped areas (in remote places) to allow analysis of core metal. By comparison, some surface analyses were carried out to assess the degree of surface enrichment (mainly loss of copper), which was, as expected, significant. Analysis of multicomponent pieces of jewellery is in general never straightforward, because the different components often have different compositions, even on one object. This is true of the pieces in the Aigina Treasure. The best that could be achieved was to analyse the largest piece of gold in each composite piece, and also some appropriate appendages, to give a range of compositions for the composite object (Table 1, p. 31). It was not possible to analyse every component of the treasure. The problems with ancient, unpurified natural gold are the variation in composition that may occur between batches of source gold that is simply 'passed on' to the objects even though these may be manufactured within a single workshop, and the recycling of scrap gold. This variation was seen across the majority of Aigina Treasure items. However, there were three cases where the composition of components from particular items of goldwork formed close analytical groups, suggesting a single batch of gold for those pieces in each group. These were, first, the five embossed gold discs (selected randomly from the total of fifty-four), which all had the same composition; secondly, the ten gold discs suspended from the pectoral with profile heads, which all had the same composition; and, thirdly, the earrings, which form two distinct pairs (Table 1, p. 31).

The composition of the four large earrings falls very neatly into the two pairs, which have already been identified from the goldworking characteristics. The higher-quality pair (763 and 765, Fig. 18) has significantly less silver, c. 12 per cent, compared with the other pair, c. 24 per cent (764 and 766, Fig. 19). Generally all of the jewellery pieces have alloys of moderate silver contents, typically within the range of the earring pairs. However, some components are much higher in silver, including the acorn necklace (c. 36% Ag) and the chain pendant owls (c. 33% Ag, while the wire contained 44% Ag). The lowest silver content appears to be in the main sheet of the pectoral with profile heads (7% Ag), while its suspended discs are different (all having c. 16% Ag).

The silver contents of the Aigina gold jewellery items are typically within the wide range of those found in natural, unrefined gold (Raub 1995; Craddock 1995; Ramage and Craddock 2000; Chapman, Leake and Styles 2002; Hauptmann, Rehren and Pernicka 1995). There are many recorded sources of gold, both ancient and recent, large and small, which can have a wide range of gold/silver compositions even within a single deposit, as determined from the analysis of alluvial gold grains obtained from geological surveys (Chapman, Leake et al. 2000; Lehrberger 1995). Hence, much early gold jewellery made from unrefined gold would typically have a range of moderate to high silver contents (e.g. 30%) (Primas 1995, Montero and Rovira 1991), as we appear to find in the Aigina goldwork. This compares with later Greek jewellery, which can have relatively low silver from a wide geographical area (Meeks 1998), presumably having been made from refined gold. The copper content in nearly all the Aigina objects is quite low (0.3%–2.2% Cu), with the exception of some components of the acorn necklace (up to 4.8%). Some of the copper content is probably a little higher than most natural, unrefined gold, which is generally found to be below 1 per cent (Hauptmann, Rehren and Pernicka 1995; Raub 1995; Craddock 1995). A low percentage of copper is therefore at the threshold between its natural occurrence in alluvial gold, its deliberate addition to the melt (Tylecote 1987, Raub 1995, Eluère 1982), and its entering the melt unintentionally from the addition of recycled gold alloys (Perea and Rovira 1995, Northover 1995) that may include solders containing copper. In practical terms, copper concentrations of around 2 per cent lower the melting point of gold by about 42°C (Lyman 1973), which is significant once the melting process begins, and therefore may have been deliberate. It is barely high enough to alter the colour of the pale silver-rich gold, but it would have a slight effect on the alloy hardness (Rapson and Groenewald 1978). Thus, the range of gold compositions found in the Aigina Treasure jewellery is not unexpected and does not preclude the items coming from a single hoard. No modern gold alloy compositions (which typically have much higher copper content and lower silver) were found in the treasure.

Analyses were made of various solder joins on sheet or wire, in order to try to determine the composition of solders. Although accurate analyses of cleaned solder joins were compared to adjacent cleaned gold components, no significant compositional differences were obtained. However, this is often the case with such analyses, where it is only possible to analyse clean surfaces and not to analyse a cross-section deep within joins, which would represent the residue of original solder. During soldering the immediate interdiffusion between the molten solder alloy and gold alloy to be joined causes any original concentration differences between gold and solder to be quickly dispersed. The only elements found at solder joins were gold, silver and low copper.

Platinum group element (PGE) inclusions in gold components

Like many items of ancient gold jewellery from the Mediterranean regions, some of the treasure pieces have small, hard metallic PGE inclusions of osmium/iridium/ruthenium of various compositions, and most have a little platinum and iron (Table 1, p. 31) (Ogden 1977, Meeks and Tite 1980). These are particularly noticeable in some sheet items such as the pectoral with profile heads, for example disc no. 1 (Fig. 41 left), discs on earring 764 (Fig. 21), the thin gold band (Figs 66 and detail 70); and on thicker wire such as the plain wire hoop (Fig. 99) and shield ring (690). The presence of these inclusions is common to many alluvial sources of gold used in the ancient world. These inclusions are of very high melting point (>c. 2400°C, Lyman 1973) and pass unaffected through crucible melting of the gold, which is the first stage of any goldworking activity, and end up in the gold objects. Their presence can make jewellery making more difficult for small and thin items of gold which require extensive hammering as the intractable, hard inclusions do not deform with the gold and create weak points (Fig. 70). Their presence also shows that the gold is unrefined, an activity that has its origins in the time of Croesus in Lydia, c. 550 BC (Ramage and Craddock 2000), considerably later than the Minoan date of the Aigina Treasure.

Carnelian beads and lapidary work

All the carnelian beads in the treasure are of a similar high standard. The carnelian is of good colour and highly polished (Fig. 103). This is particularly noticeable on both sets of earrings, but true of the other pieces too. The long, carved beads of the dog leads of one earring pair (Fig. 34) have a direct association with similar beads on the carnelian and amethyst necklace (Fig. 30). This suggests one batch or source of beads and their use in one workshop. The smallest beads on the earring gold discs are only about 2 mm in diameter, with a suspension hole drilled through the middle, and these are also highly polished. Some beads are essentially spherical, while others are long and have a characteristic biconical shape (Fig. 29) achieved through the rotational grinding and polishing process between flat surfaces. The beads all have suspension holes drilled through their central axes using hollow drills, for which there is clear evidence from the central peg remaining in misaligned, abandoned drill marks on some beads (Figs 82 and 107). The long beads have accurately aligned drill holes passing through the narrow conical apexes of the beads (Fig. 29). All beads are drilled from opposite ends, the hole meeting around the middle.

The drill holes, particularly of the long beads, taper towards the middle where they meet and are thus biconical, the holes being slightly wider at the surface due to the drill rocking slightly during drilling (Fig. 29). They are drilled from both ends to avoid chipping around an exit hole: a risk if they were drilled straight through. Some perforations in longer beads were straightened by secondary working. The alignment of tiny drill holes in the narrow ends of long thin beads and the successful drilling from opposite ends must have been difficult to achieve. Stocks (1989) describes experimental practicalities of bead drilling in the manner of the Egyptian New Kingdom period.

The drill holes have concentric striations consistent with the effect of the mechanical drilling action of a bow drill (Grace 1989). The holes and pegs left in misaligned, abandoned drillings show that the tubular drills used were of very small diameter, c. 1.5 mm, with the tube walls being c. 0.3 mm thick. The drills were probably made of either copper or bronze and used with abrasive. A hollow drill resists bending much better than a solid drill of the same diameter and the abrasive will cut quicker because it only has to cut a thin cylindrical hole, leaving a solid core which can be easily broken off. Tubular copper drills were employed to perforate hard stones outside the Aegean area in the second millennium BC. Gwinnett and Gorelick (1993) found evidence for the use of drills of similar size and shape in Egypt during the Middle Kingdom, 2040–1780 BC, and New Kingdom, 1560–1080 BC. Further afield, in the Indus Valley, Kenoyer (1997, pp. 270–1) noted the use of tubular drills for perforating small agate beads during the late Harappan period, sometime around the beginning of the second millennium until 1700 BC, and adds that tubular copper drills currently used in Khambatt have a slit along one side to allow the addition of abrasive slurry. Tubular drills could have been made by hammering sheet around a thin rod, which was removed after shaping.

Lapidary experiments (Sax *et al.* 1998) have demonstrated that it is only possible to perforate a material as hard as carnelian with a copper or bronze drill by charging the tool with an abrasive such as quartz, or harder emery.

Provenance of the gemstone materials
Fig. 115 shows a group of geological samples of the materials used to make the gemstone beads in the Aigina Treasure. It is not possible to provenance the gemstones used in the Aigina Treasure with any certainty. However, possible sources suggested in the literature are listed below:

Carnelian
The carnelian used for the beads in the earrings and necklaces may have come from known ancient sources such as Egypt, India or various parts of Europe (Ogden 1982). India has some of the finest carnelian (Webster and Read 1994). Kenoyer (1997) reported a carnelian bead-working site in Harappa, Pakistan, which was probably using similar drilling techniques for the bead holes, dating from *c.* 3300 to 1700 BC and thus coming down to the period when the Aigina Treasure is thought to have been made. Lucas and Harris (1962) and Aston *et al.* (2000) reported the occurrence of carnelian in Egypt. Aston *et al.* (2000) suggested that it may have been heated to redden the colour. Moorey (1994) names western Arabia, Iran, Oman and Anatolia in Turkey as other sources of carnelian. Higgins (1979) suggested that the carnelian may have been locally available in Crete, although he does not mention a source in Crete in his later book (Higgins and Higgins 1996).

Amethyst
Good-quality amethyst has been found in Russia near the Urals, and amethyst is also found in India and Sri Lanka (Webster and Read 1994). Higgins (1979) suggested that the amethyst may have come from Egypt, and Lucas and Harris (1962), Moorey (1994) and Aston *et al.* (2000) all name known Egyptian sources of amethyst. Moorey (1994) also names Iran and Anatolia as other possible sources.

Green jasper
Higgins (1979) suggested that the green jasper may have come from Egypt, while Lucas and Harris (1962) and Aston *et al.* (2000) name known Egyptian deposits. India is also a possible source (Webster and Read 1994).

Lapis lazuli
Lapis lazuli is a relatively rare rock in nature. Higgins (1979) suggested that the lapis lazuli may have been imported from Badakshan in north-east Afghanistan, which is generally accepted as the main ancient source for lapis lazuli (Herrmann 1968). Coggin Brown and Dey (1955) reported lapis lazuli sources in Myanmar (Burma). Lake Baikal is a lapis lazuli source that was not exploited until the nineteenth century (Webster and Read 1994). While Iran has been mentioned as a possible source there is no evidence to support this claim (Herrmann 1968).

Rock crystal
Rock crystal is found all over the world (Webster and Read 1994). Higgins (1979) suggested that the rock crystal may have been locally available in Crete, but he makes no mention of a source in Crete in his later book (Higgins and Higgins 1996). Other sources have been suggested, including Egypt (Lucas and Harris 1962; Aston *et al.* 2000), and India, Iran, Turkey and Cyprus (Moorey 1994).

Discussion: Manufacturing links between jewellery pieces and evidence for a single workshop
The apparent discovery of the treasure as a single hoard is documented by Higgins (1979) and updated by Williams in this volume (pp. 11–16). Details remain elusive, and so one of the primary objectives of the technological study of the Aigina Treasure was to establish whether there was scientific evidence to confirm the association of any, or many, of the pieces of jewellery in an original single hoard – or indeed whether they could be assigned to a single workshop. By comparing the craftsmanship of different pieces of jewellery it was hoped to find significant similarities between some items to show, with a degree of certainty, that those pieces had a common origin as a coherent group from a single workshop. With the group as a whole, where several features occur together, the probability for association increases. The process was therefore one of trying to establish links between the goldwork and items with beads and mixed materials.

As a general summary, as we have seen above, the Aigina Treasure is made from a variety of components of flat and embossed sheet, hollow sheet beads, wire, chain and gemstone beads. The gold components are joined together by soldering, fixing mechanically with twisted wire or suspending from chains. The quality of all the carnelian beads in the treasure is of a high standard, with highly polished carnelian of good colour.

However, these general jewellery characteristics are not unique to the Aigina Treasure. Many similar goldsmithing traditions and technologies manifest themselves in gold jewellery over a long period of time and over a wide geographical area. Thus we have to be confident that any comparative observations of association made between the Aigina Treasure pieces have a high probability of being significant, and not simply generally characteristic of gold jewellery of the period. Thus comparisons have to be made at a detailed and subtle level.

Technological comparisons between the earrings and different items of jewellery

The four earrings are the largest and most complex of the jewellery pieces, and are the benchmark against which all the other pieces of jewellery are compared. As described above, the overall design and manufacture of the four earrings are essentially identical, and within the four there are technologically two recognizable pairs, which have clear similarities and differences between them. Similarities in design and manufacture of components found in the earrings exist as elements in many of the other pieces in the treasure, although clearly not all pieces have all the elements. Thus several of the pieces have direct similarities with the earrings, while others have similarities that are less direct but are linked, perhaps more tenuously, via other pieces with which they do have some features in common. The major features of the jewellery pieces are summarized below for comparison:

- *Earrings*: Hollow sheet body (front and back), turned-up edges, part-soldered, pierced main body with wire fixing, discs integral with hammered wire secured by twisting, chased or punched lines for decoration, hollow sheet owls formed in mould, chains and variable wire, high-quality polished carnelian beads, carved cylindrical carnelian beads.
- *'Master of Animals' pendant*: Hollow sheet body (front and back), with turned-up back sheet edges, part-soldered, pierced main body with wire fixing, discs integral with hammered wire secured by twisting, chased or punched lines for details on geese, serpent and figure, punched dot decoration on discs.
- *Pectoral with profile heads*: Hollow relief heads, strong double sheet body, front and back fully soldered, soldered suspension rings, gold discs and integral wire secured by twisting, chased hair lines (overall the gold workmanship is perhaps of higher quality than the earrings).
- *Lion's head ornament*: Birds formed in moulds, chased or punched toolmarks, variable wire chains, hollow seed-shaped beads, soldered filigree wire decoration.
- *Chain pendant*: Birds, carnelians, chains with variable wire and solder blobs.
- *Owl pair*: Two halves of one object, similar to owls of the less detailed earring.
- *Fifty-four gold discs*: Sheets embossed into mould, chased or punched lines and dots.
- *Carnelian and amethyst necklace*: High-quality carnelian beads, carved cylindrical carnelian beads, off-set abandoned hollow drill hole in spherical bead, triple-drilled amethyst spacer beads.
- *Green jasper necklace*: Off-set abandoned drill hole in bead, soldered halves of each gold bead.
- *Double-arc necklaces*: Leaves in two identical halves, well-soldered edges, punched decoration.
- *Gold bead necklace*: Chains, soldered halves of each gold bead, seeds similar shape to lion ornament seeds.
- *Carnelian, lapis and gold breast/hand bead necklace*: Combined materials of gold, carnelian and lapis lazuli, abandoned off-set drill hole in carnelian bead. All beads were made in one workshop (identical design and size).
- *General wire*: Range of hammered wire, strip twist and block twist, 'early' wire technology. Simple, single loop in loop chains, variable wire thickness and link size, solder blobs on some links.
- *General embossed sheet*: Main and repeat components formed in moulds.
- *General carnelian quality*: High polish and colour of gemstones, drilled from each end.

The four large earrings are, not surprisingly, manufactured as a group in a single workshop. They have many features of essentially identical workmanship in common, including the use of a single symmetrical mould for working the front and back sheets of gold to form the main rings, and another symmetrical mould for making the back and front sheets of the animal motifs. But they also form two distinct pairs by way of clear differences in workmanship between the owls, the punched details on the animal features, and the use of carved carnelian beads on one pair. It is reasonable to assume that this is evidence that within the workshop the hands of two goldsmiths, at least, were involved. Perhaps the most important object with which these earrings have direct manufacturing similarities is the 'Master of Animals' pendant. Similarities are seen in the sheet-work with its punched decoration, the part-soldering of back and front, and the piercing for mechanical joining and disc suspension. The only significant difference is that the gold discs on the 'Master of Animals' pendant have a dot-punched decoration, which the earrings do not.

The next group of objects that have common technological and stylistic characteristics with the earrings includes the lion ornament, the chain pendant and the pair of owls. It is the design and manufacture of the birds suspended on chains that are particularly similar. But it is only the lion ornament that is (nearly) a complete object; the other pieces are parts of objects that are missing from the treasure. The chain pendant and owl pair may represent only one missing object as the birds are all of similar form, and are most like those of the less detailed earrings.

The pectoral with profile heads is more difficult to assign to the above groups. This is mainly because of the apparent higher quality of workmanship, shown both in the curved body, with its fully soldered front and back sheets, and the skilfully chased features of the heads and hair. However the plain, suspended gold discs are very similar to those of the earrings, although they lack the carnelian beads of the earring discs. The discs on the head pectoral are suspended from well-soldered suspension loops on the curved body, in contrast to the rather crude piercing on the four earrings and on the 'Master of Animals' pendant. The fine qualities of the workmanship perhaps suggest the hand of another goldsmith, although this does not preclude the pectoral from being a product of the same workshop as the other pieces.

The gold bead necklace can be compared with the lion ornament because they both have similar (but not identical) shaped and fabricated pendant seed-shaped beads suspended from chains with similar link wire. The embossed gold beads on this necklace are made from soldered, moulded sheet halves in the same way as those of the green jasper bead necklace, but this is common in gold beads from antiquity over a wide area and over a long time period. Similarly, the two palm-leaf gold necklaces compare well with each other, having beads of similar form and manufacture, but of slightly different design and size. However, it is again difficult to assign any particular feature as being specifically characteristic for comparison with the other pieces. Certainly the individual gold beads are each made from two halves of sheet embossed into a single mould (one for each bead type) and soldered together, but again this method of manufacture is common to many ancient gold beads.

The fifty-four embossed gold plaques are all essentially identical, having been pressed into a single mould, with chased and punched decoration added. Apart from the use of a single mould (which is not unique to this treasure), there is again no particular characteristic that can positively link these simple discs to the other pieces of the treasure. The gold cup also has no special characteristics to associate it specifically with the other treasure pieces – apart from its interconnecting spiral design decoration, which is also seen on the fifty-four gold plaques and on one gold diadem (as punched dots).

There is a strong link between the carnelian and amethyst necklace and the large earrings, not only because of the similar quality and colour of the carnelian beads, but specifically because the two carved cylindrical beads that appear on one pair of earrings are undoubtedly from the same batch as the three on the necklace, and made by one lapidary. This makes a conclusive association of these jewellery items with a single workshop dealing with both gold and gemstones. The chances of finding such similar beads in non-associated jewellery are remote. A misaligned, abandoned hollow drill hole in one carnelian bead in the necklace is similar to one on the green jasper necklace and also to one on a carnelian bead in the mixed-bead necklace, which may suggest origins in a single workshop. However, the hollow drill technology is not unique to the treasure, so this link might be regarded as tenuous.

The mixed-bead necklace with carnelian, lapis lazuli and gold beads all of the same unusual hand and breast design of matching size must surely have been made together in one workshop (Fig. 79). Clearly this was a jewellery workshop working on a range of materials, and this is an important fact for the consideration of links between different pieces of the treasure. For example, the four lapis lazuli finger rings have no obvious technological features in common with the other pieces, apart from basic goldworking, but the existence of a workshop making other composite jewellery including lapis lazuli adds strongly to the possibility that the rings could have been made in the same workshop as other pieces. These rings are each of different, distinctive design and construction so it is difficult to say whether or not they are associated with each other. However, three have in common the use of cut blocks of lapis lazuli inlaid into cloisons and burnished into place. The fourth ring (692, fluted) is the most different, with the lapis lazuli cut and inlaid into a three-dimensional curved shape, rather than used in flat blocks. Thus, the use of lapis lazuli in a multidisciplinary workshop, as shown by the mixed bead necklace, could arguably be the one link between these rings and the majority of the jewellery of the treasure. The fifth ring of sheet gold is completely different from the other rings, but it has chased toolmarks, perhaps similar to some other items of jewellery.

The gold cup is only of simple raised sheet construction, and there are no diagnostic features that can be used to link it to the other pieces of treasure, though of course this does not necessarily mean it is not linked. The interconnecting spiral design is also seen on one diadem (as punched dots) and on the fifty-four gold discs, though this stylistic link is fairly tenuous.

The rock crystal bead does not appear to have any obvious relationship to any of the pieces of jewellery in the treasure, though it seems to be from a piece of jewellery that is missing. The drill holes are of the same form as those of the other beads, but this was common technology.

Conclusions

The Aigina Treasure jewellery all appears to be ancient. There are a few minor repairs of which some are ancient and others modern, but with only a little restoration. The main damage appears to be the loss of three chain pendants from earrings and a part-missing gold disc on one. Stress corrosion cracking is a problem suffered, in particular, by the gold discs and their integral suspension wires on the earrings and 'Master of Animals' pendant, and it is these that have most repairs. One lapis lazuli ring has restoration. The body material of the lion ornament is missing. Three small components have come from other larger pieces of jewellery that are now missing from the treasure, and two have characteristics similar to other pieces, suggesting they were part of the original group.

The technological results show that there are significant similarities of workmanship between certain major objects that allow us to conclude that real associations of manufacture exist, and these are sufficient to suggest the products of an individual workshop. By comparison, analysis has shown variable composition between pieces and even components on composite objects, but this is essentially a reflection of the variable composition of unrefined natural (alluvial) gold. There are instances where components have a very closely similar composition, indicating a batch from a single crucible melt. However, in general, comparing the composition of different pieces is not particularly informative. This is commonly the case with early jewellery of unrefined gold.

The four large earrings are, not surprisingly, manufactured as a group in a single workshop. They have many features of essentially identical workmanship in common between them. They also form two distinct pairs by way of clear differences in workmanship. It is reasonable to assume that this is evidence for the hands of two goldsmiths within one workshop. The most important object with which these earrings have direct manufacturing similarities is the 'Master of Animals' pendant. Although there are no carnelian beads on this for comparison, the sheet goldworking characteristics, the soldering and suspended discs (albeit with punched dot decoration) are all very similar. The next group of objects that appear to have common technological links with the earrings in particular are the lion ornament by way of the suspended chains and birds, the chain pendant and the pair of owls. The gold bead necklace also has features that can be compared with the lion ornament.

The pectoral with profile heads is more difficult to assign directly to the above groups. This is mainly because of the apparent higher-quality workmanship and strength of the well-soldered back and front sheets and the soldered suspension loops, although the plain suspended gold discs are similar in overall form to those of the earrings and to the 'Master of Animals' pendant.

The two palm-leaf gold necklaces compare well with each other, but they are of common goldsmithing technology, so it is difficult to assign any particular feature as being specifically characteristic for comparison with the other pieces. The same applies to the fifty-four embossed gold discs. However, this does not necessarily mean they are not linked.

There is a strong link between the carnelian and amethyst necklace and the large earrings, not only because of the similar high quality and colour of carnelians beads, but specifically the two carved cylindrical beads that appear on one pair of earrings are no doubt from the same batch as the three on the necklace and made by one lapidary. The mixed-bead necklace with carnelian, lapis lazuli and gold beads all of the same design and size must have been made together in one workshop. Clearly this was a jewellery workshop working on a range of materials, which forms another strong link between different pieces of the treasure, and therefore this mixed-bead necklace could have been made in the same workshop as other pieces.

The four lapis lazuli finger rings have no obvious technological features in common with other pieces of the treasure, apart from basic goldworking, but the existence of a workshop making other composite jewellery including lapis lazuli adds credibility that the rings could have been made in the same workshop as other pieces.

In summary, there is strong technological evidence that the main Aigina Treasure pieces with essentially identical technologies are from an original single hoard, and indeed a single workshop. These are the four earrings, the 'Master of Animals' pendant, the lion ornament, the chain pendant, the carnelian and amethyst necklace, and the two owl halves. The following are probably from the same workshop: the mixed-bead necklace, the gold and green jasper necklace, and the gold bead necklace. The following are possibly from the same workshop: the pectoral with heads, the lapis lazuli rings, the fifty-four gold plaques, and the palm-leaf necklaces. Those with less definable manufacturing links or few comparable features could arguably be either from the same hoard or not: the gold cup, the quartz bead and the simple gold items not examined (diadems, gold wire rings and bracelet). Certainly there are missing pieces of jewellery, indicated by the few fragmentary items, so the treasure is incomplete.

Overall, the technological examination of the Aigina Treasure shows that there is strong evidence that some of the main pieces are directly related technologically by characteristic features of workmanship that would appear to be more than a coincidence, and there is a strong possibility that these were made in a single jewellery workshop, producing composite material items of gold and various gemstones. There is evidence for the workmanship of at least two goldsmiths – possibly three if the pectoral with heads is included. This piece is perhaps the most competently made and finished piece of goldwork and this does set it apart from the other major pieces of the Aigina Treasure, although it is not necessarily from an unrelated workshop or period. The earrings are the most complex pieces in the Aigina Treasure, and perhaps best symbolize the unity of the group in techniques and materials. Attractive as the earrings are, they could not have been worn easily because there are no fixing points and the chains would hang in an untidy clutter. This suggests they were not used, but probably made as burial gifts.

There can be little doubt that the majority of the pieces in the treasure should indeed be viewed as a group, unified by raw materials and by technique of manufacture. The paper by Williams in this volume outlines what can now be said about the treasure's discovery and strengthens the possibility that it was found in a Middle Helladic tomb. The archaeology of the island increasingly shows how important the Kolonna site was in this period, and how rich some of the inhabitants were, as is demonstrated in the essays in this volume by Felten (pp. 32–5) and Hiller (pp. 36–9). The results of this technical study can be interpreted as supporting the possibility that the treasure was at least mostly made in a workshop on Aigina, and some of the parallels adduced for the treasure would indicate the possibility of a Middle Helladic date (see the essays in this volume by Fitton, pp. 61–5, and by Markowitz and Lacovara, pp. 59–60). While uncertainties remain, the technical study has certainly advanced our understanding of the Aigina Treasure.

Table 1
Aigina Treasure analyses
Results are given as combined composition ranges of the components for the composite pieces of jewellery

	Cat. no.	Au%	Ag%	Cu%
Earrings (carved bead type)				
all components (main sheet/dog/monkey/wire/owls/disc)	763	86–88	11–13	0.8–1.6
all components (main sheet/dog/monkey/wire/owls/disc)	765	87–92	7–13	1–2
Earrings (round bead type)	764 and 766			
main sheet/dog/monkey/wire/owls/disc		71–77	22–26	1–2
owl wires		84–87	12–15	0.6
'Master of Animals' pendant	762			
discs		67–78	21–32	0.7–1.2
sheet		71–74	25–27	1–1.5
Egyptian-style pendant	761			
discs		83.4	15.8	0.8
sheet		91	7	2
Lion ornament	746			
all components		78.8	18–21	0.8–2.0
Chain pendant	752			
owls		64–66	32–34	1.4–1.8
owl wire		87	12	1
bead wire		55	44	1
Acorn, jasper, necklace	754A			
gold beads, cups, wire		58–65	33–38	1.2–4.8
Mixed-bead necklace	756A			
2 gold beads		87–88	12–13	0.3
2 gold beads		79–81	18–20	0.7
Gold plaques (5 of 54)	692–745			
all plaques		85.0	14.5	0.5
Lapis lazuli rings				
cross-hatch gold ring	888	62.5	35.8	1.7
lapis lazuli shield ring	690	81.0	18.7	0.3
lapis lazuli meander ring	693	82.6	15.2	2.2
lapis lazuli fluted ring	692	86.7	12.5	0.8
lapis lazuli reef-knot ring	691	88.7	10.0	1.3
Gold cup	768	80.5	18.4	1.1
Gold bracelet	767	71.1	27.5	1.4

Platinum Group Element (PGE) inclusions in several gold objects

	Cat. no.	Os%	Ir%	Ru%	Pt%	Au%	Fe%
Earring	764						
inclusion in disc 1		27.8	65.0	5.5	–	1.0	0.7
inclusion in disc 2		42.7	37.1	18.1	1.9	–	0.2
Shield ring, inclusion	690	34.1	63.3	0.7	1.3	–	0.6
Gold band, inclusion		31.4	63.0	0.9	3.2	1.0	0.5
Gold hoop	751						
inclusion 1		32.8	21.9	44.8	–	–	0.5
inclusion 2		61.2	21.8	12.5	4.2	–	0.3
inclusion 3		43.1	40.1	16.2	–	–	0.6
inclusion 4		35.5	62.2	–	2.1	–	0.2

These hard small silver/grey coloured inclusions are common to early unrefined alluvial gold (Ogden 1977). The compositions of those found in the Aigina goldwork varied widely in the three principal elements osmium, iridium, ruthenium, and again this is common to such inclusions (Meeks and Tite 1980)

(EDX analysis Precision, ± 0.3% relative for major elements; Accuracy ± 0.5% absolute. Minimum detection limits 0.15% Cu, 0.3% Ag and Au. No other significant elements were detected in the goldwork.)

4
Aigina–Kolonna in the Early and Middle Bronze Age

Florens Felten

As a rule the importance of a city or region in prehistoric Greece – especially in the Late Bronze Age – can be estimated by the wealth of mythical–historical tradition connected with it in later literary sources. So it comes as no surprise at all when places such as Mycenae 'rich in gold', Tiryns, Pylos, Athens and Thebes are the source of rich and precious finds.

Similar finds at places that cannot boast of such rich literary traditions – and Aigina is an example – by contrast provoke astonishment and occasionally even suspicion. I think that discussion of the Aigina Treasure might have taken a less tortuous path had it been found in a place better documented in literature.[1]

In fact Aigina is comparatively poor with regard to mythical–historical associations. In the *Iliad*, for example, Aigina is mentioned only peripherally. However, the little we learn there and in later sources demonstrates one fact quite clearly. Although there are essentially only three names that are connected with the mythical early history of the island – Aiakos, Telamon and Peleus – these three names carry considerable weight. Aiakos, the first king of Aigina, is a son of Zeus. In a period of disastrous drought it is to him that the Greeks come to ask for help. Moreover, together with Apollo and Poseidon, he erects the walls of Troy. His sons Telamon and Peleus, Aiginetans at least by birth, are the fathers of the greatest Greek heroes at Troy, Ajax and Achilles, and in the first Trojan war it is Telamon who, together with Herakles, takes the town.[2]

The importance of these figures in itself cautions us against underestimating the early history of Aigina because of the overall scantiness of literary tradition. But they perhaps also allow another conclusion. They all refer to a period before the second Trojan war; could it be that they constitute a reminiscence of an older tradition, which goes further back and is based on the importance of the island in the preceding periods? At all events, a pre-eminent position for the island is certainly attested by the archaeological finds unearthed there in excavations that have continued – though with major interruptions – from the 1920s to the present day.

A promontory on the western side of the island, protruding nearly 200 metres into the sea and rising about twelve metres above sea level, ends in a headland protected on three sides by steep cliffs. This headland, in historical times the site of the acropolis of Aigina with the temple of Apollo as its main monument, saw the evolution of the most important settlement of the island by, at the latest, the fourth millennium BC (Fig. 116).[3] Indeed, it was the most important settlement not only of the island but also apparently of a much more extensive region. This anticipates the state of affairs emphasized by J. Rutter when he says, 'Aigina–Kolonna has emerged as a Middle Helladic site without peer in the Greek Mainland'.[4] Now we may add that the same, or nearly the same, is true for the preceding Early Bronze Age.

The first clearly recognizable settlement (which does not necessarily represent the beginning of habitation on the headland) belongs to the final phase of the Late Neolithic Period (Aigina–Attica–Kephala culture), as is attested by characteristic pattern-burnished bowls and red-burnished biconical jugs with collar necks (Fig. 118). This phase increasingly proves to be a transitional phase to the Early Bronze Age. Already Aigina can boast of an extended and at least partially stone-built permanent settlement.[5] A number of remains of walls, built in a very distinctive manner with a single row of stones (Figs 117, 119, 120),[6] attest to the existence of both rectangular and curvilinear houses, which covered, in fairly close density, an area corresponding roughly to the later Early and Middle Helladic settlements. In spite of the general increase in known sites with finds of this period in southern Greece, solidly built permanent settlements are quite a rarity. So, on the basis of the archaeological data available, some scholars have developed a picture of a society changing from an economy dominated by agriculture to a system of transhumant pastoralism, and also connected to a wide interactive market or a trade/exchange network.[7]

In the case of a small island like Aigina, we surely can exclude a system of transhumant pastoralism, but the Aiginetans may have played a role in the second postulated economic factor.

A number of more or less naturalistic human clay idols, predominantly male, belong to this settlement (Fig. 123).[8] Conical caps repeatedly appear as male headgear. If we are right to interpret these as helmets, we may catch a glimpse of the Aiginetan way of life. The inhabitants of the headland settlement seem to be characterized as warriors, implying a seafaring occupation. In all probability this means sea trade, possibly connected with piracy. Perhaps we see here the starting point of a tradition which is documented again much later by quite singular Middle Bronze Age representations of seafaring Aiginetans.[9]

The most characteristic feature of the following Early Helladic settlement, whose beginnings are still rather obscure, is the occurrence of the monumental corridor houses, which were situated – in a chronological succession – at the southern edge of the settlement area (the so-called 'Haus am Felsrand' and 'Weisses Haus' ('White House')).[10] With regard to their ground plans, elevations and huge dimensions (c. 160 m^2), these correspond to the monumental buildings of this type in Lerna, Akovitika and Thebes.[11] However, just as in those cases the urban setting of these buildings on Aigina was difficult to elucidate. It seemed that in the eastern sector of the EH settlement area of Aigina–Kolonna there were only two buildings contemporary with the 'White House', both much smaller and simpler, with only one storey, and at some distance away. This gave the impression of an architectural hierarchy, in which the 'White House' – isolated and of exceptional dimensions – played a dominant role.

Inevitably this impression gave rise to some speculation about a similarly elevated function.[12] But after the excavations of the last few years the picture has changed somewhat. Quite a number of EH II wall remains have been uncovered north and north-west of the 'White House', notable among them the antae-adorned front wall and the western door-post of the main entrance door of the so-called 'Färberhaus' at the northern edge of the Kolonna hill under the later 'House 22' (Figs 117, 119).

These new discoveries change the picture in two important ways. First, we get the impression of a much greater density of buildings than previously thought. Secondly, we can now calculate quite accurately the width of the 'Färberhaus' as at least eleven metres. If we reconstruct its length according to the proportions of the 'White House', we get a ground plan of nearly 250 m^2, and that is considerably bigger than the 'White House'.

Even if this building was not two-storeyed, it can hardly be called secondary in importance in comparison to the 'White House', which thus loses much of its singularity and therefore its hierarchical aspects. Moreover, in the excavation of summer 2000 in the area north-west of the 'White House' (area of 'House 19'), we came upon the remains of an EH II building, which again has walls of a thickness (c. 80 cm) that suggests a second storey (Figs 117, 119, 127). So the general impression changes from that of a clearly stratified social hierarchy to that of an accumulation of more or less homogeneous self-sufficient units. Further excavations will surely shed more light on this question, which remains open.

A new chapter in settlement history and a break with older patterns certainly begins in the EH III period. After the abandonment of the large EH II houses and a still rather obscure intermediate period, we see a totally new start in town planning and building with Aigina V.[13] Evidently on the basis of a general masterplan, a new city with fortification walls was erected. The main feature of the newly created settlement pattern is the fact that we have to deal now not with separate houses, loosely dispersed over the headland, but quite evidently with houses joined together in 'insulae' and enclosed by a city wall strengthened with towers (Fig. 116).

It seems quite clear that a general masterplan of this kind, and the extensive common building activity necessary to realize this quite ambitious programme, demanded some sort of centrally organized administration. It seems that we are here on the verge of a development that brought the emergence of the 'first Aegean "state" outside of Crete', as W.-D. Niemeier called it,[14] at a time when most other Bronze Age settlements went through a phase of serious decline.

But even Aigina did not remain untouched by the disturbances that affected so many of the other roughly contemporary settlements. Aigina V was destroyed by an extensive conflagration, seemingly inflicted by a hostile invasion.[15] At any rate, the future history of Aigina–Kolonna is marked by permanent efforts to reinforce the fortification walls as heavily as possible. Settlement VI, still dating to the EH III period, shows these efforts quite clearly (Fig. 116). The main rebuilding activities after the conflagration concentrated on the partial reinforcement of the old fortification wall, which had basically survived, and the erection of an additional fortification behind the old one, which used the front row of the insulae houses as a kind of skeleton for a new massive city wall with solid rectangular towers on both sides of the city gates.[16] We are not altogether sure about the extent of the rebuilding activities in the burnt houses of the inner town. It seems, though, that a number of curved walls, found in recent years in the area west of the archaic temple[17] where Gabriel Welter had excavated before the Second World War, belong to this phase (Figs 117, 119). The picture still remains rather hazy, but it does not seem probable that they represent isolated apsidal houses such as those known from Lerna IV, but rather irregularly curved house combinations as seen, for example, at Poliochni, Thermi and Kastri.[18]

The sense of imminent danger, which is so obviously demonstrated by the erection of the massive fortification walls of Aigina VI, must have remained acute in the times of the early MH Towns VII and VIII (Fig. 116).[19] The unease of the inhabitants is certainly shown by the twice-repeated reinforcement of the intact fortification walls of Town VI: in the end they reached a thickness of about eight metres. It is even more apparent in their efforts to protect the city gates. In an increasingly sophisticated manner the former straight, frontal gateways became more and more elongated, turning into narrow and curved corridors which clearly were much easier to defend. Evidently the need for protection was the main concern of these times, but the building activities also extended to a new urban concept. It is at this period that the regular system of straight, narrow streets running east–west and flanked by long rows of houses with common separation walls was introduced,[20] and this can still clearly be seen today (Figs 117, 119, 121). In spite of the obviously dangerous circumstances, the settlement of Aigina–Kolonna was certainly flourishing. This is attested by increasing imports from different production centres – mainly Crete and the Cyclades – and growing exports of Aiginetan vessels to many find-places outside Aigina.[21]

The most significant feature, however, which must have been the result of a flourishing economy, is the fact that at the end of MH I the number of inhabitants had grown so much that the old area of the settlement was no longer sufficient. So, in the time of Town IX, new rows of rectangular houses were built in the area east of the fortification walls (Fig. 116). These were used at least partially as workshops: a potter's kiln was found in one of the houses.[22]

Although this first extension of the town was fortified again, the old city wall apparently still played a major role in the general fortification system. On top of the old city wall of Aigina V, which was still in use up to the period of Aigina VIII as a kind of fore-wall, the Aiginetans erected a new strong rampart with a slanting surface.[23] This emphasizes the separation of the old town from the new part, and the reason for it becomes especially clear in the southern gateway.[24] In an extensive levelling operation the lower, southern part of the old town was filled in with a substantial layer of earth. This meant that at this point the level of the settlement, together with the southern gateway, was raised up more than 1.5 metres. In this way a kind of upper and lower town came into being – an innovation that obviously originated above all for defensive purposes.

Once again the realization of such a fundamental change in a basically functioning fortification system and settlement pattern seems to demand a central authority. And indeed the existence of a local elite is proved by the so-called 'shaft grave' which was built in this phase immediately to the east, in front of the city wall of the lower town (Fig. 122).[25] This burial has remarkable features. It was in a stone-built and tumulus-covered tomb, in direct contact with the settlement, in an area that was not otherwise used as a necropolis. The grave gifts clearly show both wealth and power, and also demonstrate the existence of inter-Aegean relations: there are Aiginetan, Cretan and Cycladic vessels in the grave. It must have belonged to a member of a generally accepted leading elite. And the acceptance of this elite apparently remained intact for some time, because in a later stage of Town IX this grave, which certainly seriously reduced the effectiveness of the fortification wall, was partially rebuilt and surrounded by a massive bastion. This strengthened further the wall of the lower town.[26]

It seems only reasonable to look for traces of this leading elite in the urban context too, and indeed there is a structure which was first mentioned in this connection by H.J. Weisshaar.[27] In a central position in the upper town is a building with a ground plan that differs from the usual house ground plans in many ways (Figs 117, 119). Obviously a number of originally separate houses were united to form a monumental structure. This was achieved partly by circumwalling the older outer walls with a new wall – thus creating the double thickness which in all probability indicates a second storey – and partly by erecting new walls on foundations of big, roughly hewn blocks of a kind unknown in the context of the usual houses.[28]

The most astonishing feature of this new building, however, is that by uniting pre-existing houses it blocks the course of the important west–east road which led to the northern gate. It seems impossible to explain this fundamental alteration of the existing city plan simply as the private initiative of a nouveau-riche inhabitant. Rather it is tempting to see in this building the residence of the local leader, who then was buried in the above-mentioned grave.[29] That they are at least roughly contemporary is shown by the vessels found in the grave and the pottery from the monumental building (Fig. 124), which Welter by chance had left partially unexcavated.[30]

For the following period – the end of the Middle Bronze Age and the beginning of the Mycenaean era – the evidence becomes scantier. This is not, however, because of a decrease in the importance of the settlement; rather it is a consequence of the extensive levelling operations of archaic and later times. Indeed, at the end of the MH period we again see an extension of the settlement area to the east (Fig. 116), and, connected with it, the erection of a new massive fortification wall, of which substantial remains survived on the north-eastern edge of the hill, behind the archaic temenos wall (Fig. 126).[31] Simultaneously with this new stronghold at least the northern part of the upper town fortification, which lay outside the lower town wall, was reinforced again: a new slanting rampart was erected in front of the older one.[32] We have no reason to assume a period of decline or a basic change in the life of the settlement, even if the above-mentioned monumental building seems to have been in some way rebuilt in this phase.[33] But we know nothing about its successor and only very little about the general structure of the settlement. Nevertheless its date seems quite clear: the evidence of the pottery connected with the second town extension – for example bichrome Aigina bowls and red- or brown-slipped goblets (Fig. 125) – demonstrates its place at the end of the MH III period and the beginning of the Shaft Grave period.[34]

With regard to the history of the following Late Helladic settlement, we depend almost exclusively on unstratified sherds from Kolonna and the old finds from the nearby necropolis on Windmill Hill,[35] which may also have supplied the famous Aigina Treasure (but see the essay by D. Williams in this volume, pp. 11–16). Although they testify to an unbroken continuation of life on the Kolonna hill for some centuries, the scantiness of architectural remains still prevents us from drawing a more detailed picture of the development of the settlement in the second half of the second millennium BC. It is therefore preferable to stop here and to return to a question which in the course of this summary of Aiginetan prehistory has had to be asked repeatedly: what can be said about the character and the social structure of the community that lived on the headland of Aigina–Kolonna? Until recently tangible evidence could only be gained from the 'shaft grave' and perhaps the monumental building of Town IX, but the excavation of summer 2000 brought new evidence which seems relevant to this question and is in some way connected with the theme of this volume. It deserves a preliminary presentation in this context in spite of the fact that it still needs restoration and detailed study.

In the area of 'House 19' in the inner town (Figs 117, 119, 127), we came upon a building in which the former excavations of Welter had reached only the MH strata and left the earlier layers untouched. At this point, on a floor of a deeper-lying house, we recovered a quite remarkable assemblage of vessels of clearly EH III date (Fig. 128) – remarkable not only because of the number of vessels in a fairly limited area, but above all because of the character of the pottery assemblage. In contrast with the finds from EH III houses previously excavated, the usually numerous dark polished bowls, tankards and cups were here restricted to very few pieces, while the majority of vessels had dark-on-light pattern decoration (Fig. 129), which otherwise occurs only occasionally. Some of the pieces are evidently of Aiginetan manufacture, while a dark-on-light patterned duck vase and a splendid red-slipped and polished jug with neck handle and trumpet mouth (Fig. 130) are at least inspired by Cycladic or eastern Aegean prototypes.[36] A collection of this kind of fine-patterned and red-polished local and foreign-looking ware is quite a novelty for EH III Aigina. It invites speculation about the function of the building, which is situated very centrally in the EH III settlement area. And speculation is intensified by a discovery made in the area immediately west of this house, in connection with the stratum of a still deeper floor. This bore clear traces of severe burning and, on the evidence of the associated pottery, can be dated to an earlier EH III phase. Here we came upon a new 'Aigina Treasure' (Figs 131, 132).[37]

It consists, as far as it is possible to say at present, of four unusually long, deliberately bent golden pins with loop terminals (Fig. 133); three similar golden pins and one golden bracelet with oval heads;[38] a silver bracelet, perhaps a spiral or separate bangles;[39] and an uncertain number of necklaces. The necklaces include golden ring-shaped disc beads, silver disc beads, silver double-axe-shaped beads and variously shaped beads (barrel-shaped, tubular, biconical, polygonal) of gold, silver, rock crystal and carnelian. Among these is a bead with etched circular decoration (Fig. 132).[40] A great number of small faience beads possibly belong to another necklace. On the front and on the back the tangle of jewellery is covered by golden disc pendants, one with embossed decoration, the other with a soldered wire decoration of a double volute (Fig. 134).[41] Beneath the embossed disc pendant there can be seen the edges of one further golden disc pendant and several silver examples.

A thorough study of the jewellery will have to wait for the restoration of the ensemble, but even now it seems clear enough that the new hoard, which in all probability was hidden before the big conflagration of Town V, is a mixed deposit, whose single items show affinities to types of rather different provenances. It documents the existence of a leading local elite with far-reaching connections in the Aegean area already in the EH III period. Furthermore, find complexes such as the London Aigina Treasure and the contents of the MH 'shaft grave' must now be seen as part of a long local tradition.

Notes

1. cf. Higgins 1979, 12 ff., 45 ff.
2. Sources for Aiginetan mythology: Welter 1962, 1 ff., 88 ff., Zunker 1988, passim.
3. Walter and Felten 1981, 10 ff.
4. Rutter 1993, 780.
5. Walter and Felten 1981, 10 ff.; Weisshaar 1994, 675–89; Alram-Stern 1996, 157–9, 219–20; Maran 2000, 179 ff.
6. Felten and Hiller 1996, Beibl. 65 f., figs 23, 24.
7. Douzougli 1998, 145 ff.; Alram-Stern 1999, 7 f. with lit.
8. Felten and Hiller 1996, 77 (pl. 1) fig. 2; 89 (pl. 7) fig. 3; 91 (pl. 8) fig. 1.
9. Rutter 1993, 778, fig. 13; 779, fig. 14.
10. Walter and Felten 1981, 12 ff.
11. Themelis 1984, 335 ff.; Aravantinos 1986, 57 ff.; Shaw 1987, 59 ff.; Shaw 1990, 183 ff.; Wiencke 1989, 495 ff.; Cosmopoulos 1991, 23 ff.
12. Recently with lit; Maran 1998, 193 ff.
13. Walter and Felten 1981, 28 ff.; Konsola 1986, 16; Forsen 1992, 114 ff.; Maran 1998, 209.
14. Niemeier 1995, 73 ff.
15. Walter and Felten 1981, 41.
16. Walter and Felten 1981, 43 ff.
17. Walter and Felten 1981, 35 ff. and 47, fig. 12.
18. Lerna: Caskey 1966, 144 ff.; Forsen 1992, 31 ff.; E.C. Banks in Rutter 1995, 3 ff.; Poliochni, Thermi, Kastri: Sinos 1971, pl. 28 ff., fig. 69 ff. and pl. 37, fig. 90; Renfrew 1972, 128 ff.; Kouka 1997, 469 ff.; Bossert 1967, 53 ff.
19. Walter and Felten 1981, 50 ff.
20. Walter and Weisshaar 1993, 293 ff.; Felten and Hiller 1996, 30 f., 50 f.
21. Hiller 1993, 197 ff.; Reinholdt 1992, 57 ff.; cf. Rutter 1993, 125 ff., fig. 12; Kilian-Dirlmeier 1997, 123 ff.
22. Walter 1983, 124, 133 ff.; Walter and Weisshaar 1993, 293 ff.
23. Walter and Felten 1981, 75 ff.
24. Walter and Felten 1981, 72 ff.
25. Kilian-Dirlmeier 1997, 67 ff.
26. Kilian-Dirlmeier 1997, 71 f.
27. Walter and Weisshaar 1993, 297.
28. Felten and Hiller 1996, 40 ff., fig. 10.
29. cf. Niemeier 1995, 78; Kilian-Dirlmeier 1997, 111.
30. cf. Kilian-Dirlmeier 1997, 57 no. 10; 58, fig. 27; 64, fig. 32; and Felten and Hiller 1996, 79 (pl. 2) fig. 3.
31. Walter 1983, 139; Walter and Weisshaar 1993, 293 ff; Wohlmayr 1989, 151 ff.
32. Walter and Felten 1981, 83.
33. Felten and Hiller 1996, 40 ff., fig. 9.
34. Wohlmayr 2000, 135 ff.
35. Hiller 1975, 9 ff.
36. Jugs with trumpet mouth: Milojcic 1961, 46, pls 13, 1–2; 19, 1–3; 27, 4; 39, 6; 42, 15–16; 43, 14; 47, 13; cf. red-polished and dark-on-light patterned ware from Kalymnos, Benzi 1997, 384 ff., pl. 1f., pl. 4a.
37. The excavation of the treasure was supervised by S. Hiller. It will be published in detail by C. Reinholdt, to whom I owe valuable information with regard to the preliminary presentation. For preliminary reports, see Reinholdt 2004, 113–19, and Reinholdt 2003, 260 f.
38. For chronology and distribution of the 'Rollenkopfnadel', cf. Branigan 1974, 178 f.; Kilian-Dirlmeier 1984, 25 f.; Seeher 2000, 60; pins and bangles with oval heads, cf. Lamb 1936, 166, pl. 25, 30.33; Blegen 1950, 42, 119, fig. 215, 37.735.
39. Silver bangles or spiral bracelets, cf. Tolstikov 1996, 180, nos 236, 238 from 'treasure N'; cf. Branigan 1974, pl. 33.
40. Ring-shaped disc beads and disc-shaped beads, cf. Reinholdt 1993a, figs 4–6 from the 'Thyreatis-hoard' in Berlin with parallels; double-axe-shaped beads, Branigan 1974, pl. 19, nos 2296–9; carnelian beads, cf. Tolstikov 1996, 172, from 'treasure L'; Siebenmorgen 2000, 291, nos 221, 222; natrium carbonate etching of carnelian beads is a specific decoration technique in Mesopotamia and the western Indus Valley, cf. Woolley 1934, 366 f., pl. 129, 134–5, 220c.
41. Disc pendants as part of late Neolithic jewellery tradition come from the Balkan area, from northern Greece and from western Anatolia; cf. Demakopoulou 1998; Rudolph 1995, 26 f., 30 f., 40. The post-Neolithic disc pendants with embossed decoration in Greece belong to an MH/MS I context; cf. Reinholdt 1993a, 36, fig. 41a–c.

5
Ornaments from the warrior grave and the Aigina Treasure

Stefan Hiller

To compare pieces of jewellery from the Aigina Treasure, now in the British Museum, with the objects from the Aigina warrior grave discovered in 1981 cannot be claimed to be a very original procedure. It came to Reynold Higgins's mind immediately when the discovery of a stone-built grave on Aigina, together with its contents, had come to his attention through a preliminary report which appeared in the *Athens Annals of Archaeology* in 1981.[1] This grave contained the burial of a warrior equipped with a set of weapons. At Reynold Higgins's request I sent him a picture of the gold band from this tomb (Fig. 135) – as, some time before, I had sent him a picture of Aiginetan pottery sherds painted in the Kamares style which he requested for inclusion in his book on the Aigina Treasure.[2]

Before entering into the comparison of the two find groups to be discussed here, I may give some brief remarks regarding the Aigina Treasure as judged from my perspective:

(a) I am convinced that it was found on Aigina, and that it represents a Late Bronze Age tomb robber's cache. To the list of late nineteenth- and early twentieth-century witnesses quoted by Higgins[3] may be added Christos Tsountas, who explicitly declared: 'There is no doubt that objects of gold – probably a part of this treasure – were found in a tomb there' (that is, on Aigina).[4]

(b) I am inclined to believe that the treasure may not be homogeneous with regard to the date of its individual pieces. In my view, for instance, the gold cup, which is usually compared to Late Bronze Age I specimens from Knossos and Mycenae, is likely to belong to the period contemporary with MM II pottery and with the Tod Treasure. This was also envisaged as a possibility by Sinclair Hood.[5] This chronological diversity does not, however, necessarily imply diversity in the treasure's final topographical provenance (by which I mean the find-place rather than the place of manufacture). I shall come back to this aspect below.

(c) Leaving aside some features which are unparalleled and therefore difficult to place in terms of cultural affinities, the treasure exhibits an obvious Minoan(izing) background in its typology and iconography, while at the same time including clear Egyptian influence. The latter is a well-known feature of Minoan jewellery. Along with other Egyptian elements in several pieces of the treasure, the appearance of figural beads may also, in my opinion, reflect Egyptian inspiration.[6]

Apart from various observations regarding the Aigina Treasure's Egyptian features, three minor and, perhaps, so far unrecorded instances testifying to the deep impact of Egyptian goldwork on Minoan jewellery may be mentioned here:

(a) The first is a pendant in the shape of a fish from Knossos (Fig. 136);[7] this is a rather unusual motif in terms of Minoan jewellery while it is frequently attested in Egypt (cf. Fig. 137).[8]
(b) An Egyptian 18th Dynasty necklace consisting of duck-shaped beads (Fig. 138)[9] is, by this very motif, comparable to the necklace worn by the goddess from Thera/Akrotiri, Xeste 3 (Fig. 139).[10]
(c) The small discs below the papyrus flowers on the hair-pin from Mycenae, Shaft Grave III (Fig. 140),[11] are undoubtedly an Egyptian design (cf. Fig. 141).[12] Here P. Warren's conclusive remarks on this outstanding piece of jewellery from Mycenae may be recalled. It is 'very probably a Minoan work. It depicts the great goddess of Minoan religion with her papyrus–lily garland. S. Marinatos plausibly derived this representation from Egyptian symbolism, of which the verbal text would be, he argued, "numerous years of joyful life", here seen as the Minoan goddess bringing continued fertility to the natural world. The Egyptian background of the *waz* or papyrus stalk in relation to the Minoan "sacral ivy" motif had already been set out by Evans.'[13]

The fact that, at least until the end of the Shaft Grave period, Egyptian influences and/or imports reached mainland Greece exclusively via Crete is more or less generally accepted. Thus the question of how we have to judge the phenomenon of Minoan elements on Aigina remains, in particular in connection with the Aigina Treasure. The suggestion that these Minoan(izing) elements are also symptomatic of the much wider process of the advancing cultural Minoanization of the Aegean during the Middle Bronze Age will hardly be questioned. More controversial, however, will be the issue of Minoan residents dwelling on Aigina, to be faced here.

As I have briefly discussed in my paper 'Minoan and Minoanizing pottery from Aegina', presented at the Wace and Blegen conference at Athens in 1989, there is plausible evidence in favour of a Minoan colony on Aigina.[14] Besides a Minoan potter's wheel identified and discussed long ago by Gabriel Welter, we know of specific ritual elements testifying to Minoan residents on the island.[15] I was able to identify two Minoan stone *kernoi* (or gaming boards) and a Minoan ritual stone hammer from the Kolonna site.[16]

In sum, a small Minoan community colony (in accordance with K. Branigan's definition),[17] perhaps not bigger than an extended family, is indicated by these features as well as by the Minoan(izing) pottery found on Aigina. This I take to have been produced locally in order primarily to supply the requirements of Minoan residents on Aigina, but also to have been appreciated by the island's native inhabitants. This Minoan colony is likely to have had its own tomb(s) there. And, as is well attested on Minoan Crete, Minoan communal tombs could be used for many generations. Therefore robbing the contents of such a tomb will have resulted in an assemblage of jewellery exhibiting features of chronological diversity such as is met with in the Aigina Treasure. This explanation has also been proposed by Higgins.[18] Provided this is correct, the Aigina Treasure would testify to remarkable prosperity among the Minoan residents there, and at the same time would throw some light on their civic position within the powerful Bronze Age settlement on the Kolonna hill.

Passing now to the gold objects from the warrior grave, first its chronological position has to be briefly reconsidered. Here much depends on how we judge the two so far unrestored (and, perhaps, no longer restorable) matt-painted amphorae mentioned above.[19] Because of their relatively reduced decoration, consisting merely of simple circle ornaments painted on their shoulders, they are likely to be rather late within the Middle Helladic period; an MH III date is by no means excluded.[20] The MM II bridge-spouted jar, coming from the filling of the grave and perhaps from a supposed mound heaped up above it, will in this case represent an heirloom.

The ornaments made of gold sheet which were found in the tomb are as follows (Fig. 142):

(a) A head band (avoiding the expression 'diadem') mentioned above.
(b) A razor mounting in the shape of two animals.
(c) A hexagonal ornament.[21]
(d) The gold mounting of a sword. This comprises (1) the disc that covered the pommel; (2) the gold ring to cover the joint between the hilt and the pommel; (3) the nail that connected the pommel and the hilt; and finally (4) the mounting of the hilt. Of this, however, only very little was preserved from the point where it ended on the blade.[22]

Coming to the comparison of the ornaments from the warrior tomb with the Aigina Treasure, severe restrictions arise. Since the treasure does not include any weaponry and, vice versa, a warrior's equipment includes hardly any jewellery, there does not in fact remain much for direct comparison. As already mentioned, the main objects to be compared are the gold bands, which were discussed by Reynold Higgins. He, correctly in my opinion, took them as evidence supporting the local origin of the Aigina Treasure. It must, however, be conceded that gold bands, as well as dot ornamentation in the repoussé technique, are a widespread phenomenon occurring in Bronze Age Greece, on Crete, and also in the Balkans.[23] Moreover, a minor difference arises from the fact that the ornamental patterns are not the same: whereas on the gold band from the treasure we see a curvilinear pattern in the form of an ivy chain, a frieze of diagonal crosses is encountered on the specimen from the warrior grave. As observed by Reynold Higgins, the ivy chain has Cretan parallels.[24]

As a matter of fact, though, there is no doubt that Crete was leading the development of weaponry production within the Bronze Age Aegean. As a consequence we have to regard production in Middle Minoan Crete as having been an essential factor in the rise of metal weapons on mainland Greece. Spectacular specimens with gold-mounted hilts are known from MM II deposits at Mallia.[25] The gold-mounted razor and the gold pommel disc of the sword from the Aigina warrior tomb must be attributed to the impact of Minoan Crete.

Looking for closer correspondences, however, we have to acknowledge that there are no further specific points of comparison. As I understand it, when considered from the stylistic point of view, there is nothing in the gold ornaments from the warrior grave that might be judged as being particularly Minoan as opposed to Helladic. The patterns on both the hexagonal ornament and the head band, which are the most striking ornamental features, show a strict geometric style, such as is characteristic of Middle Helladic matt-painted pottery. This observation is no less valid for the animal heads which adorn the shoulders of the razor blade. They are characterized both by the rigid stylization of their basic shape and by their strictly geometric ornamentation which consists of zig-zag bands running straight from the animals' muzzles to their necks.

With this rigorous stylization, the animal heads on the razor differ considerably from the much more naturalistically rendered lion head which is part of the composite pendant of the Aigina Treasure. This puzzling object has been supposed by Higgins to have been originally the head of a 'ceremonial axe-head, like the one from the Palace at Mallia, made about 1700 BC'. Closer relatives may be compared to the lion head of the pendant: the gold lions from Ahhotep's tomb[26] and Shaft Grave III at Mycenae.[27] The latter I regard as being of Minoan workmanship.[28] The nearest parallel to the animals on the razor might be represented by two animal heads of gold sheet which are placed in a comparable position on the shoulders of a sword from tomb Delta, Grave Circle B, at Mycenae; these also show a relatively strong degree of stylization.[29]

We must, however, be cautious when arguing from stylistic observations. Stylistic arguments are no less fluid than stylistic development is itself: protopalatial Minoan vase painting is a highly stylized artistic system. And what might an MM sculptural lion head have looked like? In any case gold beads representing double lion heads which belong to a 12th Dynasty Egyptian necklace from the tomb of Sithathoryunet[30] are hardly less stylized than the animal heads that adorn the Aiginetan razor.

Nevertheless, I think that, generally speaking, a characterization of the style of the gold ornaments from the warrior grave as falling within mainland stylistic categories is basically no less appropriate than it is to assign a prevailing Minoan stylistic character to the Aigina Treasure.

The above brief reconsideration of possible relations between the gold ornaments from the Aigina warrior grave and those from the Aigina Treasure thus points in two directions. First, with regard to the issue of the reputedly Aiginetan provenance of the material in the British Museum, this probability is strengthened rather than weakened by the existence of one common type of jewellery in both contexts. This is represented by the joint appearance of gold bands. These are, indeed, the only type of ornament to be expected, at this early phase, to be common to both a jewellery hoard and a Middle Bronze Age warrior's equipment. Other possible matches such as necklaces or finger rings appear only within mainland warrior tombs at a slightly later period than that represented by the Aigina warrior grave.[31]

The main result emerging from our comparison is that, when regarded from a stylistic point of view, the two find groups represent two different traditions of art. Accordingly two different workshops should be supposed, one of which is rooted within the Helladic sphere of style, the other within the Minoan. Both meet and overlap in the Aegean, and workshops belonging to either of them may have co-existed at sites such as Aigina. Just as two different traditions of pottery styles are attested on Aigina, one Minoan, the other Helladic, a parallel situation might also be supposed for jewellery production.

It has repeatedly been stated that a specific feature of the Aigina Treasure is a certain 'provincial' quality when it is compared with original Cretan gold ornaments. This observation might be summoned to support the argument for a local Aiginetan origin. This, though, may be too simplistic a view. As the MM II bridge-spouted jar from the warrior grave indicates, native Aiginetans may also have admired and acquired Minoan objects.

Finally, we might glance towards the recently discovered Early Bronze Age treasure.[32] I was in the happy position of being the first to catch sight of this when it was brought to light by our workman Antoni in the trench under my supervision on the rainy morning of 13 September 2000. After I had informed my colleagues about this unexpected, most exciting find, it passed very quickly from my to their hands.

As is easily recognized, and as I was aware immediately at this great moment, the treasure as a whole has clear affinities with Early Bronze Age jewellery such as is known particularly from the north-eastern Aegean. At the same time it reflects traditions rooted beyond this region and before this epoch as it includes specific elements that connect it with the Copper Age of the Balkan region and the Black Sea. Thus three different cultural zones are reflected by three different gold hoards discovered so far on Aigina: the Pontic–Balkan–Anatolian, the Minoan and the Helladic. Together they testify to this island's continued far-reaching external relations, on which its long-lasting prosperity was founded. This calls to mind Higgins's statement that the jewellery found on Aigina 'would suggest that this island was even more important in the period in question than is usually believed'.

Addendum

In summer 2000 we were given permission to rearrange the finds transferred for safety reasons in 1993 from the storeroom of the excavation house to the magazine in the Museum at Kolonna. In the course of this work I could reidentify the sherds belonging to the matt-painted amphorae from the warrior tomb (first documented by me in 1981), and also to mark the joins between them; they were, however, not restored during my participation in the Kolonna excavations (including summer 2003). Lately I have been informed that the two vessels were mended in 2004 and exhibited in a showcase dedicated to the finds from the warrior tomb on the occasion of opening new showrooms in the Kolonna Museum.

Notes

1. Walter 1981, 182–4; Higgins 1987, 182 Table 5a.
2. Higgins 1979, 53, fig. 54. At the time I was preparing the publication of this grave, as well as two further volumes on the pottery found at Aigina–Kolonna, covering the Minoan(izing) and Cycladic pottery respectively. I was not able to finish the publication of the grave, mainly because two big matt-painted Aiginetan amphorae which formed part of the group of offerings deposited together with the warrior had not been restored, despite my repeated requests. Moreover, after a break-in at the Museum in 1993 the finds were not accessible until spring 1998. I learned that I. Kilian-Dirlmeier was going to do the publication only when her book was advertised in the publisher's offering list (Kilian-Dirlmeier 1997). The two matt-painted amphorae just mentioned are conspicuously absent in her publication. Two sherds, *op. cit.*, 3, 77, fig. 42, might, on the basis of their decoration, belong to the vessels in question. If so they are wrongly described as coming from the filling of the tomb. To my still greater surprise I recognized that Kilian-Dirlmeier's book also included the Minoan(izing) and Cycladic pottery, the greater part of which I had previously identified and collected from the boxes with unstratified sherd material left from the pre-war excavations of G. Welter. Similarly Kilian-Dirlmeier made extensive use of the excellent drawings which C. Reinholdt had produced for the book under our common preparation, of which he was destined to be co-author because of his superb graphic work. In connection with a study on Aegean Bronze Age moulds on which he was then working, he was authorized to give a preliminary discussion of a spear head (of the so-called shaft-shoe type) from the grave (Reinholdt 1993b, 43 Abb. 12).
3. Higgins 1979, 12 f.
4. Tsountas and Manatt 1897, 396, Addendum 388.
5. Hood 1978, 155: 'A gold cup from the so-called Aigina Treasure in the British Museum, with elegant repoussé decoration of running spirals on the body, and a rosette on the base like some of the silver cups from Tôd, appears to be a Cretan work of the seventeenth or sixteenth century...'.
6. Here, for instance, the necklaces with cowrie shells from the 12th Dynasty (Andrews 1990, 6 fig. 1, 55 fig.39) may be compared with the collier composed of beads that represent a hand grasping a woman's breast. Higgins 1979, 34, fig. 33.
7. Evans 1930, 411 fig. 274.
8. cf. for example, Andrews 1990, 55 fig. 39, 142 fig. 125; Stevenson-Smith 1981, 209 fig. 206; Sahrage 1988, 137 fig. 63.
9. Andrews 1990, 172 fig. 158.
10. Marinatos 1984, 70 fig. 49.
11. Marinatos and Hirmer 1973, pl. 200, left.
12. After Appelt 1930, 153–7 (153); 'die Beispiele (a) und (c) stammen vom Pavillon Ramses III in Medinet Habu, (b) aus den Kriegen Sethos I, Karnak'. The disc symbolizes, as already pointed out by Evans 1935, 910, 'the rosette (or facing papyrus)'; cf. also Koch-Harnack 1989, 25 fig. 3.
13. Warren 1995, 1–18(1).
14. Hiller 1993, 197–9 (199).
15. Welter 1937, 24.
16. The *kernoi* are still unpublished; the ritual hammer was published by C. Reinholdt (by way of what may be called anticipating attentiveness, some time after I had asked him to draw this object for me): Reinholdt 1992, 57–62; the bibliography given there is to be completed by two major contributions, which escaped Reinholdt's attention: Eliopoulos 1991, 48–61; Manti-Platonos 1981, 74–83. There is, on the other hand, a striking absence at the Kolonna site of conical cups, which are notoriously omnipresent wherever Minoans settled. I cannot explain this strange fact in any other way than by assuming that, like all other undecorated pottery, these specific vessels too were not kept by former excavators on Aigina.
17. Branigan 1981, 23–33; Branigan 1984, 49–53.

18. Higgins 1979, 53 f: 'I do not believe that the Treasure is too rich to have been the property of one or more well-to-do Cretan families on Aegina.'
19. cf. note 2 above.
20. For their reduced decoration cf. the amphoras from a warrior tomb at Thebes: Kasimi-Sotou 1980, 100 fig. 7 (unpainted); and from Mycenae: Mylonas 1972, pl. 206a.
21. Its connection with the razor handle as suggested in the reconstruction remains doubtful; its exact find-spot was not recorded.
22. The remaining piece of gold sheet is, as I understand it, a remnant of a complete gold covering of the hilt such as is shown, for instance, on the gold dagger from Pylos (Marinatos and Hirmer 1973, pl. 38, middle). Clearly the sword had been damaged at some time before it was put into the grave, and had subsequently only partly been repaired by the addition of a second set of rivets, but without re-doing the gold sheet, which originally had covered the entire hilt.
23. For Greece cf. Branigan 1974, 37 ff., 183 ff.; for the Balkans cf. Makky 1989, pl. 83 f; Kalicz 1970, 71. To my knowledge, the closest parallel to the band from the warrior tomb is from Pelikata on Ithaka, cf. Branigan 1974, pl. 20. 2155, classified there (p.183) as EM II/III.
24. Supra note 1, where he comments on the band from the warrior tomb that 'it would, however, be rash to see this diadem as Mycenaean rather than Minoan, since the method of looping the ends is standard in a number of gold ornaments of Minoan, or presumed Minoan, origin'.
25. cf. the golden cover disc of the pommel depicting an acrobat, Hood 1978, 171, fig. 175; Vandenabeele 1992, 55 fig. 51; on the date Pelon 1983, 679–703; for a gold mounted dagger from Quartier Mu, cf. Vandenabeele 1992, 69, fig. 64; Detournay *et al.* 1980, frontispiece.
26. cf. Bietak and Hein 1994, 262 no. 360.
27. Marinatos and Hirmer 1973, pl. 199 above.
28. cf. also the comparison between the lion ornaments from Ayia Triada and from Mycenae, Shaft Grave III, drawn by Hood 1978, 198 figs 194, 195.
29. Marinatos and Hirmer 1973, pl. 170 below; Hood 1978, 176 fig. 173 ('possibly Cretan work of Middle Minoan IIIB'). For a comparison of Minoan and Mycenaean lion ornaments from Mycenae Shaft Grave III and from a tomb at Ayia Triada, respectively, cf. also Hood 1978, 198, figs 194, 195.
30. Andrews 1990, 142, fig. 124; cf. also the lion necklace from the tomb of Mereret, *op. cit.*, 125 fig. 4a.
31. For the increase of both jewellery and weapons as a feature indicating chronological phases cf. Graziado 1988, 343–72; Graziado 1991, 403–40; Taracha 1993, 7–34; Kilian-Dirlmeier 1986, 159–98.
32. For preliminary reports on the Early Bronze Age treasure found in 2000, see Reinholdt 2004, 113–19, and Reinholdt 2003, 260 f. (stressing the Near Eastern connections).

6
The Aigina Treasure: the Mycenaean connection

Robert Laffineur

I confess that I felt some anxiety at the prospect of contributing to this volume in which other essays emphasize the foreign connections of the Aigina Treasure in the Near East and Egypt, when I was suggesting an approach that concentrated on the Mycenaean connection. But this feeling soon disappeared when I considered that my concern was certainly not to favour the idea of the Aigina Treasure as exclusively Mycenaean, and when I realized that, most probably, the concern of my colleagues was not to favour an exclusively Minoan, or Egyptian, or Levantine origin – with the soothing result that we could all be right. I have in fact long been thinking of the Aigina Treasure as a non-homogeneous collection of precious objects, and it is ultimately not surprising that Minoan, Anatolian, Egyptian, Levantine and Near Eastern influences are observable on items in the treasure. This would be a matter of surprise only for one who thinks in terms of a unique origin, in which case my own suggestion of connections with Mycenaean Greece would certainly add to the complexity of the picture, or even lead to real confusion. On the contrary, however, the large variety of regional parallels makes it more probable that the collection of objects that we call the Aigina Treasure consists of items originating from different parts of the eastern Mediterranean, and dating from slightly different periods as well: items that have been put together at some time in antiquity or later, under unspecified circumstances. I think that the term 'treasure' in itself may be misleading in this respect, since it does not refer only to the precious material used for manufacturing the objects, but also, even if implicitly, to the concept of some kind of hoarding at a period that is relatively close to the date of manufacture. The reader should visualize the term 'Aigina Treasure' as if in quotation marks – I want to make this quite clear from the very beginning of my essay.

The so-called Aigina Treasure in the British Museum has long been considered as providing evidence for Minoan jewellery and goldwork at the transition between the Protopalatial and Neopalatial periods, c. 1700 BC.[1] Convincing reasons for such an interpretation – and dating – are given by the similarities between objects in the treasure and the few finds in precious metal from Minoan contexts of that period that have been preserved.

Most frequently mentioned are the typological and technical affinities, mainly the openwork technique and the type of disc pendants that are common to the most significant items in the treasure (761–6).[2] These are well attested in finds from the 'necropolis' of Chrysolakkos at Mallia[3] as well as in closely related objects from Crete in the British Museum,[4] in objects from Kythera,[5] and in pieces in the Mitsotakis Collection in Athens.[6] Bird-shaped pendants must also be included as comparative elements linking the Aigina Treasure (746, 752 and 763–6) with finds from Chrysolakkos.[7] The gold cup in the treasure (768) has a counterpart, in both shape and decoration, in a silver shallow cup from the Palace at Knossos.[8] Other iconographic similarities have been noted; for example, the gold, carnelian and lapis lazuli beads in the shape of a hand grasping a woman's breast (753) may be compared to an Early Minoan clay vessel from Mochlos in the shape of a goddess holding her breasts,[9] while the ornaments in the shape of a lotus flower on the gold pendant with the 'Master of Animals' (762) relate to the identical design on a gold pendant from Chrysolakkos.[10] Equally, the human heads with spiral curls of hair that terminate the gold 'pectoral' (761) may be compared with the head of a sphinx on a Cretan seal in the Ashmolean Museum[11] and on a moulded terracotta relief from Quartier Mu at Mallia.[12] Overall, perhaps the most striking of these iconographic similarities lies in the heraldic presentation of motifs. Such similarities have been considered so marked that the treasure has often been viewed as having been robbed from an original context in Crete, most probably a funerary context, before finding its way to the island of Aigina in Mycenaean times.[13]

Dissimilarities between the Aigina Treasure and Minoan goldwork, however, are worth mentioning, among which the absence of granulated decoration and the use of precious or semi-precious stones in addition to gold are certainly significant, as are the many examples of identical designs made by hammering of the gold sheet into a hollow mould – palm-leaf necklace beads (758–9), fifty-four gold discs (692–745), the small bird pendants on the ornaments (763–6) – a technique that is unknown in Crete before LBA I and that remains rather unusual on the island.[14] They deserve special attention when considered together with signs of extra-Aegean affinities that have been observed on objects in the treasure. Charles Gates has been the first in recent years to offer an analysis of affinities with Egypt and the Near East, and these are somewhat indirect ties, contributing to the identification of some of the items in the treasure not as imports from the east, or as copies of eastern objects, but as 'readaptations by Aegean artists into what now strike us as curious hybrids',[15] or as a 'blend of Egyptian, Syrian, and Levantine features with better known local traits'.[16] The first instance is provided by the 'Master of Animals' pendant (762). Although otherwise represented with a typical Minoan pose and dress, his feathered headdress is described by Gates as 'an abstracted version of the common *atef* crown worn notably by

Osiris'.[17] He suggests that the two omega-shaped frames on the pendant were perhaps intended 'to recall the horns that form the outer frame of the *atef* crown', or 'to suggest two motifs at the same time, not only the *atef* horns but also snakes'. The frames would thus be 'echoing the Egyptian *uraeus* motif',[18] rather than referring, as suggested earlier, to the popular Levantine motif of the 'hemline of the skirt lifted by the fertility goddess as she reminds onlookers of the source of her power',[19] an equivalent of which could be found in the kind of cord that the Minoan goddess is holding on the gold-plated pin head from Shaft Grave III at Mycenae.[20] Other examples of 'the loose adaptation of Near Eastern and Egyptian themes and forms' are the human heads on the Aigina 'pectoral' (761), with originally inlaid eyes and eyebrows and with spiral curls of hair, two features that are closer, according to Gates, to Levantine and Anatolian than to Minoan images and practices – as perhaps is the comparable sphinx appliqué of the vase from Quartier Mu at Mallia.[21] This last view has been supported recently by John Younger and Paul Rehak, who list additional signs of Anatolian and Syrian influence at Mallia, including the well-known leopard stone axe from the palace, the decorated weapons, and the eagles or falcons on terracotta mould-made lids from Quartier Mu. For them 'the profile head terminals on the gold collar from the Aegina Treasure show more Syrian [and Anatolian] than Aegean affinities', as does the appliqué sphinx just mentioned and its counterpart on an ivory from Acemhöyük.[22] Their conclusion is very similar to that of Gates, namely that 'Minoan visitors to the coast of Syria or Anatolia in the first half of the second millennium must have been exposed to these artistic influences', and that 'perhaps artistic creations resulted that employed a mix of traits'.[23]

As for several other questions of primary importance that are outside the scope of the present essay, the recent finds made at Avaris/Tell el-Dabʿa in the eastern Nile Delta have provided new evidence for a significant reappraisal of the nationality of the gold pendants in the Aigina Treasure. I am referring to the gold pendant in openwork technique and with animal decoration of antithetic type excavated in a tomb of early 13th Dynasty date, *c.* 1780–40 (Fig. 184; see Schiestl in this volume, pp. 51–8). The jewel was originally considered as probably Minoan, because of its many affinities with pieces in the Aigina Treasure.[24] Among the comparisons drawn by Gisela Walberg, I should like to stress the close similarity between the antithetic animals on the Dabʿa pendant, identified as dogs, and those on the four ornaments (763–6) in the Aigina Treasure, probably dogs as well – rather than jackals, as suggested by Hopkins[25] – especially the common detail of collars and leashes. It is worth emphasizing in addition the similar coiled tail. Such affinities are truly significant and they are confirmed by the technique of backing the ornament with a flat sheet of gold (Fig. 185), also found on the 'Master of Animals' pendant in the Aigina Treasure. These affinities would lead to the conclusion of a common origin for the Dabʿa pendant and most of the Aigina pendants, if not a single workshop, but the location of this cannot be specified from the evidence uncovered at the capital city of the Hyksos. The similarities between the Dabʿa pendant and its counterparts in the Aigina Treasure, however, definitely strengthen the case for a Bronze Age date for some components in the latter, as opposed to the ninth- or eighth-century BC date originally proposed by Evans[26] or the seventh-century BC date suggested by Demargne,[27] Becatti[28] and Hopkins.[29] More recently, the Dabʿa pendant has been studied by Joan Aruz, who, arguing from parallels from Syrian glyptic, proposes to identify it as a Canaanite ornament, made in the Delta or the Levant 'by a craftsman versed in the Syrian animal style'.[30] The problem is that this new identification is based on iconographic similarities only – some of them rather general – and that such elaborated ornaments as the type discussed here are not attested at all in Canaanite or Levantine jewellery.

A further comparison concerns the shape and ornamentation of the fifty-four gold discs in the Aigina Treasure (692–745), which Aruz relates to a circular design on seal impressions from Karahöyük and Acemhöyük.[31] The particular design to which Aruz refers is also attested in Minoan glyptic,[32] as is the much closer motif of a central element outlined by a circle of running spirals.[33] Very close examples of the latter appear on gold ornaments from the Shaft Graves at Mycenae (Figs 143 and 144),[34] a comparison that finds corroboration in the eight-petalled rosettes made of dotted lines in the centre of the discs (692–745) and their exact counterpart on a gold band from Shaft Grave IV (Fig. 145).[35]

This brings us to a consideration of other Early Mycenaean features in the Aigina Treasure, the most relevant of which are:

- The palm-leaf gold necklace beads (758–9), which have parallels on necklaces from Kythera[36] and Peristeria,[37] and exact equivalents in Grave Omikron of Circle B at Mycenae (Figs 146 and 147).[38]
- The long and narrow gold bands (683–691) that correspond to a late Middle Helladic type (Fig. 148)[39] – an early date confirmed by the dotted decoration of one of the specimens (691), which has an exact correspondence on a matt-painted polychrome jug from Shaft Grave II at Mycenae (Fig. 149).[40]
- The gold strap bracelet (767) with rolled-up edges and its equivalent in Grave Alpha at Mycenae (Fig. 150).[41]
- The plain gold rings (751) with an equivalent in a context of transitional date at Asine.[42]
- The gold cup with spirals (768), the profile of which has a direct echo in a gold-stemmed cup from Shaft Grave V at Mycenae (Fig. 151)[43] and on two-handled or one-handled gold cups of transitional date, respectively from Peristeria in Messenia (Fig. 152)[44] and in the Stathatos Collection, Athens.[45]

Further evidence of affinities with Early Mycenaean jewellery comes from the technique of manufacture of a series of items by hammering the gold sheet into a hollow mould, as pointed out above. A link with earlier mainland production is provided by the flat cylindrical rock crystal bead (757) and its related shapes in gold in the Early Helladic treasure from Thyreatis in Berlin (Fig. 153).[46] A final relationship could be provided by the gold finger rings with inlaid decoration,[47] which correspond to later Mycenaean types and techniques.[48] The affinities are probably closer, however, with the Late Minoan I finger ring with cloisonné decoration excavated at Poros[49] – and this gives another significant link with Crete.

This last observation emphasizes the fact that the Aigina Treasure exhibits features that are not only characteristic of different geographical areas, but also of different periods, which means that it certainly cannot be considered a homogeneous group. As far as chronology is concerned, the impression is that the objects range from a medium phase in the Middle Bronze

Age (a date provided by the comparison of the four ornaments, 763–6, with the pendant from Tell el-Dabᶜa)[50] to an early Late Bronze Age date (judging from the inlaid finger rings) and this is in fact a fairly short timespan. A wider chronological extent is not excluded, however, if we consider the above-mentioned Early Bronze Age parallels for the flat cylindrical rock crystal bead (757). As evidence for a possible extension at the other extreme, I would be inclined to consider the necklaces (753, 754 and 760), which do not apparently fit into late Middle Bronze Age or early Late Bronze Age material, but which seem rather to correspond to much later types. I would also include the strange gold ornament (746) with a lion's head, usually interpreted as an earring: its ornamentation in filigree is quite unique in the treasure and might be viewed, together with the type of the lion's head itself, as favouring a date as late as the orientalizing period. However, the small bird-shaped pendants attached to it are reminiscent of the similar pendants on the four ornaments (763–6) and of the small owl pendants on the fragmentary ornament (752). In connection with the possible extension to later dates, I would refer in addition to the ajouré pendant of Late Geometric date from Khaniale Tekke near Knossos, and its similarities with the four gold ornaments (763–6).

It ultimately proves impossible – and the attempt is quite idle – to identify a single, precise geographical origin for the collection of gold items reputedly found on Aigina. This is in agreement with Joan Aruz's conclusion: 'I believe that the enigmatic objects in the "Aigina treasure" are a varied collection and do not appear to be explainable as works in a uniform style from a single original context or of a single date.'[51]

The final impression is in this respect very much the same as that provided by a close examination of the Tod Treasure, which does not appear to consist of strictly contemporaneous items, as traditionally accepted, but proves to include objects belonging to at least three geographical areas and three chronological phases, as I have argued in an earlier paper.[52]

The above-mentioned chronological span also confirms that the Aigina Treasure, if really found as a whole before being purchased by the British Museum, has probably never existed as such, but is the result of a secondary assemblage. A similar interpretation should apply, in my opinion, to other famous treasures of Aegean Bronze Age date, such as the so-called 'Zakro Treasure' in the Heraklion Museum and, most probably, to the so-called 'Troy Treasure(s)' that are now for the most part in the Pushkin Museum in Moscow. But these are other questions that I will keep for further investigation.

Notes

1. A complete bibliography on the treasure and detailed information on its provenance and conditions of purchase is in Higgins 1979.
2. The objects in the treasure will be referred to by their inventory number in BM Cat Jewellery, nos 683–768.
3. Demargne 1945, pl. 66 (the bee pendant) and no. 562, pl. 22 and 67, 1.
4. BM Cat Jewellery, no. 815.
5. Coldstream and Huxley 1972, 261, no. 1 and pl. 84, 1.
6. Marangou 1992, 190, no. 226.
7. Demargne 1945, pl. 67, 3.
8. Evans 1930, 387, fig. 221a.
9. Marinatos and Hirmer 1973, pl. 10, top.
10. Demargne 1945, no. 588, pls 22 and 67, 1.
11. Higgins 1979, 28, fig. 23.
12. Detournay *et al*. 1980, 116–18 and figs 164–5.
13. On this, see Higgins 1979, 51–4. The latest study of Minoan jewellery, however, does not include the Aigina Treasure (Effinger 1996).
14. One of the rare examples is provided by sheet gold beads from Poros; Muhly 1992, 90, 124, fig. 21 and pl. 27. On this technique, see Laffineur 1996, 92–100.
15. Gates 1989, 221.
16. Gates 1989, 224.
17. Gates 1989, 218.
18. Gates 1989, 219. The omega-shaped motifs are quite similar to the so-called 'snake frames' attested on Mycenaean seals and finger rings: CMS I, nos 144–5 (lentoid seals from chamber tomb 515 at Mycenae) and 189 (gold finger ring from the tholos tomb at Dendra).
19. Gates 1989, 220.
20. Karo 1930, no. 75, pl. 30.
21. Detournay *et al*. 1980.
22. Younger and Rehak 1998, 234.
23. Younger and Rehak 1998. Additional evidence is provided by silver vessels from tombs at Byblos and from the Tod Treasure. This will be commented on *infra*.
24. Walberg 1991a, 111–12. On the affinities with the Aigina Treasure, see also Laffineur 1998, 57.
25. Hopkins 1962, 182–4.
26. Evans 1892–3, 195–226.
27. Demargne 1947, 126 (Phoenician origin for the treasure).
28. Becatti 1955, 38–9.
29. Hopkins 1962.
30. Aruz 1995b, 44–8. See also Morris 1998, 282–4, and the discussion in Cline 1998.
31. Aruz 1995b, 44, with figs 41–2.
32. CMS II 5, nos 153–4 and 165 (sealings from Phaestos).
33. CMS II 5, nos 191 and 193 (sealings from Phaestos); CMS V 2, no. 464 (EC II sealing from A. Irini); CMS X, no. 53 (MM 'Petschaft' in Basel).
34. Karo 1930, nos 12–13, pl. 29 and nos 696 and 698, pls 64–5.
35. Karo 1930, nos 236–9, pl. 39. The comparison has been made by Higgins 1979, 31.
36. Coldstream and Huxley 1972.
37. Korres 1976, 499 and pl. 263g.
38. Mylonas 1972, pl. 181.
39. See the examples mentioned in note 40.
40. Karo 1930, no. 200, pl. 174, and colour illustration in Demakopoulou 1990, 272, no. 213 with fig. (Polychrome Mainland Ware, type IB-1 for Dietz 1991, 217). Gold bands with similar decoration are known from Asine (Dietz 1980, 31, figs 20–1), Corinth (Blegen *et al*. 1964, 8, nos 2–12 and pl. 3), Aghia Irini on Keos (Caskey 1972, 386, no. E40 and pl. 89) and Aigina (Kilian-Dirlmeier 1997, 54–7 and 19, figs 6, 9). The evolution in the decoration of thin gold bands and the like seems rather clear at first sight. Some specimens from Grave Circle B at Mycenae (Mylonas 1972, pl. 28a, 87 and 159a–b) and from Argos (Protonotariou-Deilaki 1990, 77, fig. 16) belong to the style called 'boss-and-dot style' by Dickinson (Dickinson 1977, 85), a style which appears characteristic of the Middle Helladic late phase and which could be considered, from the finds of continental goldwork now available, as an intermediate phase in the general development on the mainland from a pure Middle Helladic 'dot style' to the less linear and more plastic style of the beginning of the Mycenaean period (especially illustrated in the finds from Grave Circle A). While providing a precise date for gold band 691, the jug from Grave Circle A mentioned above indicates, however, that the two styles situated at the beginning and the end of the supposed evolution are likely to have been used at about the same time.
41. Mylonas 1972, pl. 21a.
42. Dietz 1980, 60, fig. 69.
43. Karo 1930, no. 656, pl. 126.
44. Korres 1976, 495–7, fig. 8 and pl. 263a–b.
45. Picard and Sodini 1971, 16–17, no St. 700 and pl. III.
46. Reinholdt 1993a, 10, fig. 13 (with reference to a similar type in the EM material from Mochlos).
47. BM Cat Finger Rings, nos 690–3.
48. Laffineur 1996, 96 (with reference to specimens from Mycenae [chamber tombs], Vapheio, Volos, Thebes, Aidonia). The technique is attested for the decoration of weapons in the Shaft Grave period (Karo 1930, pl. 87).
49. Muhly 1992, 90, 123–4 and pl. 26.
50. Caution, however, is necessary, as pointed out by S. Morris: 'The presence of Kamares sherds in the same stratum (not the same tomb, robbed of most of its contents) was adduced as further support for an Aegean provenance for this Delta discovery, although there has been disagreement as to the precise date of these sherds'; Morris 1998, 283, quoting MacGillivray 1995, 81–5.
51. Aruz 1995b, 44.
52. Laffineur 1988, 17–30.

7
The Aigina Treasure: Near Eastern connections

Dominique Collon

Introduction

For island-hopping sailors, Aigina presented a safe haven on a journey from Anatolia to the Greek mainland and vice versa. It is not surprising, therefore, to find that most of the Near Eastern parallels for the Aigina Treasure are with Anatolia. They seem to cluster in the earlier part of the eighteenth century BC, and the site of Acemhöyük has provided more of these parallels than any other excavated site.

Acemhöyük[1] lies at the south-east end of the great Salt Lake in central Turkey, a few kilometres north of the present main road linking the cities of Konya, south of the lake, and Kayseri, farther east. This road is dotted with Seljuk caravanserais of the thirteenth century AD and was already a main highway in Late or Neo-Hittite times in the first millennium BC and probably during the second millennium BC and earlier. In pre-Hittite times, Acemhöyük may have been the city of Burushhanda, known as an important emporium in the nineteenth to eighteenth centuries BC. It is mentioned in texts of the merchant colony established by Assyrians at Kanesh (now Kültepe), just north-east of the present city of Kayseri around 1920 BC. This colony was one of several trading posts in Anatolia at this time and most of them, including Acemhöyük and Boğazköy (later to become the Hittite capital Hattusas), were destroyed in violent conflagrations around 1740 BC.

Acemhöyük was excavated in the 1960s and 1970s by Professor Nimet Özgüç whose husband, Professor Tahsin Özgüç, was meanwhile excavating the houses of the Assyrian merchants at Kanesh. A comparable merchant colony has yet to be identified at Acemhöyük, but excavations on the main mound have produced material contemporary with Level Ib at Kültepe/Kanesh (c. 1800–1740 BC). Two large palaces have been excavated. The final conflagration that destroyed them was so intense that the impression of the end of a beam was completely preserved in the molten mud-brick. Unfortunately the tentative dating by dendrochronology of the felling of this tree is unreliable. The final publication is still in the course of preparation, so it is not yet clear how the timbers relate to the material in the ground-floor (or perhaps basement) storerooms that interest us here. It is probable that we shall have to adopt a Low Chronology in due course, but until the dating established by dendrochronology and ice cores has been confirmed, it seems premature to change. I am therefore using dates according to the Middle Chronology generally adopted for convenience in Mesopotamia,[2] but these may eventually have to be lowered by some fifty-six or more years.[3]

Some of the storerooms contained sealed clay bullae which had been attached to goods and seem to have been kept as part of a recording system; they provide evidence for long-distance trade. One has a design of a wheel of monster heads executed in the local Anatolian style. At precisely this period the same design is found, executed in the Gulf style, on seals from the island of Bahrein, and in the Harappan style on an uncharacteristic circular seal excavated at Mohenjo-Daro in the Indus Valley.[4] The design is otherwise extremely rare in time and space, reappearing only in the Achaemenid period in the fifth to fourth centuries BC. A bulla with the impression of an Egyptian or Palestinian scarab seal was also found.[5] Links with the west are demonstrated by rock-crystal and obsidian vessels and vessel fragments from Acemhöyük, which have good parallels in the Aegean.[6]

Close dating is provided by bullae naming Shamshi-Adad I, king of the Assyrian-dominated kingdom of North Mesopotamia, and of known contemporaries such as King Aplahanda of Carchemish. Shamshi-Adad died in 1776 BC (according to the Middle Chronology), and the bullae probably belong to the first part of the eighteenth century BC.

The Aigina pectoral

The Aigina pectoral (Fig. 41) ends in human heads in profile which have hair tucked behind the ear and falling in two curls. This is not a woman's hairstyle at this period and, in his booklet on the Aigina Treasure, Reynold Higgins suggested that the heads on the pectoral might be those of sphinxes.[7] Several bullae from Acemhöyük bear this out (Fig. 154).[8] One of the Acemhöyük bullae, naming Aplahanda of Carchemish, is sealed with a distinctive type of seal which depicts rows of heads.[9] This enables us to date to the early eighteenth century BC a seal with a similar design at Yale that includes a row of beardless heads with several curls (Fig. 155);[10] these provide a close parallel for the heads of the gold pectoral from Aigina. A seal impression from Tell Atchana (ancient Alalakh), between Antakya and Aleppo, belongs to the same distinctive group as the Yale seal,[11] but here the heads have only one curl (Fig. 156).

Another parallel is provided by seated ivory sphinxes (Fig. 157).[12] These were acquired together with some bullae in the 1930s, long before the excavations at Acemhöyük began, and are now in the Metropolitan Museum of Art in New York.[13] The bullae match exactly those from Acemhöyük, and related ivorywork has also been found at the site, thus confirming the provenance of these sphinxes and dating them to the nineteenth to eighteenth century BC. They may have been gaming pieces and furniture fittings.

At Karahöyük near Konya, where there was a contemporary emporium, a sherd was found depicting a sphinx with curls in relief (Fig. 158).[14] Curls continued to be associated with Anatolian sphinxes in later Hittite art, notably at Alaca Hüyük in the fourteenth century BC[15] and in thirteenth-century Hattusas – the Hittite capital.[16]

The Aigina earrings
The four gold earrings from Aigina (Figs 18 and 19) have several features that can be paralleled in the Near East. Little seated monkeys, often with their hands held up to their mouths, are a common feature of Near Eastern seals from around 2000 BC onwards. Just before the sack of the city of Ur in southern Mesopotamia in 2004 BC, Ibbi-Sin, the last king of the 3rd Dynasty of Ur, was presented with a monkey. His empire was under attack from all sides and this was the best thing that happened in his twenty-third year, which was therefore recorded as 'The year in which that land brought to Ibbi-Sin, king of Ur, a weighty monkey'. This seems to have inspired literary creations such as *A Letter from a Monkey to its Mother* and to have started a fashion in monkeys, which became a status symbol for the newly sedentarized Amorites. Every Amorite petty king had to be shown with a monkey before him. The fashion spread, and King Aplahanda of Carchemish is shown on his daughter's seal together with a monkey (Fig. 159).[17]

In Anatolia the monkeys often look very unrealistic and have been described as resembling 'foetal calves' or 'Madagascar lemurs' (e.g. on Fig. 154).[18] The Acemhöyük monkeys on the stamp seal shown in Fig. 160, with rather dog-like lions similar to the animals on the Aigina earrings, are somewhat more realistic, as are those on impressions of a stamp cylinder, also from Acemhöyük (Fig. 161).[19]

Reynold Higgins suggested that 'the overall design [of these earrings might] well have been inspired by some piece of Egyptian jewellery such as a gold pectoral', and he illustrated an example dated around 1850 BC with two hawk-headed lions, each one trampling a prisoner and resting a fore paw on the head of another.[20] On an obsidian seal belonging to the king of Buzuran near Mari, and dating to around 1760 BC, a sphinx is trampling prisoners but rests its paw on a monkey (Fig. 162).[21] I have suggested that this seal was made in a Levantine workshop, perhaps located at Byblos, which specialized in exotic stones, especially green jasper – a material that also appears in the Aigina Treasure (Fig. 101, lower).[22]

The Aigina beads
The barrel-shaped carnelian beads on the earrings and on a necklace from Aigina (Fig. 101, upper) may well have originated on the west coast of India, around the Bay of Cambay, where such beads were made for millennia using the same techniques and, indeed, are still being made, although the techniques are changing.[23] They have been exported in large quantities, and the similar beads that appear in the Royal Cemetery at Ur around 2600 BC, together with distinctive etched carnelian beads, must also have come from western India.[24] The clear, dark colour of the carnelian was probably obtained by heating the stone, and similar beads occur at the site of the ancient Syrian city of Ebla, between Aleppo and Hama, in a context dated between 1850 and 1800 BC.[25]

Spacer beads, a concept also attested at Ur,[26] are found on another necklace. They are made of amethyst and may therefore have come from Egypt (Fig. 101, centre). There is evidence for the use of amethyst for well-dated Middle Kingdom scarabs and for Old Babylonian cylinder seals and beads (e.g. from Ebla), during the nineteenth to seventeenth centuries BC, although it is almost totally absent from the Near Eastern repertory thereafter.[27]

Melon beads, attested at Ur around 2600 BC and at Ebla between 1850 and 1700 BC,[28] are also found in the Aigina Treasure (Fig. 102), but they continued to be popular for millennia and cannot be used as a dating criterion.

A rock crystal flanged bead from Aigina (Fig. 101, centre) is paralleled in shape by an amethyst knob, once attached to a lid, from a tomb at Ebla dated 1750–1700 BC.[29]

Reynold Higgins claimed that the motif of a right hand holding a breast, on gold, lapis lazuli and carnelian beads from Aigina, was of Near Eastern origin (Fig. 79).[30] The materials are those that were predominantly used in the Royal Cemetery at Ur around 2600 BC,[31] but I know of no Near Eastern parallels for the shape. The lapis lazuli came from Afghanistan and would have passed through the Near East on its way to Aigina, probably together with the carnelian and perhaps the gold. Ebla, in northern Syria, may well have been a transit point since beads in all three materials are found there (see above), and 22 kg of unworked lapis lazuli was found in the destruction level of an earlier palace.[32]

The Aigina finger rings
Reynold Higgins drew attention to the similarity of the gold and lapis lazuli finger rings from Aigina to those from the Royal Cemetery at Ur of around 2600 BC. In both cases, little pieces of scrap lapis lazuli were used (Fig. 163). A chronologically closer but more elaborate parallel is provided by an Egyptian gold cloisonné ring inlaid with a glass paste scarab imitating lapis, from a tomb at Ebla dated to between 1750 and 1700 BC.[33]

The Aigina pendants
The hanging discs and birds, which are such a feature of Aigina jewellery, are found on an unprovenanced necklace which is reputedly from western Turkey, in the Department of the Middle East in the British Museum (Fig. 164).[34] At Aigina, however, the birds hang upside down.

The Aigina gold roundels
The eight-petalled rosette on the gold discs from Aigina differs from the fifteen-petalled rosette on the gold cup (see below), but it is very similar to the rosette on a bronze all-metal seal ring from the Hittite capital at Boğazköy–Hattusas (Fig. 165).[35] In both cases the rosettes are surrounded by a three-strand braided design (cf. also Fig. 161). The ring has been dated to between 1650 and 1600 BC, thanks to a parallel from Alaca Hüyük that is engraved with early hieroglyphs that cannot, according to Boehmer, be earlier than 1650 BC.

The Aigina gold cup

The Tod Treasure, found at Tod near Thebes in Egypt, contained scrap lapis lazuli in the form of broken cylinder seals and amulets, some of which were centuries old, and silver bowls that had been flattened and folded so that they could be fitted into bronze boxes bearing the name of Ammenemes II (1929–1895 BC). None of these bowls is as elaborate as the gold cup from Aigina (which once had a handle), but the rosette on the base of the Aigina cup is paralleled on several of the Tod bowls, although with fewer petals.[36]

The spiral decoration on the cup is particularly at home in Syria. It appears together with the rosette on the base of shallow gold dishes in the Louvre (Fig. 166), Beirut and New York, which are said to have been found in Lebanon between Tripoli and Homs in the 1950s.[37] Altogether a dozen dishes appeared on the market. Parrot thought they were Mycenaean, but similar though more rounded interlocking bands occur on a gold disc from Ebla dated to around 2400 BC, and a more structured angular version is found on bullae from Acemhöyük. Doubt has been cast on the authenticity of the example in the Metropolitan Museum, but it should be noted that the parallels from Ebla and Acemhöyük were excavated after the dishes appeared on the market.[38]

Conclusions

It is interesting to note that the parallels come predominantly from a central Anatolian site and not from coastal areas, as might have been expected.[39] This must, at least in part, be due to the accidents of discovery, but it is remarkable none the less. However, it is scarcely surprising that the Royal Cemetery at Ur in southern Iraq in the mid-third millennium BC and Ebla in Syria in the early second millennium BC have produced so many parallels for the bead shapes and materials found at Aigina, as this is certainly due to the fact that unlooted tombs and graves were found at these two sites. The materials and shapes were popular for centuries – in some cases for millennia – but it is notable that green jasper and amethyst are absent in the Royal Cemetery and only became popular later at sites such as Ebla, thus endorsing a date for the Aigina Treasure in the eighteenth century BC, when the use of such materials is well attested.

Although the Aigina Treasure demonstrates detailed knowledge of objects of the eighteenth century BC from central Anatolia, indicating direct or indirect contact with that area, I wish to stress that I do not challenge the opinion that the Aigina Treasure was made on Aigina. In fact, the technical study indicates forcefully that the treasure belongs to a homogeneous group. What struck me, when I was able to have a close look at the treasure, was the flimsy nature of the objects. With the exception of the necklaces, they could not have been worn without getting hooked up and damaged. The earrings were intended to be seen from one side only and would have lost much of their impact if they had been worn, because all the pendant pieces would have hung vertically and got tangled instead of radiating (as in the photographs, Figs 18 and 19). The gold roundels are so thin and light that they would have become hooked up and dented had they been used to decorate a garment intended for normal wear, even in a staid ritual context.

It is unlikely that the treasure once adorned a cult statue because cult objects rarely survive, let alone as a homogeneous group showing no sign of wear and tear. It is much more likely that the objects were made especially for burial. The 'earrings' would have looked dramatic if placed or stitched down the front of a burial robe.

Notes

1. Özgüç 1966, 1–52, and Özgüç 1980, 61–99.
2. Walker 1995, 230–8.
3. Collon 2000, 7.
4. Collon 1996, 221, no. 32a–c.
5. Özgüç 1980, fig. III–13.
6. Özten 1988, esp. nos 14, 19; note that only evidence for one handle was found for no. 14 – not two as in the reconstructed drawing – thus increasing the similarity with the Aegean parallels. For the latter, see Platon 1971, 139 top right, from the palace at Zakro.
7. Higgins 1979, 28.
8. Özgüç 1971, fig. 4, with a reference to a bulla with the same impression in the Louvre: Delaporte 1923, A.842, 184, pl. 123:8; Özgüç 1980, figs III–43, 45, 47; Özgüç 1991, figs 57–10, 12–13, 36.
9. Otto 2000, no. 58.
10. Otto 2000, no. 59.
11. Otto 2000, no. 57.
12. Decamps de Mertzenfeld 1954, pls 125–8.
13. Harper 1969, 156–62.
14. Otten et al. 1992, dust jacket; I know of no publication. The original is in Konya Museum. Note that the creature has hooves rather than paws.
15. Akurgal 1961, pl. 88.
16. Akurgal 1961, pls 66–8.
17. Collon 1986a, 45–7.
18. For example Özgüç 1965, nos 10, 12, 13.
19. Özgüç 1971, 21–2, figs 2, 3.
20. Higgins 1979, 26–7.
21. Otto 2000, no. 368.
22. Collon 1986b and Collon 2001, 16–24.
23. Collon 1986a, 13.
24. Woolley 1934, pl. 133; Reade 1979.
25. Matthiae et al. 1995, 419 and 434, nos 281 and 286, dated between 1850 and 1800 BC.
26. Woolley 1934, pls 144–5, 148.
27. For the seals, Collon 1986a, 10 with references; for amethyst from Ebla dated between 1850 and 1700 BC, see Matthiae et al. 1995, no. 285, 419 and 434 and nos 389–90, 468; for green jasper, see Collon 1986b and Collon 2001.
28. For example Woolley 1934, pl. 132; for Ebla examples, see Matthiae et al. 1995, no. 284 (rock-crystal), pp. 419 and 434, dated between 1850 and 1800 BC, and nos 418–20 (gold and lapis lazuli), p. 487, dated between 1750 and 1700 BC.
29. Matthiae et al. 1995, no. 389.
30. Higgins 1979, 34.
31. For example Woolley 1934, pls 131–6; Collon 1995, 71, fig. 55.
32. Matthiae et al. 1995, no. 37.
33. Higgins 1979, 36–7; Woolley 1934, pl. 138, U.12134, U.10878, U.9778; Matthiae et al. 1995, no. 387, pp. 467, 479.
34. Collon 1995, 107, fig. 89.
35. Boehmer and Güterbock 1987, no. 143 on p. 51 and pl. 14; the Alaca parallel is illustrated on p. 51, Abb. 34.
36. Bisson de la Roque et al. 1953, pls 5–38, esp. pls 24, 35–6; only on pl. 36 is there a rosette with fifteen petals, but it covers the whole bowl.
37. Parrot 1964, 240–50, esp. figs 22–5, 27, 31, with rosettes on the base, several of them surrounded by running spirals similar to those on the Aigina bowl.
38. Matthiae 1984, pl. 38 for Ebla; Özgüç 1966, pl. 26: 1–2 for Acemhöyük.
39. The flanged beads from the new treasure from Aigina discussed on pp. 35 and 38, however, have parallels at the coastal site of Troy.

8
The Aegean or the Near East: another look at the 'Master of Animals' pendant in the Aigina Treasure

Joan Aruz

The Aigina Treasure is a jewellery hoard that is problematic for many reasons.[1] These objects appear to be a varied collection not explainable as works in a uniform style or technique, which has led to questions about their original source or sources of inspiration and their dates of manufacture and deposition.[2] Right from the start, the jewels were considered to be 'orientalizing', although the date of manufacture – either in the Aegean Bronze Age or the eighth to seventh century BC – was disputed. Attempts to derive certain foreign traits have not always been convincing and interweave stimuli from both Egypt and the Near East.

In an effort to place the Aigina Treasure in a Near Eastern context, as it were, this essay begins with a few brief and selective comments about human and animal imagery in the jewellery of Mesopotamia, Syria and Anatolia during the earlier part of the Bronze Age – prior to and encompassing the time to which Reynold Higgins and many other scholars date the manufacture of the Aigina jewels, the seventeenth to fifteenth centuries BC. We shall then turn to a discussion of some of the figural imagery presented in the hoard, focusing particularly on the much discussed 'Master of Animals' pendant, with a brief mention of the hoops with dogs and the pectoral with human-head terminals. One additional group of material with floral–geometric patterns will also be considered: the fifty-four roundels with loop borders.

Early Near Eastern jewellery with figural imagery

During the periods contemporary with the Aegean Early Bronze Age throughout the Near East, figural imagery in jewellery is largely confined to small pendants in the form of animals and divinities with animal attributes. These pendants probably served some amuletic as well as decorative function. Among the most spectacular are those that appear to have been part of a diadem from the Royal Cemetery at Ur and the lapis lazuli and gold pendants in the form of the Mesopotamian thunderbird from a number of sites, including Tell Asmar, Mari and Tell Brak. Other thin gold pendants – cut or partially cut in animal form – depict animals in a symmetrical arrangement either addorsed, as on an example from the Persian Gulf, or crossing, such as the lions on a pendant from Tell Brak.[3]

Perhaps the most intricate gold jewel with figural decoration of the period is a 3.2 cm high Mesopotamian pendant, acquired by the Louvre, which is worked in the round and exhibits a great deal of detail on the reverse (Fig. 167).[4] Depicted in openwork is the symmetrical composition of a bullman with a human torso between two human-headed bulls, all standing on a flat base. Their missing faces were perhaps originally in another material. While intricate, there is no evidence for the use of the advanced techniques of ornamentation, namely granulation and filigree, on any of these early jewels.

Possibly dating to a period contemporary with the generally assigned date of the Aigina Treasure (and incidentally the Mallia bee pendant) are jewellery hoards from the Near East – one excavated at the site of Larsa and another without archaeological provenance in the Metropolitan Museum. They consist of numerous beads (collared melon beads roughly paralleled, in fact, in the Aigina Treasure) and pendants, including discs with very fine granulated ornament, as well as representations of divinities – namely two pendants in the form of a goddess wearing a flounced garment with arms raised in supplication.[5]

Beyond greater Mesopotamia, one looks both to Anatolia and to the Levant. In Anatolia, most of the excavated pendants in figural form date to the Hittite Empire period. One of the most elaborate is a small seated sun goddess wearing a large disc-like headdress and holding a child on her lap.[6] The disc is backed with a flat sheet of gold to which the suspension loop is attached; the rest of the piece – which is worked with details also on the reverse – consists of her square throne. A small necklace, perhaps for a child, which has been discussed in connection with the Aigina Treasure, has openwork pendant falcons from which discs are suspended on short chains (Fig. 168). It was thought by Richard Barnett to come from a Hittite royal grave in western Anatolia, and this view is repeated by

Dominique Collon in her book on the British Museum collection.[7] The workmanship and design were attributed to Egypt by Edith Porada. Already in 1976 she noted the connection with the larger discs dangling, less elegantly, from pendants in the Aigina Treasure as indicating elements 'characteristic of the eastern Mediterranean jewelry'.[8] Although the discs on the Hittite piece are plain, some of those from the Aigina Treasure have punched decoration, which is typical for the Levant as well as early Anatolia. Falcon imagery – certainly derived from Egypt – is prominent in the jewellery of the Levant. Earrings from Tell el-ʿAjjul consist of embossed sheets decorated with granulation, one characteristic type in the form of a falcon.[9]

Some ornaments from Byblos are reported to have flat backs. One of particular interest is in the form of three water birds with large eyes and stippled bodies (Fig. 169),[10] which will be referred to again in the detailed discussion of the 'Master of Animals' pendant. First, however, it may be of interest to introduce another class of Canaanite jewellery: gold triangular pendants with female representations. We will concentrate on examples found in a deposit at Minet el-Beidha, the port of Ugarit (dated to LB II), and one from the collection of jewellery pendants and 'scrap' carried on the Uluburun ship.[11] While technically very different from the Aigina Treasure 'Master of Animals' pendant, neither being openwork nor exhibiting its complexity of concept and design, they are similarly unrefined in finish and combine iconographic elements that may be relevant to our discussion (Figs 170 and 171). With these plaques one may find a key to understanding some of the imagery on the Aigina Treasure pendant in Near Eastern terms, including the theme of mastering animals itself, the composition, and details of physiognomy and of hairstyle, as well as floral elements.

The 'Master of Animals' pendant: connections with the Levant
From the time of Sir Arthur Evans's initial suggestions in 1892–3 regarding the subject matter on the Aigina Treasure pendant, many scholars have considered the image of a man with legs in a striding posture and holding two water birds, standing on an element that looks like a boat, to be an allusion to Egyptian scenes of fowling in a marshy setting. Those, such as Giovanni Becatti, who dated the piece to the Orientalizing period have cited Phoenician art as the filter through which such Egyptian motifs came to the Aegean.[12]

On first examination the imagery on the pendant (Fig. 11) looks incoherent. It appears to have been produced in an eclectic style with iconography exhibiting an interpretation of elements deriving from various sources.[13] Perhaps the best place to start is with the male figure himself, for it is largely his appearance that has led many scholars to accept a Minoan seventeenth- to fifteenth-century BC attribution without question. Are we in fact looking at a typically Minoan figure, or does this lithe, slender figure derive from an eastern type, found both in New Kingdom Egypt and later in Phoenician depictions?

The 'Master of Animals' stands in a rather static posture, his head and torso frontal with arms bent at the elbow and outstretched, placed on top of but not actually holding the large water birds. The posture is not typical for Minoan art and lacks the torsion of images seen, for instance, on Aegean seals, rings and sculpture, as on the Hagia Triada boxer rhyton (Fig. 172). The torso, while rather flat, does taper to a wasp-waist, but then there is an abrupt transition to a profile view of the figure in a striding pose with one leg extended backwards. The curving line of this leg achieves some movement, as on the Boxer rhyton. Paul Rehak astutely noted that the figure's garment – a kilt with overlapping edges, belt and a 'peculiar tassel' consisting of a vertical band divided into segments that may represent beadwork – 'is reminiscent of Egyptian costume, perhaps filtered through Syrian eyes, and may not be representative of typical Aegean garb'.[14] Such a garment is worn by a rather stiff striding, conquering pharaoh represented twice on an Egyptian Middle Kingdom pectoral from Dahshur (Fig. 173).

In further exploring the association with the Levant, one can turn to the triangular plaques (Figs 170 and 171). While sharing neither stylistic similarities nor identical subject matter – which make them look quite different at first glance – there are none the less a surprising number of features suggesting in the Aigina pendant some allusion to 'Mistress of Animals' depictions on Canaanite jewellery. We have evidence that such jewellery was travelling to the west, at least in the late fourteenth century BC, based on the one discovered in the Uluburun shipwreck.[15]

Let us begin with hairstyle. The nude goddesses on the Canaanite plaques, with the exception of the Uluburun example (Fig. 171), wear Hathor wigs. The Aigina Treasure 'Master of Animals' has a similar hairstyle with large discs or disc-like curls at the shoulders, which Evans, back in 1892–3, may have correctly interpreted as hair but others have called earrings.[16] Charles Gates has drawn the parallel with the image of a nude goddess from Karahöyük in central Anatolia, but here again the discs at the end of the hair may also represent Hathor curls, as on sphinx-shaped ivory furniture legs apparently from Acemhöyük.[17] Another comparison for the hairstyle of the Aigina 'Master of Animals', as well as his facial type, can be found in the Levant on a sheet gold plaque from Byblos (Fig. 174).[18]

On the pendants from Minet el-Beidha and the Uluburun wreck (Figs 170 and 171), one notes that above the head of the female figure is a wide ribbed headdress below a wide ridged suspension loop (a typically Canaanite form of attachment). Both are paralleled on the Aigina Treasure pendant, where the male figure appears to wear a tall crown with four round-tipped feathers. Some scholars have derived this headdress from the Egyptian pharaonic crown consisting of two large plumes with a distinctive upper outward curve above horizontal ram and bull horns (see Fig. 184). The Near East, however, provides parallels of both Bronze Age and the early first millennium BC date that are more appropriately proportioned. The feathered headdress is worn by nude females on some of the so-called 'Astarte' terracotta plaques of the Late Bronze Age (Fig. 175)[19] and on Syrian-style ivories from Megiddo (Fig. 176) and later from Nimrud.[20] Crowns composed of numerous individuated feathers are also worn by sphinxes on the Mari 'Investiture' wall painting, and by male warriors depicted both on a group of controversial bronzes and on cylinder seals.[21]

Returning to the goddess on the elaborate triangular pendant (Fig. 171), she also wears jewellery on the neck, arms and ankles. Similarly, the Aigina Treasure 'Master of Animals' wears spiral bracelets on his wrists and arms, but no pectoral – as is common on images of men in Egypt and as seen on some of the Canaanite pieces. The goddess's attributes and significance may perhaps be even better understood when looking at her depiction on a more monumental scale – on votive stelae of the 18th to 20th Dynasties, depicting the nude goddess Qudshu or

Qadesh, identified by inscription with Anat-Asherah (Fig. 177).[22] As is typical for Ishtar, she stands on a lion. The goddess has a flat element below the sun-disc on her head, wears a Hathor wig, is frontal with arms outstretched to hold lotus and serpent, and is approached by Min at left with a tall feathered headdress and Reshef at right in a kilt, who may be represented as an Asiatic in such scenes. It is of interest that many of these elements come together on the 'Master of Animals' pendant in a way not seen elsewhere.

The head and torso of the goddess on the Levantine pendants are frontal, with arms bent at the elbows and extended, and they may grasp animals in a symmetrical composition (Figs 170 and 171). On some examples gazelles are held upright by the feet. In some respects this parallels the position of the 'Master of Animals' and brings up the issue of the origins of the general theme and its introduction into the Aegean.

The theme of a central male human figure dominating animals in a symmetrical composition achieves its full expression in Late Uruk-style images of the late fourth millennium BC, as seen on the Gebel el-Arak knife handle from Egypt.[23] Tentative renderings of the subject are very rare in the Aegean before the Late Bronze Age, with some instances on Minoan seals, including one from Mallia (Fig. 178). The Mallia seal and others from pre- and protopalatial contexts on Crete suggest that, by the onset of the Middle Bronze Age, this theme must have been transmitted to the Aegean from the Near East.[24] Some of the best examples are seen on Late Bronze Age glyptic found both in the Aegean and on Cyprus, one on a famous cylinder seal found at Enkomi. Probably dating from the fourteenth century BC, the seal depicts a male figure standing between two large birds and two lions, his arms extended in a posture characteristic of Aegean heroes (Fig. 179). The bent arm posture is more common on Near Eastern cylinder seals.[25] Regarding specifically the symmetrical scenes with water birds, this is one of the most unusual features on the Aigina Treasure pendant (Fig. 11). The water birds are very large and, like geese in Egyptian art, are distinctive enough to be identifiable. According to experts at the American Museum of Natural History in New York, they are similar to the waterfowl represented on the marsh scene that adorned the Tomb of Nebamun in Egyptian Thebes, and belong to the species called Egyptian Goose.

On the Aigina Treasure pendant the geese are not held by the feet, as is usual in Egyptian renderings of birds caught in the marshes, nor by the throats as on an Aegean seal from Vapheio with a central female whose arms are bent in the Near Eastern manner.[26] Rather the hands of the man are simply placed over the necks. In Near Eastern art, there appear to be no close parallels for this type of scene. What comes to mind are the first millennium BC bronze plaques of the Phoenician period, perhaps horse cheek pieces, probably from the Iberian peninsula (Fig. 180).[27] Other features associated with the water birds on these plaques are lotuses, depicted on the necklace of the goddess who holds either sistra or perhaps an instrument for fowling as in the original Egyptian marsh scenes, and the bird bodies form a boat-like shape. Earlier Canaanite jewellery, specifically the gold ornament from Byblos (Fig. 169), shows three Egyptian Geese comparable to the Aigina Treasure examples (and may share some technical similarities).

This brings us to the subject of another feature of the 'Master of Animals' pendant that it is difficult to explain: the bow-shaped extensions protruding perhaps from behind his kilt and extending upwards, similar to the 'snake frames' held up above the heads of Minoan 'Mistresses of Animals' on Late Bronze Age lentoid seals. On one Minet el-Beidha pendant (Fig. 170) there are two snakes crossing each other and emerging from behind the figure at the pelvic area. Does this suggest then that the ridged extensions from the sides of the Aigina Treasure hero are really reptilian?

In his 1989 article Gates mentions various explanations for these elements. He alludes to snake imagery and to the *uraei* on a Byblos plaque above a boat-like form, as well as to horns, in this case the ram's horns that form part of the Egyptian *atef* crown. Margaret Gill's suggestion that they are bovine horns – backed up by Hägg and Lindau's belief that they were horns of sacrificed bulls – is also suggested on a sealing from Pylos where a goddess, like Near Eastern deities, wears the horns as part of her headdress (Fig. 182).[28] Usually the Aegean goddess holds the elements above her, the horned element suggesting perhaps the adaptation of the eastern sign of divinity. In other cases, quadrupeds sit above forms that resemble unstrung composite bows or perhaps horns of already sacrificed animals. With such a variation in placement, however, there continue to be many interpretations of this element.[29]

The unique position of the 'frames' as emerging from the kilt of the Aigina Treasure figure led Gates to suggest parallels with depictions of one type of nude goddess on Syrian cylinder seals of the early second millennium BC. She holds in both outstretched hands the two ends of an arc-shaped ridged element with bud-like tips.[30] Although often interpreted as a deity lifting the hem of her transparent garment to reveal her nudity, the representation on a plaque from Alalakh (Fig. 181) seems to suggest a divinity framed by vegetation. It is of interest that the one Aegean jewel most often cited in connection with the Aigina pendant, found in Mycenae Shaft Grave III, also depicts a goddess framed by lotuses.[31] Therefore, in considering the thematic content of the Aigina pendant, one may interpret them the way that Evans did – as lotus buds which the geese seem to nibble.

Thus, in attempting to understand the iconography of the Aigina Treasure pendant, one can only say that its elements relate to and appear to derive from Syro-Canaanite imagery on jewellery and glyptic of the middle to late Late Bronze Age.

This view can only be enhanced by this author's interpretation of one piece, which has been shown to share a number of features with the Aigina jewel: the gold pendant from Tell el-Dabʿa (Fig. 190). This pendant was found at the Nile Delta site in a 13th Dynasty plundered tomb, and the attribution to Minoan manufacture by Gisela Walberg is now widely accepted.[32] The features of the Tell el-Dabʿa pendant that most closely relate to the Aigina Treasure 'Master of Animals' pendant are its technique, also found in the Levant,[33] and its ground-line with three raised circular elements. However, is this an argument that the Dabʿa pendant is Aegean or that the Aigina Treasure pendant is even more closely connected to the art of the Levant?

As I have already argued, the gold pendant from Tell el-Dabʿa seems most likely to be a Canaanite piece, made locally at Tell el-Dabʿa itself or in the Levant by a craftsman versed in the

Levantine animal style. While Walberg states that the Dabʿa piece 'does not show any Egyptian, Egyptianizing or Oriental features',[34] in fact the style and postures of the animals, with their near hind legs extended back – thereby providing a sense of stability – look very Near Eastern, and are more closely paralleled on Syrian seals (Fig. 183)[35] than on any examples from Crete. The collars and harnesses of the animals on the Tell el-Dabʿa pendant appear to suggest that they are dogs rather than lions, and canines are sometimes represented in Syria with open jaws.[36] Their postures, however, are more common for images of felines in the Levant.

Dogs are represented in the Aigina Treasure on the large and unusual gold hoops (Figs 18, 19), where they are also in heraldic posture. One foreleg is extended outwards in a version of the Old Kingdom victory posture for royal sphinxes and griffins – a stance that is evident on a Middle Kingdom pendant, openwork in technique but otherwise very different technically from the Aigina Treasure jewellery (Fig. 184).[37] This posture was transmitted to Syria in the Middle Bronze Age and is evident on seals with other Egyptianizing elements. Now we also have the extraordinary silver pendant of confronted hawk-headed griffins, discussed fully in this volume and referred to below (Fig. 192).

In Aegean art dogs are generally shown engaged in the chase or at rest. One Late Bronze Age lentoid seal from Mycenae shows two dogs facing one another (Fig. 186),[38] but they are still part of the hunt, as they are seen flanking their victim, a wild goat, and are not detached as symbolic elements as we see in oriental art. Further support for a Canaanite attribution for the Dabʿa pendant (and, by association, the 'Master of Animals' pendant) was revealed in the Aigina Treasure conference in 2000 by Robert Schiestl, although the presenter came to a different conclusion. Schiestl made a startling discovery in the Petrie Collection of a second Dabʿa-type pendant with symmetrically placed Egyptianizing griffins standing on elements very similar to those on the other two jewels (Fig. 192). Characteristic Egyptian aspects of the Petrie griffins include the falcon head, the wig lappets that are typical for animal gods, the wing folded against the body, and tails upcurved with feathers displayed, elements familiar from Middle and New Kingdom depictions.[39]

These features were combined in various ways on the griffins (and sphinxes) carved on Syrian cylinder seals.[40] The horns on their heads may, like those on Syrian-style griffins from Kültepe and attributed to Acemhöyük, represent a variation of a divine Egyptian headdress, the latter with three tiny feathers and spiralling horns deriving from the *andjty* crown (see Figs 184 and 185). On the Petrie pendant they may come from the headdress associated with Hathor, as rendered on an ivory plaque from Byblos, which also displays a ridged element (Fig. 187). Such features, while at home in the Near East, are foreign to the Aegean, as is the static stance of quadrupeds with feet aligned, effectively immobilizing these felines even in the most dynamic of Levantine styles.

The interpretation of the Petrie Collection silver pendant and the Tell el-Dabʿa gold ornament as oriental rather than western would then reinforce the view that the 'Master of Animals' pendant is of eastern Mediterranean creation or inspiration. It is possible that the Dabʿa and Petrie ornaments were in fact created in the Nile Delta, where a local, somewhat more dynamic Syro-Canaanite style appears to have developed, as is clear from the image on a seal impression from the site.[41] The other possibility is the southern Levant. This appears to be the direction we must follow to resolve some of the difficulties in interpreting the Aigina Treasure jewel as well.

Aigina pectoral and golden roundels: connections with Anatolia

Connections between the Aegean and central Anatolia may also be demonstrated in the Aigina hoard. Although the link between these regions during the early second millennium BC is not yet proven in the archaeological record, certain art-historical studies – of vessel shapes, the form of the Mallia leopard axe, the origins of the Minoan griffin, and possibly the iconography of libation ritual in both areas – may suggest that contacts existed.[42] Similarly, a number of Aegean seal shapes and motifs may have parallels in the trading colonies or *karums* at Kültepe, Acemhöyük, Boğazköy, Alishar Höyük and particularly Karahöyük, subjects that I have discussed elsewhere.[43]

A small incised ivory with a griffin, attributable to the site of Acemhöyük in central Anatolia and datable to the early eighteenth century BC (Fig. 185), has features that appear later on Aegean griffin images.[44] Other ivories in the same group provide evidence for the effect of Egyptian imagery in Anatolia. Sphinxes depicted on furniture finials and plaques exhibit Hathor-like curls and have persuaded many scholars of a connection with the pectoral in the Aigina Treasure, with its inlaid eyes and brows and distinctive refined technique of manufacture (see pp. 19–20 in this volume).[45] Also of interest, the haircurls atop the head of the sphinx carved in relief on a plaque have also been thought to be an allusion to Cretan hairstyles, pointing further to intercultural connections. Parallels for the object type, a pectoral with head-shaped terminals, are found in Egypt and the Levant. Examples include the often cited larger pectorals from Byblos.[46]

One other corpus of material from the Aigina Treasure consists of fifty-four gold roundels with central raised rosettes and distinctive disconnected loop borders (Fig. 63). It is this border that finds its closest parallels in central Anatolia, adapted for a ring design of Old Hittite date (Fig. 188),[47] and commonly used on glyptic, as seen on seal impressions from Karahöyük and Acemhöyük (Fig. 189).[48]

Conclusion

Thus, in conclusion, how do we answer the questions we all pose regarding the Aigina Treasure? Certainly the objects in the hoard could all have been made within the general timeframe suggested by Higgins. While technical arguments have been made in this conference for consistency in materials and techniques of manufacture, the physical appearance of the objects themselves seems to support other possible conclusions. Some beads in the treasure look purely Mycenaean, while other more spectacular pieces display features not easily explainable in Aegean terms. Rather, elements of the treasure seem to derive from various areas of the Near East, leaving questions regarding the sources and dates of original manufacture and the identification of their craftsmen. Perhaps the finest work, the small pectoral with human-head terminals, as well as the roundels, can be most closely associated with central Anatolia in the eighteenth century BC. The 'Master of Animals' pendant, less carefully worked but more ambitious and complex in design, has characteristics that appear to relate to Canaanite imagery on jewellery. It can perhaps be best understood as a work produced beyond the Aegean, as suggested by Sarah Morris.[49] It would then be related to an early group of eastern Mediterranean works, integrating stylistic and iconographic elements from East and West, such as the frescoes and gold ornament from Tell el-Dabᶜa and Syrian seals depicting Minoan and other motifs in a dynamic Mediterranean style.

Notes

1. Higgins 1957a, 42–57; Higgins 1979.
2. Individual pieces, such as the gold cup, have been related to material of LM/LH I rather than the MM period; Davis 1977, 322, note 677.
3. Musche 1992, pl. 29; Potts 2003, 314, cat. no. 210b; Matthews *et al.* 1994, 185; Moortgat and Moortgat-Correns 1974, pl. 21:4, 5.
4. Orthmann 1975, pl. 122b; Contenau 1931, 696, figs 486, 487.
5. Lilyquist 1994, 15, fig. 19.
6. Metropolitan Museum of Art 1984, 23, no. 24.
7. Collon 1995, 108; see also Barnett 1960, 29.
8. Porada 1976, 52.
9. Tufnell 1983, 57 ff., fig. 1; McGovern 1985, 36, fig. 27.
10. Dunand 1950, pl. 138, no. 17754.
11. Schaeffer 1949, 36, fig. 10; Barrelet 1958, 34 ff., pl. 2c–e; Negbi 1970, 30 ff., pl. 4; Platt 1976, 103 ff.; for the Uluburun wreck, see note 15 below.
12. Becatti 1955, 38 ff.
13. Technical analyses reported at the British Museum conference in 2000 appear to confirm that the piece is ancient.
14. Rehak 1996, 43.
15. Pulak 1997, 243; Bass *et al.* 1989, 4, figs 3, 5 (smaller pendant with incised figure).
16. Evans 1892–3, 198. This interpretation would circumvent the problem that earrings were not shown as worn by men until well into the Bronze Age.
17. Gates 1989, 219.
18. Dunand 1950, pl. 164:9306.
19. Albright 1939, 111, nos 3 and 5, 118; see also Yadin *et al.* 1960, pl. 158: 2, 8; May 1935, 598, pl. 31.
20. Loud 1939, 175, pl. 39; Barnett 1982, pl. 44c.
21. Mari wall painting: Porada 1942, 57 ff.; Negbi 1961, 111 ff.; Parrot 1958, 163 ff. and pl. ix.
22. Cornelius 1994, 59 ff., pls 20–23.
23. Aldred 1965, 35.
24. For early versions of this theme, see Demargne 1939, 122, fig. 1; *CMS* II 1, no. 469; for the theme and its appearance and meaning in Greece, see Spartz 1962.
25. Aruz 1997, fig. 13; occasionally in the Aegean, *CMS* V 2, no. 113, the Near Eastern posture is adopted.
26. *CMS* I, no. 233.
27. Sabatino *et al.* 1988, 236.
28. Gates 1989, 219 ff.; Gill 1969, 93 ff.; Hägg and Lindau 1984, 67 ff.; *CMS* I, no. 379.
29. *CMS* I, no. 189; Hägg and Lindau 1984, 74.
30. Gates 1989, 220–1.
31. Mylonas 1983, 38–9, pl. 26.
32. Walberg 1991a, 111–12.
33. Aruz 1995a, 44–6; Dunand 1939, pl. 86: 3287, 1442; Dunand 1950, pl. 138: 17754, 7727; I thank Christine Lilyquist for these references.
34. Walberg 1991a, 111.
35. For a discussion of the differences between Near Eastern and Aegean heraldic lion postures, see Aruz 1993, 39–40. The foreleg posture for confronted (standing and couchant) lions and sphinxes in Syrian art is a variation of the Egyptian victory stance that first occurs in the Old Kingdom.
36. See the gold dagger sheath from Byblos: Dunand 1950, pl. 118; the hatched lines on the body run diagonally and may be part of the harness and not indicate animal fur, which is generally represented as a hatched band outlining the belly both on Syrian seals and also on the handle of the gold dagger sheath.
37. Wilkinson 1971, pl. 17. For heraldic compositions of canine-bodied Seth animals in Egyptian art, see *op. cit.*, pl. 20 (Middle Kingdom pectoral); Kaplony 1981, 121, pl. 170 (Old Kingdom cylinder seal). C. Lilyquist (personal communication) notes that in Egyptian art such symmetrically placed creatures do not engage; Aldred 1978, 185, pls 25, 26.
38. *CMS* I, no. 81.
39. Schiestl 2000, 127–8; Wilkinson and Hill 1983, 68: MMA acc. no. 33.8.14.
40. Özgüç 1968, pl. 20c; see also note 44 below.
41. Porada 1984, 485–8.
42. For a fuller discussion of this evidence, see Aruz 2008b.
43. Aruz 1993, 37 ff.
44. Aruz 2008a, 138, cat. no. 76. It is part of the Pratt Ivories, a collection that came to the Metropolitan Museum in the 1930s. Subsequent controlled excavations at the site of Acemhöyük produced similar pieces.
45. Poursat 1973, 111–14.
46. Montet 1928, 166, 619, pl. 95.
47. Musche 1992, pl. 55 (Fingerschmuck no. 2).
48. Alp 1968, 209, pl. 78; Özgüç 1983, 419, fig. 8; see Aruz 1995a, 44, for a discussion of this Anatolian motif.
49. Morris 1998, 283; see also Cline 1998, 210.

9
Three pendants: Tell el-Dabᶜa, Aigina and a new silver pendant from the Petrie Museum

Robert Schiestl

In W.M.F. Petrie's catalogue *Objects of Daily Use*, published in 1927, among a miscellaneous collection of jewellery, a small silver pendant is presented.[1] Even in its heavily corroded state, the pendant exhibits various features that link it closely to the well-known gold pendant found at Tell el-Dabᶜa (Figs 190 and 191), as well as to the 'Master of Animals' pendant and the dog earrings of the Aigina Treasure (see Figs 11, 18 and 19).

Petrie's brief and amazingly accurate description was as follows:[2]

> Silver. Two hawk-headed sphinxes of Mentu, facing, wearing the crown of Lower Egypt. The bases on which they stand are not clear, they look like boats. At the back was a horizontal tube at the top, and another at the base, for threading. The tails of the sphinxes curl like a dog's tail, a form which is very unusual. This pendant is made by impressing a sheet of silver in a die, and then soldering it to a flat sheet for the back. It is thus very thin and hollow; and the amount of corrosion that it has suffered prevents it being cleaned. XIIth dynasty.

Fortunately the penultimate statement has been proven wrong, owing to the marvellous work done by the British Museum conservator Marilyn Hockey. Now an in-depth look at the details of the pendant is possible and we can see what Petrie could not.

The Petrie Museum pendant

Technique and provenance
The pendant[3] (Fig. 192) is 3.2 cm high and 5.4 cm wide at the base line. It was produced by cutting out two silver sheets and soldering their edges together; the front sheet had been worked in repoussé technique, the back remained flat. Some details on the front have been added by chasing. The back sheet has been folded over at the top, thus creating a small tube for the suspension of the pendant. Three little wire loops have been soldered on along the bottom of the base in order to attach additional pendants, possibly small discs, which have not survived.

Petrie purchased the pendant in Egypt in 1912, while working at Kafr Tarkhan/Kafr Ammar.[4] Technologically, the piece does not stand in an Egyptian tradition: Middle Kingdom pendants are exclusively made in cloisonné technique, a method in which precisely cut-out semi-precious stones are fitted into cells created by metal strips soldered at a right angle to the sheet metal base.[5] The reverse side of the pendant, which was not visible when worn, was usually worked in repoussé technique and details were added by chasing. However, not until the New Kingdom do repoussé and chasing appear on the face of pendants, either as a complementary feature to the continuing tradition of inlays[6] or with the whole pendant fashioned in that way.[7]

Hence, from a technological point of view, an Egyptian manufacture can be disputed. Attempts at localizing the place of manufacture must be based primarily on an iconographic discussion. While such a discussion can never replace a lost context, essentially the same questions would be asked of the object had it been found in a known context.

Mirroring the reception of the Tell el-Dabᶜa pendant,[8] the most likely candidates for place of manufacture for the Petrie pendant are the Aegean, the Levant – in either case under strong Egyptian influence – or the north-eastern Nile Delta. While forming part of an interrelated discussion, the pendants will be treated separately: first, an attempt will be made to embed the Petrie pendant in its cultural context; secondly, the Tell el-Dabᶜa pendant will be presented in its archaeological context.

The Petrie pendant's protagonists
The antithetic creatures are Egyptian-style griffins, composed of leonine bodies and heads of hawks with short beaks. They wear a long, Egyptian-style headdress, which falls to the chest. The heads are fitted with C-spirals, the wings are folded on the body (Barta griffin type b).[9] Both griffins are shown standing with three legs on the ground and one front leg extended, which overlaps with the front leg of the opposing animal. The bases consist of horizontal bars ending in rounded elements.

Petrie's identification may have been aided by De Morgan's discovery of a pendant in 1894, from Princess Mereret's tomb in the pyramid complex of Senwosret III at Dahshur (Fig. 184).[10]

This pendant's griffins, flanking a cartouche spelling the name of Senwosret III, are shown in the Egyptian pose of 'trampling the enemies'. The Petrie griffins wear the same headdress as the Dahshur griffins; however, the latter's heads are fitted with *andjty* crowns, consisting of cow's and ram's horns, and a pair of tall feathers. The wings are folded on the body, as on the Petrie pendant. From beneath the folded wings, tail feathers emerge. This is the canonical Egyptian style of the Old and Middle Kingdom for depicting folded griffins' wings, as opposed to folded wings of sphinxes – as shown, for example, by the reconstructed reliefs from the 6th Dynasty pyramid complex of Pepi II from Saqqara (Fig. 196).[11] In the case of the sphinx, shown on the top, the wings are larger and more stylized, with a scale-like pattern, and are shown without tail feathers. While this differentiation between griffins' and sphinxes' wings was rigorously maintained throughout the Old and Middle Kingdoms, by the time of the New Kingdom it was abandoned and sphinxes are shown with tail feathers as well.[12] The Dahshur and Petrie pendants show the same wing composition of tail feathers, four and three respectively, emerging from below the wing. The adherence to such detail is remarkable and stands in contrast to the adaptation of the trampling scene. In this classic Egyptian pose, developed in the Old Kingdom, sphinx and griffin represent royal power and are, in this context, interchangeable. On the Petrie pendant, the enemies have been dropped, the griffins have been pushed together and touch at the tip of their beaks, like the snouts of the Dabʿa dogs (Fig. 190) and the Aigina dogs (Figs 18 and 19). The paws of the extended front leg have been lowered and overlap with the opposing griffin's paw. Both features are unknown in Egyptian iconography; from an Egyptian point of view the animals are too close, and there is no overlapping and rarely 'touching' in Middle Kingdom Egyptian art. Figures and signs are only adjacent to each other; they do not interact. Exceptions are small confronted bird amulets, where one does also find examples with the birds' beaks touching – for example from Khnumet's burial at Dahshur[13] and from various non-royal Middle Kingdom burials.[14] But they seem more like hieroglyphs simply pushed together until their borders touch. This still holds true for Egyptian lion amulets of the New Kingdom,[15] which show the antithetical animals barely touching.

Also removed in the Petrie pendant is the griffins' threatening regal stance, while the touching beaks and overlapping legs create an impression of harmless affability. This informality is inconsistent with Egyptian 'hieroglyphic' poses and renders the scene meaningless in an Egyptian context. But what if we consider it in an Aegean or Levantine context?

Both Levantine and Aegean art adapt Egyptian art freely, losing and adding iconographic elements and meanings.[16] Comparable variations of the trampling pose are amply known from Syrian seals, though never with griffins but always sphinxes, alone or in pairs.[17] The enemies may be depicted, or omitted, or replaced by snakes. The front paws may touch, yet there is no overlapping. A very good parallel to the overlapping of the front legs is shown by the bees of Mallia–Chrysolakkos.[18]

The bodies of the griffins on the Petrie pendant are more compact than and not as slender as the Egyptian lion's body from Mereret's pendant or as in another Middle Kingdom example showing a hawk-headed lion from the collection of the Myers Museum, Eton College,[19] presumed to be from a royal burial at Dahshur. The Syrian griffins and sphinxes also tend to have slender bodies like the Egyptian creatures. In contrast, the earliest Aegean/Minoan group has broad upper bodies, as shown by the Middle Minoan standing sphinx from a prism, probably from Sitea, in the Giamalakis Collection (Fig. 193)[20] and the earliest representations of Minoan griffins from the Phaistos sealings (Figs 194 and 195).[21] The Mallia clay sphinx[22] also displays a particularly broad upper body.

Undoubtedly, though, little otherwise links the Phaistos griffins with the ones from the Petrie pendant. The elongated beaks and upraised wings are to become trademarks of Aegean griffins; later typical features – such as spirals on the neck and upper body, adder marks on the wings, a feathered crest on the head, and spirals dangling down the back – are missing.

The wings of both Minoan and Syrian griffins are never shown folded on the body; either they are wingless or the wings are raised. Some examples of sphinxes on Old Syrian glyptic[23] show an abstract 'ladder pattern' hatching on the body, which could be interpreted as indicating folded wings. These marks, however, depict details of the fur, as shown by the griffin from the Ahmose axe from the tomb of Ahhotep,[24] which shows both raised wings and such vertical marks on the body. Folded wings are an Egyptian characteristic and neither Aegean nor Levantine.

The two C-spirals on the griffins' heads are unique. They do not fit in any of the eastern Mediterranean griffin traditions – the Phaistos sealings showing either one individual curl or three leaf-like elements. The Syrian and Anatolian griffins are also shown either with one curl, falling off to the back,[25] or wearing a sundry array of elements, presumably degenerated remnants of Egyptian crowns.[26] The horns or the tufts of hair sprouting from the Sitea/Giamalakis sphinx (Fig. 193) have also been linked to the ram's horns of Egyptian *andjty* and *atef* crowns, which on their way to Crete lost the tall central element while emphasizing the horizontal elements.[27] The Petrie C-spirals are reminiscent of the double volutes emanating from the woman's head on the plaque pin from Mycenae, Shaft Grave III,[28] or they could simply be a doubling of the single curl from the Dabʿa dogs. Yet unlike all the above-mentioned elements, the C-spirals do not emerge from the head, but seem to rest on top, like an independent element consciously added. They are symmetrical and cleanly executed, and therefore, in my opinion, do not fall into the Syrian tradition of degenerated Hathoric cow's horns. If then the spiral was added as a separate element, this also would point to the Aegean. Except for the running spiral, spirals were not common in the early second millennium BC in the Near East.[29]

Finally, the round tail is not particularly diagnostic. In Egypt it is limited to the depiction of dogs' tails; it can, however, also be found both on protopalatial seals[30] and in Levantine depictions of animals, such as on a dagger sheath from Byblos.[31]

The pendant's base

The closest link between the Aigina, Dabʿa and Petrie pendants is the base. As in the case of the Dabʿa dogs, the Petrie griffins each stand on their own flat base, which ends in a round volute. In the Dabʿa pendant and the Aigina 'Master of Animals' pendant, a third round element was added in the middle, from which, in the latter, lotus flowers sprout. The interior of the horizontal bar is decorated with hatched lines, a feature also present in the Dabʿa pendant, where the lines are more vertical. Evans, in keeping with his highly Egyptianizing interpretation of the setting as a Nilotic fowling scene, considered the Aigina base a stylized Egyptian bark.[32] To support his theory, he cites the supposedly frequent depiction of Egyptian barks decorated with lotus flowers at their prow and stern.[33] Higgins emphatically rejected the boat theory and laid the emphasis on the flowers, thus initially suggesting a marsh[34] and later a field of lotus flowers.[35] However, he ventured no suggestion as to what the base was supposed to depict. On a formal level, similarities to Egyptian papyrus barks do exist. A bark on a Middle Kingdom relief from Lisht[36] also displays a partly curled-up end, almost creating a volute. Comparable shapes, however, can also be found on Near Eastern seals.[37] These simple Egyptian barks are made of papyrus and consequently generally end in umbels of papyrus, not lotus.[38] From an iconographic point of view, the setting of trampling scenes on barks would be an oddity.

As of the New Kingdom, it becomes very popular for scenes on pectorals to be set on boats, which fill the entire width of the base of the pendant: Ahhotep's pectoral[39] is the oldest example.[40] These barks are often shown floating on stylized water and always remain enclosed in a kiosk frame. Variations on this scene, associated with the sun-god's voyage across the ocean of the sky, become very popular on private funerary pectorals.[41] Regardless of how crude the jewel may be, however, the barks, whether shown in detail or stylized, are always immediately identifiable as such. The design, even on the minute space of a scarab seal,[42] had never been experimented with to the extent of clouding the crucial messages these images were conveying. Occasionally, bow- and stern-posts end in papyrus umbels,[43] rarely in lotus flowers.[44] Other rare variations show the ends consisting of heads of gazelles[45] or snakes,[46] or topped with sun discs.[47] A non-Egyptian artisan would not have been bound by any of these formal or iconographic concerns and could have transferred the lotus decorating boats or growing wild in fowling scenes on to an abstracted bark, as well as relocating the griffins 'trampling the enemy'.

However, looking to the Aegean, another suggestion for the origin of the base could be put forward. Possibly it developed from Early Bronze Age pins with attached plaques, which rested on wire bases ending in wire spirals. Examples are the antithetic birds from Poliochni on Lemnos[48] and a pin from Troy, Treasure O.[49] While a large chronological gap separates these pieces from our pendants, the slim corpus of Aegean jewellery of the intervening centuries leaves room for the imagination. Trade in the northern Aegean in the later Early Bronze Age was extensive and lively.[50] A close link also exists between pins with plaques and pendants suspended from necklaces: Higgins, in comparing the 'Master of Animals' pendant with the Mycenaean plaque pin from Shaft Grave III, suggested the former might have originally been suspended from a pin as well.[51] A development of a quasi-generic Aegean/Anatolian base might be proposed, which could be used simply as a neutral base line, as in the case of the Petrie and the Dabʿa pendants, or – as in the case of the Aigina pendant – could be adapted through the addition of lotus flowers to create a marshy or swampy setting. Hence, the Dabʿa and Petrie pendant did not omit the flowers;[52] rather they were added for the Aigina scene.

Three wire loops are soldered on to the base line of the Petrie pendant. The holes bored through the base of the Aigina 'Master of Animals' pendant and the soldered-on loops of the Aigina pectoral with human-headed terminals (see Fig. 41), reminiscent of an Egyptian wsx-collar,[53] show that from these loops additional circular pendants should be suspended. In the Petrie pendant nothing of such appendices remains. The fondness for chain attachments has a long Aegean tradition, as Higgins has pointed out: examples come from Mochlos;[54] and, more contemporary to our pendant, the bees of Mallia–Chrysolakkos and the Middle Kingdom jewellery of Princess Khnumet from her tomb in the pyramid complex of Amenemhat II at Dahshur[55] could be added. The rare Levantine parallels for such attachments do not use wire rings but little tubes.[56]

Summing up, I ultimately suggest an Aegean manufacture for the Petrie pendant, under both strong Egyptian and Near Eastern influence. Egypt contributed the griffins, while their pose was adapted in the Near East. Although the pendant does not immediately suggest an Aegean or Minoan origin, most of the evidence – the technique, the shape of the griffins' bodies, the overlapping of the front legs, the C-spirals on the heads, the base, the loops for attachments – in my opinion points in the direction of the Aegean. A comparable item, also possibly Aegean with a high degree of Egyptianization, is an unprovenanced golden falcon ornament with wings inlaid in cloisonné technique, now in the British Museum.[57] Chronologically I would place the Petrie pendant very close to the Dabʿa dog pendant, namely the first half of the eighteenth century BC, thus hardly changing Petrie's original dating. While these individual pieces of evidence are still too singular to draw historical or art-historical conclusions, the fusion of styles and the difficulty in pinpointing the place of manufacture in some ways anticipates discussions familiar from the Late Bronze Age.[58] One object that already has opened such a debate is the Tell el-Dabʿa pendant.

The Tell el-Dabʿa pendant

Since its discovery in 1989 and first publication in 1991 by Gisela Walberg,[59] the Tell el-Dabʿa gold pendant (Figs 190 and 191) has been much scrutinized, while also serving as a focal point for wider-reaching discussions on eastern Mediterranean Middle Bronze cultural interactions. Walberg's initial designation as Aegean and presumably Minoan[60] has been widely accepted.[61] It was Joan Aruz who first voiced doubts, suggesting, mainly on the basis of comparisons with Syrian seals, that it is a 'Canaanite piece, made either locally at Tell el-Dabʿa itself or in the Levant'.[62] This idea was enthusiastically taken up by Sarah Morris,[63] who discusses the Dabʿa pendant and other 'orphans'[64] of the second-millennium BC eastern Mediterranean. Her approach also advocates a shifting of the emphasis from the great cultural superpowers of Egypt and Crete to undervalued Levantine regions such as Asiatic craftsmen in the Delta.[65] While the new focus on new regions and shifting centres is crucial, chronological questions tend to get pushed aside. Despite there being no inherent connection between the Tell el-Dabʿa pendant and the ʿEzbet Helmi wall paintings, and despite being separated by hundreds of years, the two issues are at times blended in discussions.[66] The focus here will be on the pendant and its Middle Bronze Age IIA (or late Middle Kingdom) period alone. Middle Bronze Age Tell el-Dabʿa certainly offers itself as a site for reassessing the international climate of this age. Hence, an attempt will be made to put the dog pendant into context.

The 'palace necropolis' of Tell el-Dabʿa, stratum d/1

The site of Tell el-Dabʿa, ancient Avaris, lies in the north-eastern Nile Delta.[67] In antiquity the town was situated on the Pelusiac branch of the Nile and spread out over a group of mounds, so-called *geziras* or turtlebacks, which were protected from inundation. Of these tells only one remains visible today, namely Tell el-Dabʿa. To its west is the area designated F/I, where the tomb p/17-no. 14, in which the pendant was discovered, lies. It was erected in a cemetery in the garden of a large residential building, frequently called a palace,[68] and consequently the cemetery has been termed a 'palace necropolis'. The residence and the cemetery associated with it belong to stratum minor d/1 (Fig. 198), which is dated, in dynastic terms, to the early 13th Dynasty, or about 1780–1750 BC. In the 'palace' area, in the same stratum, four sherds of Classical Kamares ware, probably all from the same cup, were also found.[69]

The cemetery extends to the south of the residence and was excavated from 1985 to 1990 by an Austrian team under the direction of Manfred Bietak.[70] To date, twenty-nine tombs, generally arranged in parallel rows running from north-east to south-west have been excavated. The full extent of the necropolis and its boundaries is not known. However, it is certainly larger than the hitherto excavated area. To the east of the residence, a second 'palatial' structure was discovered and partially excavated; it could represent an expansion of the first residence or an independent second unit. In any case, to the south of this building a similar layout of rows of tombs appears, of which to date only the southern part has been excavated.

This was a cemetery for an elite associated with the palatial residence. While the design and construction of the residence and the tombs are Egyptian, certain features designate the interred as foreigners, linking them to Syria–Palestine: the dead are buried in a contracted position and donkeys have been ritually deposited in front of the tombs. All weapons deposited in the tombs are exclusively of Syro-Palestinian type and, presumably, manufacture (see below).

The large size of the tombs, along with the fact that they were marked by prominent structures above ground and an integrated garden design, eventually contributed to a high level of tomb robbing. The area, which had been used as a cemetery before the construction of the residence, continued to be used as such after the abandonment of the residence. While some smaller tombs of the preceding and the following strata escaped plundering, every single tomb of the 'palace necropolis' was robbed, although to varying degrees. Some sections of tombs remained intact and some parts of ensembles were also *in situ*. The pendant tomb, p/17-no. 14, lies at the southern edge of the excavated area, approximately 75 m from the 'palace'.[71] A huge east–west oriented Sebakh-pit, created by farmers digging for fertile earth, cuts off the whole necropolis along its southern flank. The tomb was thus sliced in half along its east–west axis, almost completely cutting off the southern half.

The tomb's architecture and its contents

The tomb is built of sandy mud-bricks and erected in a pit 7 m long and 2.7 m wide. The orientation of the tomb, ESE–WNW, is aligned with the orientation of the residence to the north. As was the case in the row of tombs to the north,[72] a chapel-like superstructure had probably originally been built over the tomb. No substantial traces of this remain, however, except for a small row of bricks to the west of the chamber (Fig. 199, situation 1), which could be interpreted as remnants of a superstructure. In front of the entrance to the tomb to the east, a pair of donkeys was deposited (Fig. 199, situation 2), a Near Eastern funerary feature[73] very common in the tombs of this cemetery: over two thirds of the tombs excavated in this stratum have donkey burials associated with them.

The rectangular tomb-chamber (measurements on the outside 4.26 x 2.13 m) was covered with a mud-brick barrel vault, the greater part of which had collapsed when the tomb was robbed in antiquity (Fig. 199). The vault can be reconstructed as consisting of three courses of bricks (Fig. 197). While the bricks of the inner course were laid at a right angle to the axis of the chamber, in the outer two courses the bricks were parallel to it. Vaults of more than two courses at Tell el-Dabʿa can so far be documented only in tombs of the 'palace cemetery'. While these tombs are often very large, it should be noted that it was not the size of the chamber that necessitated the construction of such a multi-layered vault. Expenditure on tomb construction might have been considered one of the means of expressing status.

The robbers had entered the tomb via a tunnel in the north-western corner, and pilfered it thoroughly. The result, for us, is a very disturbed context which, in order to reconstruct some of the original arrangements, is presented here in a sequence of four 'situations' (Figs 199 and 200). These 'situations' essentially reflect the order of excavation, but it should be emphasized that they do not represent phases of use. Under the debris of the collapsed vault, the partial skeletal remains of two burials were encountered (Fig. 199, situation 2). In the western half of the chamber, the upper body of a mature man, approximately fifty to sixty years old (burial 1, B 1),[74] was found, while to the east the very disturbed and fragmented remains of the lower body of a woman, twenty to thirty years of age (B 2), were discovered. The position of the man's body, in the western end of the tomb with his head to the east, reflects the typical burial position of this and the previous stratum. Either this body was still in its original position or, if it had been moved by the robbers, this had taken place not very long after the burial, as the bones were still articulated. If the latter scenario is correct, the tomb would definitely have to have been robbed twice, as the lower body was cut off by an intrusive robber's pit. After the removal of these bodies, the disarticulated skeletal remains of the upper body of a second woman of the same age were discovered (burial 3, B 3, see Fig. 200, situation 3). It also became clear that the eastern part of the tomb-chamber had not been touched by the plundering. A small ensemble of ceramics, consisting of a Canaanite jar, two dipper juglets, a 'beer jar' (nos 13, 4, 5, 11 in tomb; see also Fig. 201, nos 7, 6, 5) and some bones of sheep and goats remained *in situ*.

Beneath the tangled bones of the young woman (see Fig. 200, situation 4) the remains of a coffin emerged. It had consisted of a simple rectangular wooden box, the wood having decayed completely and only being recognizable as a dark discoloration. Around those sides of the coffin not directly touching the northern wall of the chamber, a small supporting wall of mud-bricks had been constructed. The coffin was 50 cm wide and preserved to a length of 95 cm, its western end having been cut off by a robber's pit. It was on the floor of this coffin that the pendant lay, among 602 beads (see Fig. 200, situation 4, nos 1 and 2 in coffin). At this point in the excavation, the floor of the tomb-chamber and the coffin were submerged in water.

During analysis of the bones of the upper body of the young woman, the last bead, a large barrel-shaped bead of agate,[75] was subsequently discovered. The close association of the bones of burial 3 with the beads and the pendant are an indication that the pendant had belonged to the young woman, who was between twenty and thirty years old when she was buried. Having been deposited in the coffin, she had been the primary burial; lacking room for a second coffin, the body of the man had probably been deposited on top of the coffin. If this tomb's primary owner was a woman, it also represents the only definite donkey burial in front of a woman's tomb at Tell el-Dabʿa.[76] However, the context is obviously highly disturbed and these conclusions remain uncertain. The fact that three adult bodies[77] were buried in a chamber not planned for such a number does not imply that the tomb was used over a long period of time, as there is no evidence at Tell el-Dabʿa for this practice.

Of the original stringing of the 602 beads[78] nothing remains and any reconstruction of the original arrangement is hypothetical. On the photographs, they have simply been assembled into necklaces by material and shape (Figs 202–11). There are 391 small beads made of garnet, of which most (221) have a roughly spheroid and irregular shape (Fig. 202), whereas 180 are well-made clean spheroid and barrel shapes (Fig. 203). The sizes range from diameters of 2.8 to 4 mm. All have a central or longitudinal borehole. Of the beads, 149 are made of whitish to reddish agate. Most are in various barrel shapes, ranging from very slim (Fig. 206) to wider shapes (Figs 204, 205). While the former are roughly similar in size (lengths range from 5.5 to 8.5 mm), the latter (Figs 204, 205) show size gradations from 0.8 to 1.8 cm. Unusual are the five ribbed agate beads (length 0.6–1.39 cm), roughly barrel shaped with a spheroid, ribbed middle section (Fig. 207, top). Six plain spheroid beads of agate (Fig. 207, bottom, diameter c. 65–75 mm) and two slender elongated drop-shaped beads (Fig. 205, length 2.6 cm) are represented in small numbers. The sixty-one beads of gold or electrum can be divided into the following shapes: thirty-one very small beads (Fig. 209, diameter 2.5–3 mm) have a flattened spheroid body with five to seven grooves running parallel to the borehole. Twenty-three small beads are drop shaped, with a flattened top (Fig. 208; length 4.5–6 mm). Three are barrel shaped (length 3.5–4 mm, diameter 3 mm) and four are biconical (Fig. 208, top left; length 3 mm, diameter 3.2 mm). Some of the metal beads have a dented surface, presumably caused by wear.

All the raw materials are available in Egypt[79] and commonly used for Middle Kingdom jewellery. The spheroid,[80] barrel[81] and drop shapes[82] are very common Egyptian types, but others are more unusual and exact parallels are difficult to find. The barrel-shaped agate beads with wide, ribbed mid-section are documented in Egypt only in faience and without the ribbing[83] or in gold from a Byblos tomb.[84] The small flattened spheroid gold ribbed beads are also documented in Egypt only in faience,[85] whereas similar shapes with a collar are known from Egypt in gold.[86] Similar shapes in metal are very popular in the Near East,[87] the Levant[88] and the Aegean.[89]

While keeping in mind that perhaps not all the beads survived, it is none the less very likely that those used for the suspension of the pendant are to be found among the remaining ones.[90] The pendants of Middle Kingdom royal women are today uniformly displayed and pictured[91] suspended from necklaces using alternating drop-shaped beads and small spherical beads. However, these are all later reconstructions, based on post-excavation analysis. De Morgan as well as Petrie and Brunton were at first at a loss as to how to thread the beads they discovered. De Morgan opted for presenting the Dahshur pendants without any suspension.[92] Brunton's excavation of the treasure of Sithathoryunet at Lahun[93] remains the most careful excavation of pendant beads to date. Nevertheless, Petrie[94] and Brunton[95] were both initially uncertain of the mode of suspension and the latter was not convinced of his own suggestion of a necklace of spherical amethyst beads. Pendants found in non-royal Middle Kingdom burials offered little clarification. The tombs with pendants at Riqqeh[96] and Harageh[97] were both disturbed, but it should be noted that among the assorted beads no drop beads were found in either. Middle Kingdom depictions show pendants[98] suspended from wide bands, presumably a continuation of the Old Kingdom fashion. It was Winlock[99] who, based on Brunton's documentation,[100] sorted Sithathoryunet's beads out and presented the stringing of alternating drop beads (37 per pendant) and spherical beads. As Brunton[101] had already noted, Sithathor's Dahshur pendant was also associated with, among other beads, thirty-seven drop beads,[102] making the same suspension very likely. Subsequently, this has become the standard suspension for all Middle Kingdom royal pendants. While by no means certain, the same stringing, in accordance with the royal examples, is tentatively suggested here (Fig. 212).

The remaining finds from the tomb include a simple dagger blade, which was found near the tomb's entrance, next to offerings represented by sheep and goat bones. Of the ceramics,[103] thirteen vessels remained (Fig. 201), of which nine are of Egyptian clay and shape (Fig. 201, nos 1–5) and four are Syro-Palestinian imports (Fig. 201, nos 6–7). Of Egyptian manufacture are the hemispherical drinking cup (Fig. 201, no. 1)[104] and the ring stands of Nile B 2 (Fig. 201, no. 2) associated with the donkey burials in the entrance pit, along with the dishes (Fig. 201, nos 3, 4) and a 'beer jar' (Fig. 201, no. 5)[105] made of coarse Nile clay from the tomb-chamber. Of imported ware are two dipper juglets, with a finely combed surface and no coating or polish (Fig. 201, no. 6). The globular baggy shape has its best parallels in tombs from the Lebanese coast, for example Lebea Tomb 1,[106] Sin el Fil,[107] Beirut Kharji Tomb 1[108] and Byblos.[109] Similar examples are also known from Ras el-ʿAin/Tel Aphek[110] and Megiddo[111] and as exports to Nubia – for example at Mirgissa.[112] One dipper juglet was found still inside a Canaanite jar (Fig. 201, no. 7) for which a very close parallel in shape and size, and with the very same pottery mark on the shoulder, was also discovered in Megiddo[113] and the Beirut Kharji Tomb 1.[114] The same tomb, which was, however, reused as late as the LB, contained an MM IIA polychrome cup.[115] These links based on formal criteria have recently received petrographic support, which indicates that two imported vessels analysed from tomb 14 were produced at 'the Northernmost Israeli coast or the Lebanese coast' and one in the '(undetermined) Northern Levant'.[116]

Local production?

This sample of pottery, even though from a disturbed tomb, happens to reflect roughly the statistical distribution of Egyptian and foreign vessels in stratum d/1. Of the overall tomb material analysed so far, Syro-Palestinian imported wares constitute around 20 per cent, and Egyptian wares around 80 per cent of the ceramic corpus.[117] The Egyptian pottery of stratum d/1 fits well into the relatively homogeneous corpus of the late Middle Kingdom;[118] the Egyptian material culture still seems fully integrated into the Egyptian state/culture of the late Middle Kingdom. While the earliest Asiatics living at Tell el-Dabʿa, documented in the preceding stratum d/2, mark the tangible beginning of a continuous Asiatic presence at this site, their role need not necessarily be a continuous one and the site's evolution into the later Hyksos capital was not necessarily linear. The 13th Dynasty cannot be reduced to a period of invariable and steady decline of central government and royal power,[119] mirrored by an increasing secession of influence to 'foreigners' in the eastern Delta. There are, for example, some indicators that the people buried in the cemetery of stratum d/1 had been employed as Egyptian officials dealing with expeditions to Sinai and possibly further afield,[120] the Egyptian central government taking advantage specifically of their ties to Syria–Palestine. The economic success of the community is documented by undisputed imports of luxury goods such as the Kamares ware.

The establishment of a local identity, expressing itself in local production of symbolic goods, is closely linked to the question of integration into and identification with the Egyptian state. However, the level of Egyptianization by itself is no reliable indicator of ethnicity, and different parameters may apply to different groups of artefacts. For example, most extant Hyksos monuments display no non-Egyptian features.[121]

Detailed analyses of various groups of artefacts from Tell el-Dabʿa are currently under way or have recently been completed. Thus, diachronic observations of the technological and stylistic development of individual artefacts can be made. Imports of pottery are very limited in stratum d/1 – despite being higher than even in the region of the capital[122] – and local imitations of imported ceramic goods are only just beginning. During the MB IIA phases represented at Tell el-Dabʿa (stratum d/2=H to b/3=F; see Fig. 198), other categories of material culture offer a similar pattern of measured local adaptations of imported goods. Apart from ceramics, weaponry and scarabs will be discussed in slightly greater detail. Among the earliest ceramic shapes being produced locally are relatively simple, everyday household forms such as Syro-Palestinian cooking pots[123] (as of stratum d/2 or phase H) and dishes with incurved rims (as of stratum d/1 or phase G/4).[124] With the growth in the amount of imports in stratum c and in particular b/3[125] (phases G/1–3 and F respectively, mid-13th Dynasty to the advanced 13th Dynasty or approximately 1760–1680 BC), large-scale local production of a variety of Syro-Palestinian shapes may be noted.[126]

These observations also seem to apply to the more sophisticated production of weaponry. The weapons found in stratum d/1 tombs – narrow-bladed axes, socketed javelin heads and ribbed daggers[127] – have very close parallels in the Levant and are in this phase most probably exclusively imported from Syria-Palestine.[128] Again it is the 'post-palace' stratum c (G/1–3) that offers the first indication for local metallurgy, with the discovery of limestone moulds for casting weapons and tools, interestingly of Egyptian types.[129] Moulds for producing Syro-Palestinian types of weapons, as were found in tombs, have only been found in later contexts.[130] The distinctly different alloy composition of the earlier (stratum d/2 to c or H–G) from the later metalwork[131] could also be interpreted as corroborating a shift from imports to local production.

In the case of the scarabs, the following observations may be made. The very small group of scarabs of stratum d/1 (4 pieces) display no Canaanite features. Based on an analysis of typological features[132] of the Tell el-Dabʿa scarabs, local production or workshops for scarabs is evidenced as of stratum c (G/1–3), though still in a purely Egyptian tradition.[133] Only in stratum b/3 (F) do Syro-Palestinian features and elements such as twigs, figures shown in an un-Egyptian stance[134] or other 'un-Egyptian' features[135] first appear on locally produced scarabs. Via this detour through ceramics, weapons and scarabs, it is here argued that a comparable chronological development applies to a potential local production of jewellery at Tell el-Dabʿa. In the pendant phase (stratum d/1 or G/4), we have found as yet no artefacts visually expressing the *de facto* blend of Egyptian and Near Eastern cultures.

Summing up, I suggest 'removing' the Petrie pendant from his *Catalogue of Egyptian Objects (of Daily Use)*, and tentatively including it in a corpus of Middle Minoan jewels, together with the Dabʿa and the Aigina pendants.

Notes

I would like to thank Stephen Quirke, assistant curator of the Petrie Museum of Egyptian Archaeology, and Lesley Fitton, keeper, Department of Greek and Roman Antiquities, The British Museum, who both have been instrumental in having the pendant restored and have been very helpful to me.

1. Petrie 1927, pl. 8, no. 110.
2. Petrie 1927, 9.
3. UC 34342, currently on display at the British Museum. Schiestl 2000, 127–8.
4. Information kindly provided by Stephen Quirke. The acquisition is recorded in Petrie Notebook 99 (CD-Rom page 45, price marked as '50') and a photograph of the pendant, amid other objects, can be found on Petrie Museum Archive Negative no. 3579.
5. Andrews 1990, 88–90.
6. For example a pendant from Hildesheim; Schmitz 1994, 255–63.
7. Compare, for example, a pendant in the Antikenmuseum Basel; Wiese 2001, 88, no. 50. Middle Kingdom exceptions are 'amuletic' pendants, such as individual metal hawk amulets (Andrews 1981, 95, Appendix Q), which can be made from sheet metal alone.
8. See in particular Walberg 1991a, and Aruz 1995a, 33–48.
9. Barta 1967–74, 337.
10. De Morgan 1895, table 19, 1. See also Andrews 1990, 128–9, fig. 112.
11. The reliefs were placed in the lower part of the causeway connecting the valley temple and the mortuary temple. Jequier 1941, pl. 15.
12. For example, the sphinxes on a carved wooden panel from a chair of Thutmosis IV, MMA 30.8.45a–c; Hayes 1990, fig. 84; sphinxes on painted chest (no. 21) of Tutankhamun, Carter and Mace 1923, pl. 54.
13. De Morgan 1903, 64, pl. 5, no. 48.
14. Andrews 1981, note 396, appendix D.
15. Only known from depictions; Wilkinson 1971, fig. 49.
16. For Minoan 'iconographical transfer' see, for example, Warren 1995, 2.
17. Teissier 1996, 144–9; Otto 2000, 251–2, 257–8.
18. Higgins 1980, pl. 6a.
19. Spurr *et al.* 1999, 16, cat. no. 8.
20. Xénaki-Sakellariou 1958, pl. 4, IIIb.
21. Levi 1957–8, 122, figs 308 and 309. *CMS* II, 5, nos 317 and 318.
22. Poursat 1973, 111–14, table 10, 3.
23. cf. Teissier 1996, nos 133, 134, 256.
24. Bissing 1900–8, table 1.
25. Frankfort 1935–7, 117, fig. 19. Teissier 1996, 146–8, nos 39, 153, 163–4.
26. Aruz 1993, 35–54.
27. Dessenne 1957, 45–6, proposes a route via Syria; Aruz 1993, 37–8, via Anatolia and Syria.
28. Higgins 1980, pl. 7a.
29. Crowley 1989, 109. For the most recent discussion of spirals in Egypt see Fitton and Quirke 1997, 421–44.

30. *CMS* II 1, nos 249, 312; *CMS* II 5, no. 281.
31. Caubet 1998, 84–5.
32. Evans 1892–3, 198–9.
33. Evans 1892–3, 198, note 5.
34. Higgins 1957a, 46 and note 35.
35. Higgins 1979, 22.
36. Hayes 1990, I, fig. 108.
37. De Graeve 1981, pl. 6, no. 22, pl. 7, no. 26. Note that the latter 'boat' (PML 872) stands upright and was considered a staff by Porada 1948, 111.
38. Landström 1970, 94–7.
39. Andrews 1990, 131–2, fig. 115.
40. Another royal example being, for example, from Tutanchamun, Andrews 1990, 137, fig. 119.
41. Feucht 1971, 4, table 1, 3–15, nos 25, 33a, 34, 35, 38, 43, 46–51, 56–81.
42. Wiese 1990, 59–69.
43. Feucht 1971, table 7, 15, nos 63, 67, 92, 105a.
44. Feucht 1971, table 14, 15, 99a, 105a. Wiese 1990, 68–9, Abb. 87. Compare also boat on chair of Sitamon, Quibell 1908, pl. 36.
45. Feucht 1971, table 14, 97.
46. Hornung 1963, I, 4.
47. Feucht 1971, table 14, 99a.
48. Bernabò-Brea 1976, 285–6, table 240. Maxwell-Hyslop 1971, fig. 42.
49. Schliemann 1881, 544, no. 834. Tolstikov and Treister 1996, 182, no. 239.
50. Mellink 1986, 139–52. Buchholz 1999, 110. Broodbank 2000.
51. Higgins 1979, 22.
52. As Bietak suggested; Bietak 1995, 19.
53. Morris 1998, 283.
54. Higgins 1957a, 45–6.
55. De Morgan 1903, pl. 12. The position that tombs lying within royal precincts should be dated as contemporaneous with the reign of the king has been abandoned in Egyptology (see Williams 1977, 41–55). However, the dating of many of these Middle Kingdom burials is still under debate. For a recent redating of Khnumet's neighbouring tomb of Keminub, who had previously been considered a wife of Amenemhat II, to the 13th Dynasty, see Jánosi 1994, 94–101.
56. Montet 1928, 185–6, pl. 94, 707.
57. Higgins 1957a, 56, pl. 15g. L. Fitton in Bietak and Hein 1994, 214.
58. The literature on this topic is vast and only a selection is cited: Kantor 1947; Smith 1965; Crowley 1989; Cline and Harris-Cline 1998; Lilyquist 1999, 25–33. Note also Cadogan's suggestion of Middle Bronze Age cultural *koiné*: Cadogan 1983, 515–16.
59. Walberg 1991a, 111–12.
60. Walberg 1991a, 111–12.
61. Bietak and Hein 1994, 211–12, cat. no. 238; Warren 1995, 3; Helck 1995, 38; Fitton 1996, 142–3; Laffineur 1998, 57.
62. Aruz 1995a, 46.
63. Morris 1998, 283.
64. Morris 1998, 282.
65. Morris 1998, 284.
66. Cline 1998, 207–8.
67. Bietak 1975; Bietak 1996.
68. Eigner 1985, 19–25; Eigner 1996, 73–80. The designation as palace has been questioned lately: see, for example, O'Connor 1997, 53. Wegner 1998, 25. On the other hand, K. Ryholt has based wide-reaching historical conclusions on the definition of the residence as a palace, the seat of his 14th Dynasty: Ryholt 1997, 295.
69. Walberg 1991b, 115–17. MacGillivray 1995, 81–4. Walberg 1998, 107–8. No Kamares ware has been found in the tombs of the 'palace cemetery'.
70. Bietak 1991a, 47–75. Bietak and Dorner 1994, 15–19. Schiestl 2003.
71. For the location of the tomb see lower left corner of map by D. Eigner in Bietak and Dorner 1994, 17, Abb. 2.
72. Compare the reconstruction by M. Bietak in Bietak and Hien 1994, 40, fig. 24.
73. Boessneck and Driesch 1992, 16–19, plans 2–7, 9. Wapnish 1997, 335–67.
74. I thank K. Grossschmidt and his team for providing me with the information on the human remains. The burials were numbered when discovered; the numbering does not suggest a sequence of deposition in the tomb.
75. Inv. no. 8432a.
76. Note the depiction of a woman riding a donkey on a scarab, Berlin inv. no. 9517; D. Wildung in Bietak and Hein 1994, 165, cat. no. 151.
77. When analysing the women's bones, a foetus was also discovered. It is not clear, however, whether it was associated with burial 2 or 3.
78. Tell el-Dabʿa inv. no. 7316/1–11, Museum Cairo JE 98563. Published by I. Hein in Bietak and Hein 1994, 110, no. 42.
79. Aston *et al.* 2000, 26–7, 31–2.
80. For example, spheroid garnet beads from MK tombs: Abydos, tombs E 30 and E 45, Garstang 1901, 4–5, pl. I; and Thebes, tomb 24, Carter and Earl of Carnarvon 1912, 53, pl. 45, 2b.
81. For example Abydos tomb 416: Kemp and Merrillees 1980, 153, fig. 46; Denderah: Petrie 1900, pl. 20.
82. Haragheh: Engelbach 1923, pl. 52, type 70; Beni Hasan, tomb 487: Garstang 1907, 113, fig. 104; Lisht, Senwosret I: Arnold 1992, 67, pl. 79, nos 106–7.
83. Engelbach 1923, pl. 52, type 73 L2.
84. Tomb III: Montet 1928, 170, no. 630, pl. 95, no. 630.
85. Haragheh: Engelbach 1923, pl. 51, type 47b and f. Abydos, tomb 416, Kemp and Merrillees 1980, 151, no. 119, 6.2.
86. Haragheh, tomb 72: Engelbach 1923, pl. 22, 5, pl. 51, 47. Aldred 1978, 117, pl. 34.
87. For example Ebla: Matthiae 1981, figs 47a–b, 50a–b, 51–4. Favissae 5327: Marchetti and Nigro 1997, fig. 13. Mari, tomb 809: Jean-Marie 1999, pl. 149, no. 7. Assur, tomb 20: J. Aruz in Harper *et al.* 1995, 50–1, fig. 14, no. 3, pl. 6.
88. Montet 1928, 170, nos 631–2, 209, nos 830–1, pl. 95, 631–2, pl. 121, no. 832. 'Depot b' in Temple Syrien: Dunand 1939, 156, pl. 136, no. 2316.
89. Effinger 1996, 25, 'Kugelförmige Perlen Variante C'.
90. M. Bietak suggests 'globular amethyst beads most probably mounted between golden tunnel-beads' (Bietak 1995, 19). The garnet beads were originally thought to be amethyst.
91. Sithathor, Mereret, Sithathoryunet: see, for example, Aldred 1978, nos 19, 29, 30; Andrews 1990, 6, 24, 59, 128–9, fig. 1, 15, 43, 111–12. Saleh and Sourouzian 1986, nos 109, 110.
92. Prémier trésor, Sithathor, second trésor, Mereret: De Morgan 1895, pl. 19, 1, 20, 2, 21. For location of treasures, De Morgan 1903, pls 15–16, 1.
93. Brunton 1920, 23–4.
94. Petrie 1914, 98.
95. Brunton 1920, 28, pls 1, 7.
96. Tomb 124: Engelbach 1915, 11–13, pl. 1.
97. Tomb 124; Engelbach 1923, 15–16, pl. 15.
98. For example El Bersheh, tomb of Djehutj-hetep: Newberry 1895, 29, pl. I. Statues of Nofret: Borchardt 1925, 1–2, f. 60, nos 381–2.
99. Winlock 1934, 29–32, pls 5–7. Before the publication of Brunton's report, Winlock had suggested a suspension from all the drop beads in the tomb: Winlock 1920, 76.
100. Note Brunton's drawing of the tomb chamber, showing the pendant in area B surrounded by drop-shaped and spherical beads. Brunton 1920, pl. 12.
101. Brunton 1920, 29.
102. De Morgan 1895, 63.
103. The clays are classified according to the 'Vienna System'; see Nordström and Bourriau 1993, 168–86.
104. The vessel index of the hemispherical cup (height of the vessel divided by the maximum diameter and multiplied by 100) is 175 putting it in the range of the late 12th Dynasty/early 13th Dynasty (cf. Dominique Arnold in Dieter Arnold 1988, 140–1; Bietak 1991b, fig. 14; Bourriau 1991, 16–20).
105. For the discussion of this shape, see Dominique Arnold in Dieter Arnold 1988, 141–3; Bietak 1991b, 36, fig. 7. Szafranski 1998, 95–119.
106. Guiges 1937, fig. 3d.
107. Chéhab 1939, 804, fig. 2d.
108. Saidah 1993–4, pl. 12, 3.
109. Tombeaux des Particuliers 3: Montet 1928, 247, pl. 147, no. 932. A group of vessels from a cave tomb discovered 1955; Baramki 1973, 28–9, pl. 4, no. 3, 4.
110. Stratum II and tomb 4: Ory 1938, 113–14, 118, nos 47–8, 53, 56, 91.
111. Stratum XIII: Loud 1948, pl. 20, nos 12, 13.
112. Dunham 1967, pls 87b and 88a and e.
113. Tomb 5114: Loud 1948, pl. 16, no. 10.
114. Saidah 1993–4, 150–1, pl. 7. Bagh 2000, 91–2, 148, fig. 115.
115. Warren and Hankey 1989, 134–5, pl. 12; Hankey 1991/2, 16–17.
116. Goren and Cohen-Weinberger 2004, 74, 93, samples nos 39–41, Groups B 2 and B 3. I thank the authors for providing me with their data.
117. Here: 70 per cent local made, 30 per cent imports. Bietak 1991b, 34–6.
118. Bourriau 1991, 3–20.
119. Quirke 1991, 123–39.
120. Bietak 1991a, 64–72.
121. Compare Bietak *et al.* 2001, figs 16–18.
122. Dorothea Arnold *et al.* 1995, fig. 3.

123. Aston *et al.* 2004, 167–9.
124. Preliminary results of analysis of the settlement material; information kindly provided by K. Kopetzky, Vienna.
125. Bietak 1991b, 40.
126. Kopetzky 2000, in print.
127. Philip 1995, 66–83.
128. G. Philip, in his analysis of the Dabʿa weapons, does not address the question of place of production directly, while emphasizing the close connection of the earlier Dabʿa material with Byblos: Philip 1989, 209–10.
129. Bietak 1984, 339–41, Abb. 10. Bietak 1996, 31, fig. 28.
130. For example Hein in Bietak and Hein 1994, 162–3, cat. no. 146.
131. Philip 1995, 77.
132. Mlinar 2001, part I, 261.
133. Mlinar 2004, 133–4.
134. Mlinar in Bietak and Hein 1994, 101, no. 32.
135. Keel 1994c, Abb. 23. Mlinar 2004, no. 103: the male figure holding a stave is unique. The figure's hair seems reminiscent of the Canaanite dignitary's 'mushroom'-shaped coiffure (see Bietak 1996, fig. 17); his skirt shows an un-Egyptian diagonal hatching. The use of 'Füllzeichen' can also be considered un-Egyptian. I thank C. Mlinar for this information.

10
Egypt and the Aigina Treasure

Yvonne J. Markowitz and Peter Lacovara

It is commonly held that Egypt's contribution to ornament was one of motif and design rather than technology. Granulation, loop-in-loop chains, cloisonné enamelling and metal refining are all techniques that appear to have been developed elsewhere and imported into the Nile Valley. The exceptions include the introduction of glass eye beads during the New Kingdom and the development of champlevé enamelling at Meroe during the first century AD. So, for all intents and purposes, the Nilotic Valley was the beneficiary of material advances made elsewhere.

On the other hand, Egypt's unique iconography, incorporated into ornaments worn in life and during burial, was borrowed extensively. This is primarily because jewellery – small, precious and portable – was often bartered or given as gifts. From surviving material we know that Egyptian products were well designed, finely crafted and made of superior materials. By the end of the Pyramid Age, they had also acquired a certain magical allure. It is true that symbols such as the scarab, lotus and falcon had specific meanings and connotations within Egypt. But to those living in the shadow of the pyramids, these and other images took on the might and mystery of Egypt itself.

In examining the motifs used in the Aigina Treasure, it appears that some imagery is Egyptian in origin. For example, one motif – that of the reef knot – forms the central design element found on one of the inlaid finger rings (Fig. 88). This design configuration is particularly interesting because few jewellery historians are aware of its Egyptian derivation and it is an excellent example of what happens to a culturally specific symbol when it is borrowed.

A simple, gold bracelet with a central reef knot (Fig. 213) is part of the collection of the Museum of Fine Arts, Boston.[1] It was acquired during the 1923–4 excavation season when the Harvard University–Museum of Fine Arts Boston Expedition, under the direction of George Andrew Reisner, excavated a series of cemeteries along the east bank of the Nile in Upper Egypt. Several areas, including the site of Sheikh Farag, contained burials dating to around 2100 BC – a period of social unrest and political change after the Old Kingdom which is known as the First Intermediate Period (FIP).

The tombs from this uncertain age were largely plundered and the excavators' efforts yielded meagre results by way of grave goods. One of the few items of gold recovered – a bracelet found on the left wrist of a woman – came from a cemetery in the 5000 series. The ornament consists of two strips of thin gold sheet twisted and rolled into 1 mm wires. Each wire was then bent in half and knotted in the middle in what is typically known as a square (reef) knot. Finally, the craftsman soldered the wires at the tips. A comparable bracelet of FIP date from Mostagedda, now in the British Museum, is similar in design and construction. It was also found on the wrist of a woman.[2]

Was the knot configuration that appears in FIP jewellery merely a chance occurrence? Or is its presence meaningful and rooted in Egyptian culture?

The reef knot has universal appeal in that it integrates opposites into a satisfying whole. This role of the knot in ancient Egypt was noted by Gertie Englund in a paper exploring the treatment of opposites in Egyptian iconography and wisdom literature.[3] She observed that the knot serves a central and unifying function as represented on the side panels of royal thrones. Here the knot binds the antithetically placed and ideologically opposite figures of Horus and Seth, the personifications of good and evil or construction and destruction. The figures tug on cords formed from two plants, a papyrus and a lily – symbols of Upper and Lower Egypt and an enduring motif that endures throughout the course of pharaonic history (Fig. 215). The tendency of the 'two lands' to split or disorganize into separate entities was a legitimate anxiety, as a study of Egyptian history readily illustrates. It was only under the exercise of strong central kingship that the land along the Nile was able to maintain its integrity. In this respect the enthroned king was the mighty, magical force who bound north to south and the knot was a tangible expression of that concept.

It is interesting that the first appearance of the knot in jewellery occurs precisely at a time when Egypt is experiencing decentralization, a period of national distress dramatically described in the 'Admonitions of Ipuwer', who laments:[4]

> Crime is everywhere . . .
> The servant takes what he finds.
> Lo, Hapy inundates and none plough for him . . .
> All say, 'We don't know what happened in the land.'

And later in the text:

> Gold is lacking.
> Exhausted are [materials] for every kind of craft.
> What belongs to the palace has been stripped.

In addition to the knot, an important part of the throne image is the vertical element in the middle. It represents an animal windpipe flanked by two lungs – the Egyptian hieroglyph *sema*, meaning 'to unite'. Although the knot would later be used without this powerful emblem of unity, its earlier association only added to the symbol's ability to convey a sense of protection against disintegration and chaos.

Representations of the reef knot as a separate amuletic element are first found in burials of the FIP, including on scarabs of that date. At that time several other images associated with kingship, such as the falcon, found their way into adornments worn first by the upper classes and later by all. This democratization even extended to jewellery worn in the afterlife.

By the Middle Kingdom, knot bracelets in silver and gold, as well as clasps in the form of a knot, were common forms of adornment. The tongue-in-groove clasp was particularly ingenious in that it could be used to join two ends of a string of beads mechanically, thereby reinforcing the sense of unity, order and balance.[5] Add to this symbolism the inherent indestructibility of the gold and you have a powerful talisman. Considering the popularity of the knot in jewellery during this period, it is conceivable that a scarab or an ornament with a reef-knot clasp pendant found its way to the island of Aigina.

Although it is reasonable to conjecture that an Egyptian scarab (Fig. 214) or ornament was imported into Aigina, it is more difficult to understand why the reef knot made its way into the jewellery design repertory of the Aigina craftsman. Ancient jewellery is laden with meaning, so we can assume it was a purposeful selection. Was its connection to Egypt – a dominant force in the region – enough to see the motif as having certain powers? Or was something else motivating the selection? If Gertie Englund is correct, the motif – the unity of opposites – has universal appeal, making it satisfying to jeweller as well as owner.

Aegean motifs also seem to have made their way into Egyptian jewellery during this cosmopolitan age. The most striking example of this cross-fertilization and the one with the closest parallels to the Aigina Treasure is the jewellery group from the Dahshur burial of the princess Khnumet, a daughter of Amenemhat II (1929–1892 BC).[6]

While the assemblage of jewellery from the princess's tomb contains many traditional Egyptian items, there are some items that were either inspired by Aegean jewellery, direct imports or made by foreign craftsmen resident in Egypt. The latter seems the more likely, not only given what we now know about the production of Minoan frescoes in the Delta,[7] but also because of the unique style of the ornaments. The extensive use of granulation evident in many of Khnumet's adornments is also remarkable. Not found in earlier ornaments, it becomes a common form of surface decoration on precious metal later in the Middle Kingdom. The pendant known as the 'Medallion of Dahshur' also demonstrates Aegean influence (Fig. 216). While the recumbent cow motif on the pendant is iconographically Egyptian, the setting of the medallion with its other round, dangling elements resonates with certain decorative forms present in the Aigina Treasure.

Another striking similarity between Khnumet's jewels and the Aigina Treasure is the gold bird pendants. Ancient Egyptian representations of animals are exceptional in their attention to naturalistic detail. These birds on the pendants, however, are highly stylized and of a type not seen in Egyptian art (Fig. 217).

Other stray jewellery finds from the later Middle Kingdom, notably the Tell el-Dabʿa pectoral,[8] have affinities to the treasure as well, although the Khnumet group is the largest, and perhaps earliest, corollary to the Aigina Treasure.

The vogue for foreign styles, particularly Minoan motifs, characterized the arts of the Middle Bronze Age in the eastern Mediterranean. Even Egypt, with its own rich traditions and master craftsmen, was not immune from this influence.

Notes
1. Markowitz 1995, 142.
2. Andrews 1981, no. 276, 49, pl. 24.
3. Englund 1989, 78.
4. Lichtheim 1973, 151–2.
5. For a discussion of the clasp, including its fabrication, see Wilkinson 1971, 58–9.
6. For a discussion of the tomb and its findings, see De Morgan 1903.
7. Russell 1999, 118–21.
8. Hein in Bietak and Hein 1994, cat. no. 238, 211–12.

11
Links in a chain: Aigina, Dahshur and Tod

J.L. Fitton

The Aigina Treasure may be viewed not just within the bounds of its own purported island home, or within the sphere of Minoan Crete and the Aegean world, but also against the background of a wider stage – one that includes the eastern Mediterranean, Egypt, the Levant and Anatolia. Other essays in this volume embrace a broader approach to this enigmatic but fascinating group of material. Here an attempt is made to demonstrate some links – tenuous enough, perhaps, but feasible in terms of historical background – between the Aigina Treasure and finds of early Middle Bronze Age date made in Egypt: specifically, the Tod Treasure and Khnumet's jewellery from Dahshur.[1] These perhaps tie in with other evidence presented in this volume to suggest the possibility, at least, of an earlier date for the Aigina Treasure than the 1700–1500 BC dating that has entered the mainstream literature.

Looking from the Aegean towards Egypt makes sense for this early period, as it certainly does later in the Bronze Age, when cultural contacts were such that frescoes of entirely Minoan type could be painted at Tell el-Dabʿa. In fact, any use of sea routes from Crete would almost necessitate contacts with Egypt, which lies on the anticlockwise circular route around the eastern Mediterranean dictated by the prevailing winds and currents of the summer months. The fact that Egypt did play an integral part in east Mediterranean contacts from the very beginning of the Middle Bronze Age is shown by one particular class of evidence, that of scarabs, while the distribution of Minoan pottery shows intensification of Crete–Egypt contact somewhat later in the period.

The background: evidence from scarabs and pottery

A previous detailed survey of Egyptian scarabs and local imitations in Crete and of reciprocal influence on Egyptian glyptic highlighted certain facts.[2] The chronological implications of the Egyptian scarabs of the First Intermediate Period or very early Middle Kingdom associated with MM IA pottery in the Lenda tholos tombs have been accepted by most commentators, and these have recently been the subject of full publication.[3] Equally significant is the identification by Ingo Pini of a group of Minoan scarabs apparently produced in one workshop, or a group of related workshops, probably in the Mesara region of south Crete during MM IA (about 2100–1950 BC).[4] These scarabs are Egyptianizing in form and materials, but they are decorated in a distinctive and entirely un-Egyptian manner. What had not previously been stressed is the fact that, since the scarab type was only invented in Egypt in the First Intermediate Period, in about 2050 BC, the importation of examples to Crete and the local production of copies there must have been a relatively rapid process (as, indeed, was the reciprocal influence of spiral patterns on Egyptian glyptic). This seems to indicate direct contact between Crete and Egypt at this early stage, particularly since the phenomenon seems not to be found in western Asia, where the first copies of Egyptian scarabs date from later in the Middle Bronze Age.[5]

Pottery evidence is lacking for the very beginning of the Middle Bronze Age,[6] but the large quantity of Minoan pottery of MM IIA date from Lahun and its associated cemetery of Harageh indicates quite intensive contact at this time.[7] The quantity of sherds from this one site, the largest Middle Kingdom town to survive in Egypt, represents a larger group of Minoan pottery than the sum of all known sherds of similar date from sites along the Syro-Palestinian coast – although the absolute numbers are not large, with some thirty vases represented at Lahun and about twenty elsewhere. Nonetheless, the existence of Egyptian copies of Minoan vases at Lahun is also indicative of a certain impact.

We can summarize as follows: scarabs represent Aegean–Egyptian contacts appearing in the archaeological record in the MM IA–B period, before Aegean–Asian contacts are truly apparent; and pottery shows the intensification of such contact in the succeeding (MM IIA) period. It is against this background that we turn to the evidence from three 'treasures': the Aigina Treasure, the jewellery of Princess Khnumet from Dahshur and the Tod Treasure.

The context and date of the Aigina Treasure

The archaeological context of the Aigina Treasure is of course not precisely known. When Arthur Evans first published the treasure in 1892, he simply accepted that it had come from Aigina, and there seems no doubt that it had come from that island to the British Museum. He recognized 'Mycenaean' features in the material, but dated the group to about 800 BC. As part of his masterly reappraisal of the treasure, the main thrust of which was to underline the Minoan character of the group,[8] Reynold Higgins reconstructed as much of the story of its discovery as possible. This process has been brought up to date by Dyfri Williams in this volume (pp. 11–16). His additional evidence includes the remarkable 'x marks the spot' of the map marked by Cresswell to show where the treasure was found (Fig. 10). Although many details will perhaps never be known, it now seems likely that the treasure came from the area of the Middle Bronze Age cemetery near to the Kolonna site. The treasure may have come from a rich tomb, and this possibility is strengthened by the existence of the warrior grave discussed by Hiller in this volume (pp. 36–9).

In terms of dating, Reynold Higgins invoked both Middle and Late Minoan comparisons for the material, and felt that some pieces, notably the fifty-four dress ornaments, were best paralleled in the Mycenae Shaft Graves. The possibility of what in Minoan terms would be a protopalatial date was, though, implicit in his original suggestion that the treasure might have come from the Chrysolakkos mortuary building at Mallia, though he later reviewed his position and concluded that it was more likely to have belonged to, and probably been made by, Minoans living on Aigina. He also narrowed down his suggested date range to about 1700–1500 BC.

While the treasure is far more likely to have come from Aigina than from Chrysolakkos, it remains true that striking parallels for some elements are found among the Chrysolakkos finds. The bee pendant has similarities to the 'Master of Animals' pendant, itself now more likely to belong in the protopalatial period because of its connections to the Dabʿa dog pendant[9] and the Petrie silver pendant (see Schiestl in this volume, pp. 51–8). The golden bird from Chrysolakkos is the best Minoan parallel for the many golden birds in the Aigina Treasure (see also the discussion of Khnumet's birds, below). Higgins of course recognized the parallels, though he argued that the jewellery found in the French excavations at Chrysolakkos was most likely to date from the final period of use of the mortuary building, in MM III, as precious items would routinely have been removed as successive burials were made. The general logic of this does not, though, make it impossible that the few scraps of jewellery found at Chrysolakkos had been overlooked in earlier clearances, as they certainly had been by later robbers. In fact a gold flower pin from the complex seems to belong early in the Middle Bronze Age, and the bee pendant could equally be protopalatial in date. G. de Pierpont's study of the Chrysolakkos complex emphasized that MM II was its most important period of use.[10]

A protopalatial date for the Aigina Treasure?

All discussions of the date and nature of the treasure are affected by the findings of the technical study that forms part of the catalogue section of this volume (pp. 17–31). This tends to associate the individual items in the group rather closely in terms of manufacture and technique. It thus reduces the likelihood of different dates being possible for the items in the treasure: widely bracketed dates encompassing 250 years or so should therefore be seen as representing a timespan within which the treasure as a whole should fall at some specific point, rather than a timespan representing a range of dates for individual pieces.

If the 'Master of Animals' pendant is likely to belong in the earlier part of the Middle Bronze Age, then, can the rest of the treasure be similarly dated? It is clear that the history of Aigina itself poses no problem for such a dating, and can perhaps be said in a general sense to support it. Florens Felten (in this volume, pp. 32–5) gives us a picture of the Kolonna site flourishing particularly in the early part of the Middle Bronze Age. Moreover, his discovery of an Early Bronze Age 'Aigina Treasure' shows that some islanders had already accumulated wealth at an earlier period – and wealth represented by gold and carnelian, which are the main materials of the Aigina Treasure itself.

The four large ornaments that are probably earrings are without close parallels. However, as Higgins pointed out, there are similarities in the arrangement of their main elements with schemes found in Egyptian jewellery, and he cites specifically the openwork gold pectoral of Mereret, daughter of Senwosret III, now in the Egyptian Museum, Cairo.[11] The position of the symmetrical griffins trampling the smaller human figures on the pectoral is strikingly similar to that of the dogs and monkeys in the earrings. The earrings are, though, much simpler in design, and the position of the central cartouche in the Egyptian pectoral is taken by a single carnelian bead. While the elaborate Egyptian scene is imbued with the symbolism of the power of the pharaoh, the Aigina earrings seem to belong entirely in the natural world of snakes, dogs and monkeys. Yet the formal connections with Mereret's pectoral seem clear, and that is a piece from the 12th Dynasty, dating from about 1850 BC.

The earrings have suspended birds of the sort represented by a single example from Chrysolakkos and found in Khnumet's jewellery, discussed below. Such birds are also found on the lion's head ornament, though in this case the birds are larger and more elaborately shaped. Apart from this connection, the lion's head ornament remains a puzzle. It is difficult to imagine the nature of the perishable part that is now lost, and difficult to understand quite what the original purpose of the object could have been. Higgins suggested it was an earring, and if so this would be another indication that the treasure as we have it is incomplete, since it lacks a pair. It could perhaps have been worn as a pendant. In any case it lacks any obvious means of suspension. The absence of convincing parallels means chronological conclusions remain elusive.

The pectoral ornament with profile heads has been shown by the technical study to represent the highest-quality workmanship of all the pieces in the treasure. Although more robust than the 'Master of Animals' pendant, it is linked to it stylistically through the presence on both of pendant discs. The essay by Collon (this volume, pp. 43–5) compares the heads with bullae and ivories found at Acemhöyük, dating to the eighteenth century BC.

Some elements in the treasure show connections with the Shaft Graves at Mycenae and are perhaps precursors of some of the types of object found in those rich assemblages. Among these must be numbered the diadems. Considerable lengths of plain and narrow gold strips are included in the Aigina Treasure, and these in fact are instantly reminiscent of the gold bands in the Royal Graves at Ur, dating from the third millennium BC. The diadems that are complete, with ends designed for fastening, are also narrow. Two are plain, while a third has punctuated decoration. They seem to belong to a type that continued without much change from the Early Bronze Age, and it could be argued that they look earlier than the diadems of the Shaft Graves, which are in most cases broader and more elaborately decorated. The fifty-four dress or shroud ornaments represent a type of object found in the Shaft Graves, though their convex form is not found there. The double-curved gold beads also have Shaft Grave parallels (see Laffineur in this volume, pp. 40–42).

Other beads in the treasure are of carnelian, amethyst, green jasper and lapis lazuli. The combination of gold and carnelian (along with silver and rock crystal) is already found in EH III Aigina, as we see from the 'new' Aigina Treasure. Amethyst is particularly associated with Middle Kingdom Egypt, which may also have been the source of the jasper and the carnelian. Lapis lazuli is found in the 'hand on breast' beads, which occur also in gold and carnelian: perhaps the strongest indication that an Aiginetan jewellery workshop was working all three materials. Lapis lazuli is also used to remarkable effect in the finger rings of the treasure, which remain without close parallel – though see Markowitz and Lacovara (this volume, pp. 59–60) on a possible Egyptian association for the reef-knot motif.

The Aigina Treasure consists mainly of jewellery, but includes a single gold cup. This cup is of interest here because it bears some similarity to the silver vessels in the Tod Treasure: vessels which the original excavator thought might be Minoan, beginning a long and still inconclusive debate. As Sinclair Hood points out, the rosette decoration of the base of the Aigina cup features also on some of the Tod examples.[12] The Aigina cup is thought by Hood to be Minoan work of MM III, about 1700–1550 BC, while Oliver Dickinson suggests, presumably because of its probable Aiginetan provenance, that it may not be absolutely mainstream Minoan, but rather may indicate 'other metalworking traditions in the Aegean in the pre-Shaft Grave era'.[13] It is certainly feasible, as these two scholars suggest, that the Aigina cup is earlier than the Shaft Graves, rather than exactly contemporary with the wealth of metal vessels that they include. The cup would thus help to fill the chronological gap between the Tod vessels and those from the Shaft Graves, if the Amenemhat II date for the former is accepted (see below).

A further link with the Tod Treasure is represented by the spool-shaped bead of rock crystal which is a small, isolated element in the Aigina Treasure, but which is closely paralleled in the Tod Treasure by two silver beads of the same shape.

In view of these tenuous, yet suggestive links with the Tod Treasure, we should turn briefly to the latter to note some of its main characteristics and to explore its connection with Minoan Crete. It is very different from the Aigina Treasure, in both content and in circumstances of deposition, yet some of the problems of interpretation are common to the two groups of material.

Context and date of the Tod Treasure

It is clear that the Tod Treasure is in no sense from a sealed context.[14] The four bronze boxes in which it was contained came from a sand layer beneath paving stones of Middle Kingdom date in the Tod temple, but the presence at a higher level in this same sand layer of a Late Period Osiris hoard demonstrates that the layer could have been re-entered at any time. Nonetheless, the Middle Kingdom paving stones seem to be cut to accommodate the deposition of the boxes, two of which were labelled with the name of Amenemhat II (c. 1922–1878 BC). While parallels have been sought for some of the silver vessels among later (particularly Mycenaean) material, as discussed below, these remain controversial. In fact, most of the material in the treasure is clearly either earlier than or contemporary with the Middle Kingdom.[15] The silver cups and bowls are accepted by most scholars as forming a unified group, as they are very thin walled and technically much alike. An important reason for arguing that they were made during the Middle Kingdom, and probably not later than about 1800 BC, is the presence on one of them of a hieratic ink inscription in a Middle Kingdom hand with the name Nenitef (nn-ít.f) – a name of Middle Kingdom type. It seems therefore to be a reasonable hypothesis that the treasure is indeed a group of material from disparate sources brought together, probably though not necessarily in Egypt, and given as an offering to the god Mont at some time during the reign of Amenemhat II.

The treasure as appropriate to Mont

Silver and lapis lazuli are overwhelmingly the two main materials of the treasure. These are the only two foreign materials in Middle Kingdom Egypt not found in the adjacent deserts and therefore necessarily from very distant sources. They thus were appropriate as offerings for Mont, a deity particularly associated with foreign lands. The fragmentary and 'scrap' nature of both the lapis and the silver underscores the fact that this was essentially an offering of raw value, not of desirable finished artefacts, to the god – a fact somewhat obscured by the archaeological restoration of the majority of the silver vessels.[16]

The treasure also contains a smaller amount of gold – ten ingots, one vessel indistinguishable in form from its silver counterparts, two small flowers and some scraps – as well as a scattering of extremely small pieces of unworked semi-precious stones. These include rock crystal, carnelian, feldspar and amethyst, all found in Middle Kingdom jewellery and, in the case of amethyst, particularly characteristic of the period. Like much of the lapis the fragments were too small or too low grade to have practical value as material for reuse. In this they differ from the silver, which naturally did have the potential for melting down for reuse, thus representing the renunciation of very real value in the dedication to the god.

The lapis lazuli

Almost all of the lapis lazuli objects in the treasure were made outside Egypt. They include a large number of complete or fragmentary cylinder seals, Mesopotamian and Cappadocian, with dates ranging throughout the third millennium BC into the early second – though the latest elements are not thought to be later than Amenemhat II. Other objects include such things as beads and inlays – usually broken, but mostly Mesopotamian and dating from the second half of the third millennium BC. One Middle Kingdom scarab, five scarab fragments and one amulet in the shape of a child are the only lapis objects contained in the treasure that were clearly made in Egypt. They fit well with the early date: the child amulet is paralleled by examples from the Lisht radim at Amenemhat I's pyramid, though admittedly Late Bronze Age material was also found there. The remaining fragments were mainly poor-quality waste from lapis working.

The silver

Deposited in the treasure were 153 silver vessels, all but nine of them flattened and folded, along with thirteen tablet ingots, twenty-five chain ingots, some rolled-up silver fragments, some jewellery elements and a few other objects. The impression is overwhelmingly of dedication of a weight of silver, with the nature of the objects a secondary consideration, but after restoration the silver vessels immediately suggested Minoan origins to the excavator. With a Minoan specialist as a collaborator, he formulated the early mainstream view, which was that the vessels were closely paralleled in Minoan protopalatial pottery, and were either made in Crete or just possibly somewhere such as Byblos, under strong Minoan influence. Later commentators suggested an Anatolian origin, again generally invoking the intermediary of pottery to show the connection, and this view has many adherents today. Nonetheless, no site in any part of the world has produced overwhelmingly convincing parallels, and the question has remained controversial, with no clear consensus emerging.[17]

Among the miscellaneous silver objects in the Tod Treasure are a lion of Asiatic style, possibly a weight, and a cylindrical case or container, both of problematical origin. Two drum-shaped beads may be Aegean, and are paralleled by the rock crystal example from the Aigina Treasure, while a strong case can be made for the Minoan origin of the three-sided pendant.

The silver pendant

The first excavators cited Minoan parallels for the pendant, which has three spiders on one side and a bee/wasp motif on the other. The soundness in particular of the comparison with Minoan seals with spiders has since been reaffirmed in a short note by Paul Yule,[18] who accepts the pendant as Minoan or at the very least Minoanizing, and this is worth emphasizing here, since the presence in the Tod Treasure of at least one silver object generally accepted to show an unequivocal link with Minoan Crete makes the theory that the silver vessels are Minoan seem less isolated.

Silver is a relatively rare material among Minoan seals or amulets: only two silver seals are known, dating from MM II and MM II–III respectively, though poor survival may mean the number known is not representative. The shape of this pendant is unusual, but not unparalleled, occurring in a late prepalatial (MM Ia) seal in Paris, as Yule demonstrated, and relating to other seals of MM IB–II. The wasp motif is found on a few Minoan seals of EM II–MM II date, while spiders occur on some thirty seals of the same date range, either singly or in pairs or groups. Gold pendants with combinations of such things as spiders, wasps, snakes and scorpions occur in Minoan jewellery,[19] the association of biting or stinging creatures presumably having some amuletic significance, and it is possible that the Tod example was designed to be worn, but not necessarily to be used as a seal; to have the sealing surfaces on the sides rather than the base would be unusual, though it is not completely unknown. While precise dating of the pendant is not possible, the evidence suggests that it remains firmly in the prepalatial or protopalatial period, and would fit perfectly well with an Amenemhat II date for the Tod Treasure.

Analysis of the silver

Analysis of the silver has produced a confused picture, with a Chalkidiki/Thasos source emerging as the best candidate for the ingots, and the region of Troy as second best.[20] The analyses seem to vary chemically even within one chain – indicating melted-down objects – but are isotopically similar, indicating that the provenance of the metal was originally the same. Only two of the vessels have been analysed: the results were different from the ingots, and no suggestion for the source of the silver has yet been made. While not yet solving the problem of origin, the presence of mixed analyses and the remelting of silver indicated by the ingots perhaps supports the notion of silverworking at some distance from the silver source, in a place such as Crete or Syria rather than Attica or Anatolia, where one might expect just the local source of readily available silver to be used.

Parallels for the silver vessels

While not considering the Anatolian question closed, we shall restrict our further comments to the Aegean side of the argument, and here an interesting development has been the emergence of claims that certain elements in the treasure are best paralleled not in Minoan Crete but in Mycenaean material from the Greek mainland in the sixteenth century BC. Doubts about the security of the context of the treasure[21] seemed to give a plausible background for such arguments, allowing the possibility of later material within it. Thus, for example, it has long been recognized that the spool handle of one Tod cup is an Aegean metal vessel form par excellence, but at a time rather later than that of Amenemhat II – actually beginning in pottery in Crete in MM III, and becoming ubiquitous on metal vessels later. Similarly troublesome for the Amenemhat II date of the treasure is a close parallel in gold for one of the Tod silver kantharoi from a tholos tomb at Peristeria of about 1570 BC.[22]

It is perhaps possible both to accept the Minoan identification of vessels deposited in the Tod Treasure in about 1922–1878 BC (MMIb in Minoan terms) and to explain the presence of these apparently later Aegean features if we invoke a long and conservative tradition of metal vessel production in the Aegean with scarcely any deposition in the archaeological record before the Shaft Grave period. Very occasional survivors would include the well-known crinkle-rimmed kantharos from Gournia, of protopalatial date.[23] Another survivor that perhaps helps to bridge the gap between protopalatial Crete and the Shaft Graves is the gold cup from the Aigina Treasure, as we have seen.

The Tod Treasure and Minoan Crete

It is possible to envisage various directions for further research which may help to answer the questions posed by the Tod Treasure more thoroughly than is currently possible. In particular, scientific analysis of the silver may in future be able to determine the source in a way not yet possible. Individual items within the Tod Treasure may also be identified more securely. For the moment, many points remain unresolved. It is only possible to say that our understanding of links between the Aegean and Egypt towards the beginning of the Middle Bronze Age make it perfectly feasible that Minoan material of some value should be reaching Egypt in some quantity, though the Tod find represents by any standards an unusual preservation of a wealth of precious material. If Crete were an intermediary source of silver for Egypt this might explain the other phenomena – scarabs, pottery, influences in jewellery and so forth – that otherwise give us tantalizing glimpses into relatively intensive interconnections that we cannot fully understand.

The Aigina Treasure and Khnumet's jewellery from Dahshur

Finally, we turn to an element in the Aigina Treasure that strongly suggests a date as early as the MM IB/Amenemhat II period to which the Tod Treasure can be dated. This is the extensive use of suspended hollow golden birds. These bear a striking resemblance to similar birds found in Egypt among the jewellery buried with the princess Khnumet at Dahshur. Aegean influence has long been noted in Khnumet's jewellery, and the phenomenon is also discussed by Markowitz and Lacovara (this volume, pp. 59–60), so a brief summary here will suffice.

A rich collection of jewellery was buried in the tomb of Khnumet, a princess buried in Amenemhat II's pyramid complex at Dahshur in about 1900–1850 BC. Much was purely Egyptian in style, but palpable foreign influences in some of the pieces were summarized by Henry Fischer, who cited specifically Minoan parallels for certain items.[24] These included the pendant illustrated here by Markowitz and Lacovara (Fig. 216). He was, though, puzzled by the hollow golden birds designed to be suspended from their feet, of which he concluded, 'There is no parallel for these birds at all events, and it can only be said that they are entirely un-Egyptian in style'. In fact these birds are strikingly like the birds suspended from their feet that are such a feature of the Aigina Treasure, particularly those depending from the two pairs of elaborate earrings.

The birds in Khnumet's jewellery are foreign to Egypt, and are very likely to represent an imported Aegean idea, for which our best evidence is the Aigina birds – the only other close parallel being the single example from the Chrysolakkos funerary complex at Mallia, as we have seen. There is therefore good reason to suggest that such birds were in the Aegean repertory as early as (if not earlier than) the burial of Princess Khnumet. They certainly form another link in the chain of demonstrable Aegean–Egyptian connections in the early part of the Middle Bronze Age, and suggest a date for at least certain aspects of the Aigina Treasure that may be just about as early as the Tod Treasure itself.

Conclusions

This essay joins others in this volume that view the Aigina Treasure against a broad background of foreign influences and interconnections. We should perhaps conclude, though, by bringing the focus back to the island of Aigina itself. The considerable importance of the Kolonna site has emerged with increasing clarity since Reynold Higgins completed his ground-breaking work on the Aigina Treasure.[25] It can now be viewed as a 'peer polity' of the Cretan palatial sites in the Middle Helladic period: wealthy, influential and with wide-ranging trading connections. Our increased understanding of the nature of Kolonna is supported by specific finds, such as the warrior grave and the EH III treasure, that have direct relevance to our interpretation of the Aigina Treasure, making it seem much less of an isolated phenomenon. Rather we can state with confidence that Kolonna in the Middle Bronze Age was the sort of place that had wealthy inhabitants – some perhaps coming from Minoan Crete – and was very likely to have supported a workshop making jewellery, along with a population providing a market for such jewellery and the wish to take it with them to a wealthy grave.

Notes

1. This essay originally resulted from collaborative research with Dr Stephen Quirke. I thank him for allowing me to incorporate his work into the version presented here.
2. Fitton and Quirke 1997, 421–44.
3. Alexiou and Warren 2004.
4. Pini 1990, 115–27; Pini 2000, 107–13.
5. See now Ben-Tor 2007 on the Montet jar as early 12th Dynasty (but all the scarabs are Egyptian, and none is a copy).
6. The Minoan vase from Qubbet el-Hawa does not certainly represent a link at this time, since although it has been published as of MM Ia date it is probably an east Cretan product and may be as late as MM Ib or MMIIa. See Manning 1995, 107–8. The Egyptian context of the vase is unhelpfully broad, with material ranging from the early Middle Kingdom to the 13th Dynasty.
7. Fitton and Quirke 1998.
8. Higgins 1957a, 42–57.
9. Walberg 1991a, 111–12.
10. Pierpont 1987, 79–94.
11. Higgins 1979.
12. Hood 1978, 155, pl. 147.
13. Dickinson 1994, 104.
14. The find was published in full in Bisson de la Roque *et al.* 1953.
15. See Porada 1982 for the date range of the Tod Treasure.
16. Pierrat 1994, 18–27, convincingly makes the point that the treasure is a 'weight' of raw materials dedicated in perpetuity, and not a hoard of materials intended for reuse.
17. Davis 1977, 71–9, is an authoritative discussion that concludes in favour of an Anatolian origin: Warren and Hankey (1989) strongly restate the case for Minoan pottery parallels.
18. Yule 1985, 42–4.
19. Examples from Mount Juktas and Ayia Triadha are in Herakleion museum. The bee/wasp is most famously represented in Minoan jewellery by the confronted pair of the well-known pendant from Mallia.
20. Menu 1994, 29–45.
21. Kemp and Merrillees 1980, 290–96.
22. Maran 1987, 221–7. Laffineur 1988, 17–50.
23. Evans 1921, 191. This is the only silver vessel of the MMIb–II period to have survived in Crete, but it is overwhelmingly likely that there were originally more: with the palaces rebuilt on the same sites and the protopalatial royal tombs unknown we lack the contexts in which preservation of vessels in precious metals could be expected.
24. Terrace and Fischer 1970, 69–71.
25. Rutter 2001, 126–30, reviews archaeological research since 1979 and discusses the many factors that have emerged to show 'the economic and probably political pre-eminence of the inhabitants of Aigina during the MH period'.

Plates

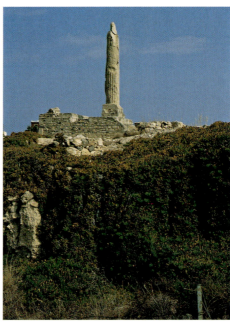

Figure 1 (top left) View of the island of Aigina.

Figure 2 (top right) The Classical Temple of Apollo, with its one remaining column, at Aigina–Kolonna.

Figure 3 (centre) The sea-turtle (*careta careta*), symbol of the island of Aigina on its famous silver coinage in the Classical period.

Figures 4 and 5 (bottom, left and right) Late Neolithic figurine of a woman, carved from shell (front and side views). Aigina, c. fifth millennium BC. (Staatliche Antikensammlungen und Glyptotek, Munich).

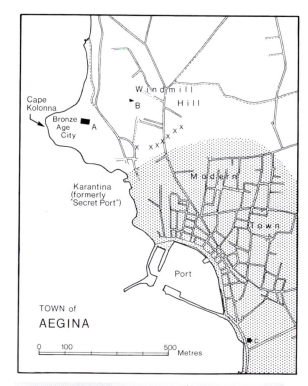

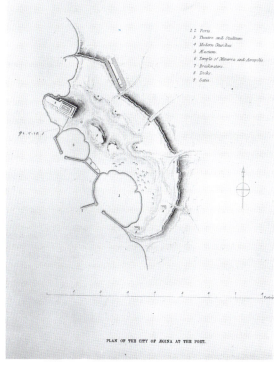

Figure 6 (top left) The Aigina branch of Cresswell Bros, c. 1891: Frederick Cresswell, seated in the centre, is flanked by George Brown on his right and Michel Emmanuel on his left; behind stand three Greek employees of the firm.

Figure 7 (centre left) Photograph of Frederick Cresswell.

Figure 8 (top right) Two Mycenaean vases and two bronze knives or scrapers from Aigina in the British Museum, which were purchased from Fred Cresswell in 1893.

Figure 9 (centre right) Map showing Aigina port and town, Cape Kolonna and Windmill Hill. A indicates the Temple of Apollo; B the Browns' hexagonal house on Windmill Hill; C indicates the Browns' principal house, now the Hotel Brown; Xs denote Mycenaean chamber tombs.

Figure 10 (bottom right) The plan of Aigina port published in C.R. Cockerell, *Aegina and Bassae* (1860), p. 1. This photograph shows the copy in the Greek and Roman Department at the British Museum with A.H. Smith's marking of the spot where Cresswell told him the treasure had been found.

Figure 11 The 'Master of Animals' pendant, constructed of sheet gold, front and back, and pendant discs.

Figure 12 The 'Master of Animals' pendant, detail of discs with dot-punched decoration.

Figure 13 The 'Master of Animals' pendant. Optical detail of the larger disc with the cut neck showing the dot decoration dipping below the pierced repair hole. Note the punched and chased decoration on the main pendant and the turned-up edges of the back sheet.

The Aigina Treasure: Catalogue and Technical Report

Figure 14 The 'Master of Animals' pendant, detail of a goose wing. Scanning electron microscope (SEM) image showing the punched and chased lines simulating feathers. Width (object detail): 7.9 mm

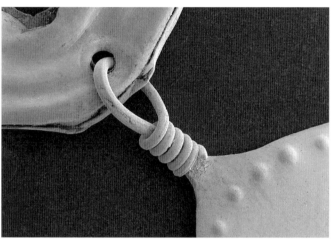

Figure 15 The 'Master of Animals' pendant. SEM image detail of a suspended gold disc showing the integral wire that loops through a pierced suspension hole in the pendant and is secured by twisting the wire back on itself. Width (object detail): 11.8 mm

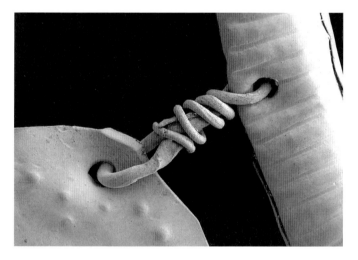

Figure 16 The 'Master of Animals' pendant. SEM detail of the larger disc with the cut neck (left in Figs 11 and 13), showing the ancient repair using wire through a pierced hole in the disc. Width (object detail): 11.8 mm

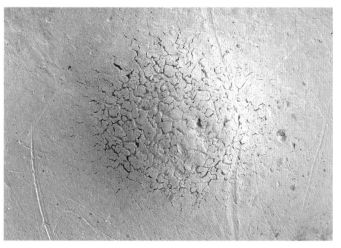

Figure 17 The 'Master of Animals' pendant. SEM detail of stress corrosion cracking on a disc where the original gold surfaces of the domed dot decoration was stretched during punching and was left in a stressed condition without further annealing, thus allowing cracking over time. Width (object detail): 1.2 mm

Figure 18 Pair of gold ornaments (763, 765), probably earrings. This is the pair with the finer details on the owls, dogs and monkeys and carved cylindrical beads for the dog leads.

Figure 19 Pair of gold ornaments (764, 766), probably earrings. This is the pair with the less well-formed details on the owls, dogs and monkeys.

Figure 20 Detail of earring 763 showing the fine details on the creatures (cf. Fig. 18). The main hoop at the top is not cut.

Figure 21 Detail of earring 764 showing the less fine details on the creatures (cf. Fig. 19) compared to earring 763. Note the broken wire 'lead' and hence the missing carnelian bead. The main hoop is cut through at the top.

Figure 22 Detail of earring 765 showing the mechanical wire attachment of a monkey to the hoop. The wire wraps over the monkey's foot and passes through a pierced hole in the main earring hoop. Note the upturned edge of the back sheet of the hoop, lower right.

Figure 23 Earring 764; detail of the wire attachment of a monkey to the hoop, which shows the mechanical fixture with the retaining wire of the overlapped hoop edges that are not soldered.

Figure 24 Earring 763; detail of the centre of the earring showing the carved cylindrical carnelian beads on the dog leads.

Figure 25 Detail of earring 765 showing a pair of well-decorated owls and a disc, typical of those suspended from the main ring. Note the tiny carnelian beads on the chains adjacent to the pendants.

Figure 26 Detail of earring 764 showing a pair of the less well-decorated owls and a disc, typical of those suspended from the main ring. Note the tiny carnelian beads on the chains adjacent to the pendants, which are of the same high quality as on the other earrings (763, 765).

The Aigina Treasure: Catalogue and Technical Report

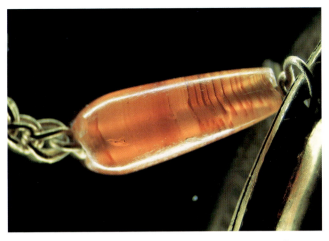

Figure 27 Polished, elongated carnelian bead from a chain on an earring, showing the translucent orange-red colour in transmitted light and the dark-coloured banding. Note the two internal drill holes that meet towards the right end of the bead, rather than in the centre.

Figure 28 Round bead of coloured, crackled quartz from the dog lead of earring 764.

Figure 29 Long carnelian bead in the centre of earring 764, in transmitted light showing the drill holes from each end of the bead that meet in the centre.

Figure 30 The three carved cylindrical carnelian beads on the carnelian and amethyst bead necklace which are very similar to the carved dog lead beads on earrings 763, 765. Seen in transmitted light.

Figure 31 SEM image of typical chain links on one of the owl chains on an earring showing the uneven strip-twist wire and a blob of solder on one link, upper left. Width (object detail): 6.2 mm

Figure 32 SEM image of a typical pierced hole in the edge of the main hoop ring of an earring from which chains are suspended via a twisted wire. Width (object detail): 7.7 mm

Figure 33 Round carnelian bead on the dog lead of earring 766. Note the unmelted snippets of solder wire partly fused to the dog head around the wire ear.

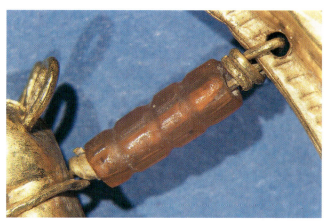

Figure 34 Cylindrical carnelian bead on the dog lead of earring 765, with carved grooved decoration similar to beads on the necklace of carnelian and amethyst beads in Fig. 30.

Figure 35 Front of the sheet gold owl (also seen in Fig. 48, right) showing the embossed features of the face and wings. The pierced hole is for a suspension chain.

Figure 36 Reverse of the sheet gold owl showing the concave features and the upturned sheet edges that would form the hollow owl when the two halves were originally part-soldered together at points along the edge.

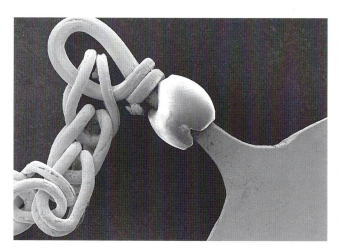

Figure 37 SEM image of the small carnelian bead on one of the discs of an earring. The bead is 2.1 mm in diameter. Note the disc gold is hammered into wire that passes through the tiny bead and chain loop then twists back on itself to secure the components. Width (object detail): 11.6 mm

Figure 38 SEM detail at high magnification near the edge of the owl showing stress corrosion cracking at the grain boundaries of the silver-rich gold. Width (object detail): 0.2 mm

Figure 39 SEM image of a cylindrical carnelian bead on earring 765 showing longitudinal and short tangential grooves filed into the carnelian. Width (object detail): 11.6 mm

Figure 40 SEM detail of the cylindrical carnelian bead in Fig. 39 showing the short, tangential file marks across the bead. Note how the longitudinal groove (upper) has a parallel 'starter' groove below, where the cutting tool began the groove but slipped and then took hold, thus forming the deeper main groove. Width (object detail): 4.6 mm

The Aigina Treasure: Catalogue and Technical Report

Figure 41 Pectoral ornament with twin profile heads and ten suspended discs.

Figure 42 Pectoral ornament; detail of one of the profile heads showing the chased features and hair lines, the cut-out eye and eyebrow and the soldered loop on the chin.

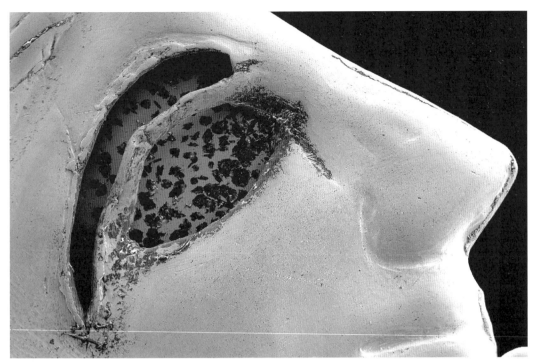

Figure 43 Pectoral ornament. SEM detail of the profile head showing the hollow space behind the cut-out eye and eyebrow, which may have earlier been inlaid. Details of the nose and mouth are chased. The edge of the soldered back sheet is seen around the nose and mouth. Width (object detail): 12 mm

Figure 44 Pectoral ornament. SEM detail of the chased hair lines and tool marks forming the decoration. Width (object detail): 5.8 mm

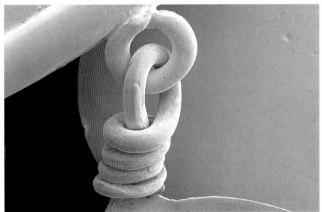

Figure 45 Pectoral ornament. SEM detail of a suspension loop soldered to the pectoral and showing the suspended disc wire passing through the loop and twisting back on itself. Width (object detail): 10 mm

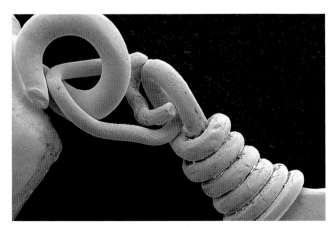

Figure 46 Pectoral ornament. SEM detail of the suspension loop on the chin of one profile head, showing that the disc and its twisted wire loop are attached by a separate piece of ancient wire, rather than directly. Width (object detail): 7.9 mm

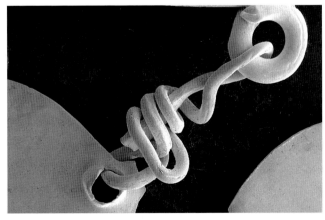

Figure 47 Pectoral ornament. SEM detail of one of the repaired discs showing the broken wire neck on the disc and that the original wire has been re-used to suspend the disc, which has been pierced for the repair. Similar to the disc repair of the 'Master of Animals' pendant, Fig. 16. Width (object detail): 11.8 mm

The Aigina Treasure: Catalogue and Technical Report

Figure 48 Left to right: lion's head ornament with the two stub-winged ducks and seed-shaped beads on chains from the head, and three swept-wing ducks from the base; the twin owl and carnelian ornament (see also Fig. 53); the two sheet gold owls (see also Figs 35 and 36).

Figure 49 Detail of the naturalistic swept-wing ducks suspended from chains of the lion's head ornament. Wingspan of ducks: 22 mm

Figure 50 Lion's head ornament; detail of the head and suspended ducks and seed-shaped beads. Note the central wire that joins the head to the base.

Figure 51 Detail of the two types of gold duck on the lion's head ornament.

Figure 52 Bottom of the lion's head ornament which is hollow, has a central wire suspending it from the head and has three soldered loops from which the swept-wing ducks are suspended.

Figure 53 Twin owl and carnelian ornament from a more elaborate piece of jewellery. The two owls hang from chains attached to their tails in the similar manner to other pendant birds. The owls are the smallest in the treasure with stubby wings and of the less well defined type. Also seen in Fig. 48 right. The gold fittings on the carnelian are similar to those of the base of the green jasper acorns (cf. figs 102 and 105).

Figure 54 Lion's head ornament. SEM detail of the bottom showing the chased tool marks mimicking the lion's mane. Width (object detail): 12 mm

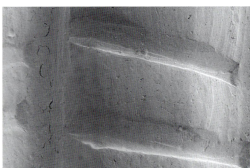

Figure 55 Lion's head ornament. SEM detail of the chased tool marks on the base, showing the original curved tool profile at the ends of the grooves. Width (object detail): 2.2 mm

Figure 56 SEM detail of the chain link and soldered suspension loop on one seed-shaped bead from the lion ornament. Note the duck wing behind with a gap at the edge where the front and back sheets were not soldered together. Width (object detail): 11.6 mm

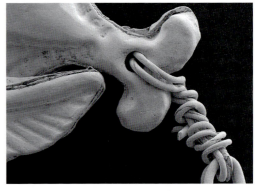

Figure 57 Lion's head ornament, pierced suspension hole on a duck's tail for the chain attachment using a double strip-twist wire. Note the overlapped edges of the sheet tail and wing. Width (object detail): 11.6 mm

The Aigina Treasure: Catalogue and Technical Report

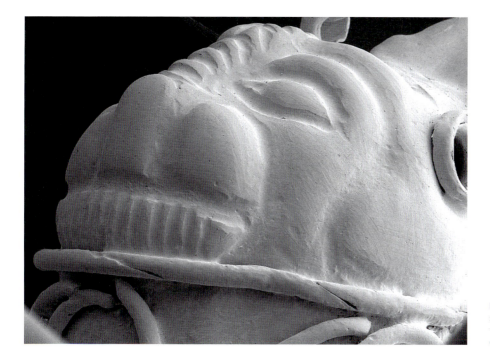

Figure 58 SEM detail of the lion's head showing the punched decoration forming the features of the face, and the strip-twist wire collar. Width (object detail): 11.6 mm

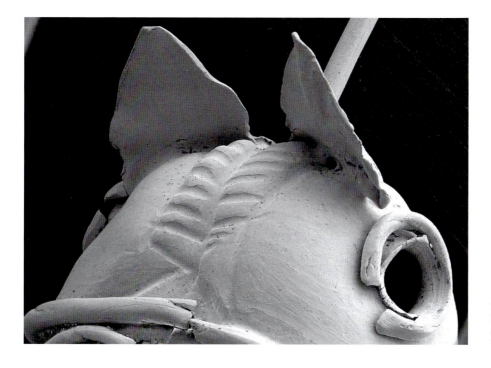

Figure 59 SEM detail of the back of the lion's head showing the sheet ears soldered in place and the chased grooves forming the mane. Width (object detail): 11.6 mm

Figure 60 Lion's head ornament; SEM detail of the chains suspending the three ducks, showing the loop-in-loop, strip-twist chain links. Width (object detail): 11.6 mm

Figure 61 Twin owl and carnelian ornament; chains showing the variable thickness of the strip-twist wire of the links, some with large blobs of solder. Width (object detail): 11.8 mm

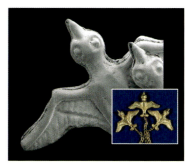

Figure 62 Lion's head ornament, superimposed optical images of the three swept-wing ducks on the SEM detail of a pair of the ducks. Note the naturalistic representation of the birds' heads, feathers and bone structure of the wing leading edge. Wingspan of ducks: 22 mm

Figure 63 Gold plaques. Five representatives of the fifty-four similar plaques of sheet gold with punched and chased decoration.

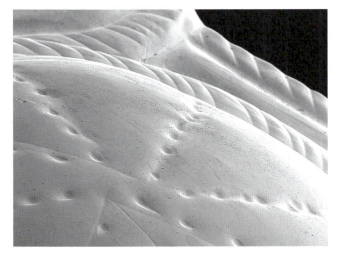

Figure 64 Gold plaque; SEM image showing detail of the punched decoration and the scored guidelines on the surface for alignment of the dot punch marks. Width (object detail): 9.8 mm

Figure 65 Gold plaque; pierced edge for attachment to clothing. Width (object detail): 9.8 mm

The Aigina Treasure: Catalogue and Technical Report

Figure 66 The three sheet gold diadems and one of the fragments of plain gold band (at top).

Figure 67 The twisted wire end of one diadem is continuous with the sheet. The whole object was formed by hammering from a gold rod.

Figure 68 Detail of the punched dot decoration on a gold diadem, seen from the punched side.

Figure 69 Detail of the punched dot decoration on a gold diadem, seen from the reverse side.

Figure 70 SEM detail of the smooth surface of a diadem and showing a double osmium/iridium/ruthenium inclusion (right centre) that passes through the sheet and appears on both sides. They are very hard and resist deformation during hammering the sheet gold. Width (object detail): 0.17 mm

Figure 71 Gold bracelet. Side view showing the tapered ends and the slightly concave outer section.

Figure 72 The upper and middle necklaces are the sets of double-arc-shaped hollow gold beads (upper 759a, middle 758a; see also Fig. 73); the lower is the gold bead necklace (cf. Figs 74, 77 and 78).

Figure 73 Detail of the double-arc-shaped bead necklaces (upper 759a, middle 758a; cf. Figs 75 and 76). Each bead is made from two similar halves soldered together.

Figure 74 Detail of two suspended oval pendants on short chains from the gold bead necklace shown in Fig. 72, bottom.

The Aigina Treasure: Catalogue and Technical Report

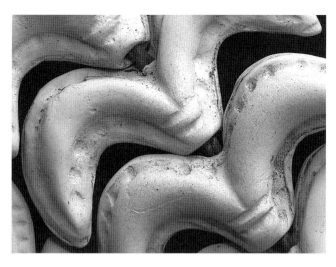

Figure 75 SEM detail of the beads of necklace 759A showing soldered edges of bead halves and attention to the punched detail producing very regular patterns between all beads. Width (object detail): 11.8 mm

Figure 76 SEM detail of the beads of necklace 758A showing larger beads of similar construction, regularity and punched details to the other necklace. Width (object detail): 11.8 mm

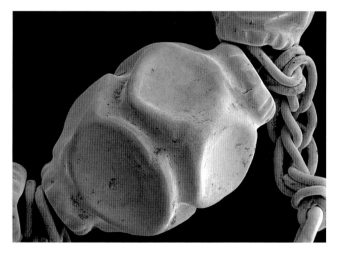

Figure 77 SEM detail of one of the well-made geometrical beads on the gold bead necklace. Note the soldered seam joining the identical bead halves together, indicated only by the small unjoined gap, top right. Width (object detail): 11.6 mm

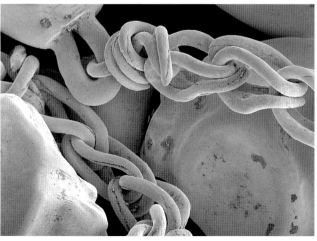

Figure 78 SEM detail of part of the gold bead necklace showing a wire loop soldered into an oval pendant, and the twisted wire connecting this to the chain link. Note also the twisted grooves in the chain link wires, typical of strip-twist wire manufacture. Width (object detail): 8.5 mm

Figure 79 Alternating carnelian, lapis lazuli and gold bead necklace. The beads are all in the form of a right hand holding a woman's breast. The very similar designs of all the beads (essentially identical and possibly unique) show that a single workshop was the origin of the manufacture of the beads of different materials.

Figure 80 Gold and lapis lazuli beads viewed edge-on showing the hollow tubular gold bead and the drilled lapis lazuli bead (connected by modern cord).

Figure 81 Sample of lapis lazuli rock with the typical mixture of blue lazurite, white diopside (rather than calcite in this case) and gold coloured pyrite.

The Aigina Treasure: Catalogue and Technical Report

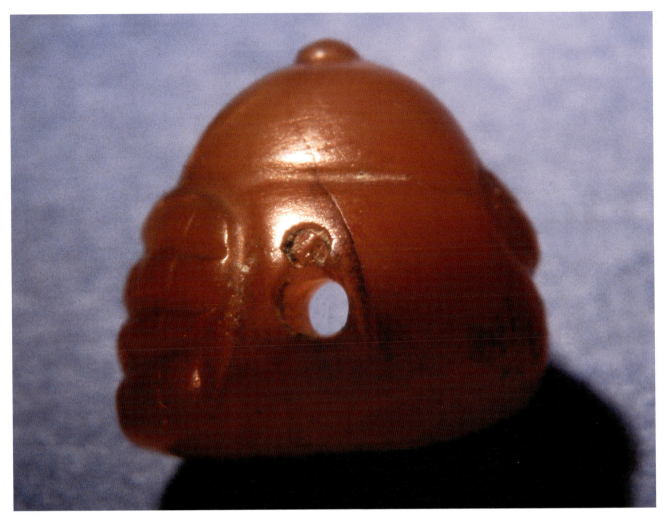

Figure 82 Translucent orange-red carnelian bead from the side showing the drill hole through the bead, above which is the off-set abandoned start of a drill hole, still with a core showing a hollow drill was used.

Figure 83 Translucent orange-red carnelian bead seen from the back in transmitted light, showing the vivid colour and some dark inclusions.

Figure 84 Translucent orange-red carnelian bead from the front in partly transmitted light, showing the grasping right hand.

Figure 85 Three gold finger rings: the upper is of thin sheet with chased cross-hatch decoration; the ring at lower left is shaped in the form of a reef knot with inlaid lapis lazuli; and the ring at lower right is in the shape of a double-axe or shield with inlaid lapis lazuli and with a thick solid finger loop.

Figure 86 Gold finger ring inlaid with dark lapis lazuli in a meander pattern.

Figure 87 Gold finger ring with an inlay of lapis lazuli with carved decoration of fluted design.

The Aigina Treasure: Catalogue and Technical Report

Figure 88 Reef knot ring, left side, showing the deep cloison channels made from soldered strips of gold, revealed where lapis lazuli is now missing.

Figure 89 Reef knot ring, right side, showing lapis lazuli in the finger loop to the right. Note the gap in the soldered join between the cloison wall and bottom sheet, left of centre.

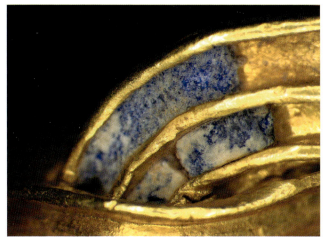

Figure 90 Detail of the reef knot ring showing oblong blocks of lapis lazuli cut to fit the deep channels in the ring. Note the blue and white colours of the natural rock mineral. Detail of Fig. 88, top left.

Figure 91 Reef knot ring; SEM detail of the cut and polished blocks of lapis lazuli inlaid into the gold channels. The gold has been burnished to spread the edge over the lapis lazuli to hold it in place, but some is missing.

Figure 92 Gold double-axe or shield design finger ring with blue lapis lazuli inlaid into cloisons, with some missing.

Figure 93 Detail of the gold double-axe or shield design ring. The lapis lazuli inlays have been cut to shape to fit the curved cloison walls. The gold is burnished to spread the edges over the lapis lazuli to hold the pieces in place.

Figure 94 Meander-pattern ring showing the darker blue coloured lapis lazuli, the colour possibly created by heating. The central rectangular block of lapis lazuli is 0.8 × 1.5 mm and accurately cut to fit the gold cloison cell.

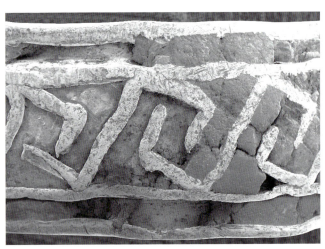

Figure 95 SEM detail of the gold finger ring with inlaid lapis lazuli in the meander pattern. Pieces of blue lapis lazuli are seen to be cut to the shape of the gold cloisons and inlaid and the gold burnished over the edges to hold the gemstone pieces in place. Some pieces are missing. Width (object detail): 8 mm

Figure 96 Detail of part of the fluted lapis lazuli ring showing the rounded convex profile of the inlaid lapis lazuli at the top and illustrating the oblique decoration. An area of damage and missing lapis lazuli shows the depth of the inlay, and the gold sides curve in to retain the gemstone.

Figure 97 Fluted lapis lazuli ring showing a wide gap between pieces of inlaid lapis lazuli, and another thin circumferential join line between pieces laid around the ring, bottom right.

Figure 98 SEM detail of the edge of the fluted ring showing the oblique, carved, decorative grooves in the lapis lazuli. Note also the small indents in the gold rim (left) to hold the inlaid pieces in place. Width (object detail): 5.4 mm

The Aigina Treasure: Catalogue and Technical Report

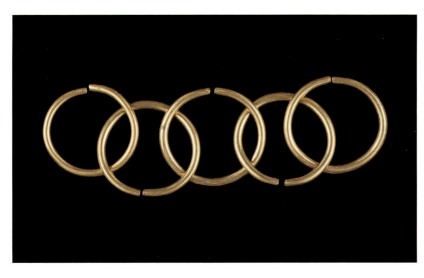

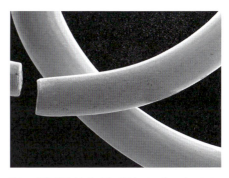

Figure 100 SEM detail of the thick wire of overlapping rings. Note the tapering of the wire and evidence of faceting from hammering to shape the wire. Width (object detail): 11.6 mm

Figure 99 Five plain wire gold rings.

Figure 101 Lower: the gold and green jasper bead necklace; middle: the carnelian and amethyst bead necklace; upper: the alternating carnelian, lapis lazuli and gold bead necklace; top centre: the single rock crystal bead.

Figure 102 Detail of the gold and green jasper bead necklace showing the manner of spacing and suspension of the green jasper beads in the gold acorn cups, and the pigtail-twisted gold wire keeping the beads in place.

Figure 103 Detail of some of the carnelian beads on the carnelian and amethyst necklace shown in Fig. 101, centre. In transmitted light the rich orange-red colours show dark inclusions and thin banding. Each bead is drilled through the centre from both sides to meet in the middle.

The Aigina Treasure: Catalogue and Technical Report

Figure 104 Gold and green jasper bead necklace; SEM detail of several melon-shaped beads showing the soldered seams joining bead halves, and two flattened wire suspension loops of acorn cups (top left and bottom right). Width (object detail): 11.6 mm

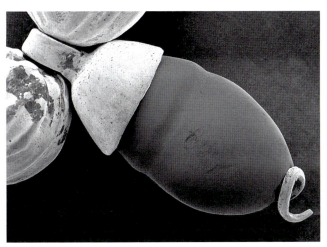

Figure 105 Gold and green jasper bead necklace; SEM detail of one green jasper bead in a gold acorn cup. Note the grooved waist carved around the bead, and that the pigtail twist of the securing wire that passes through a central hole in the bead is soldered to the gold cup and passes through it to form the suspension loop. Width (object detail): 11.6 mm

Figure 106 Carnelian and amethyst necklace; detail of one of the amethyst beads. Note that the bead has three suspension holes, and each was drilled from both ends to meet in the middle. Also note how the drill holes taper towards the centre due to slight rocking of the thin drill during use that widens the outer ends of the hole.

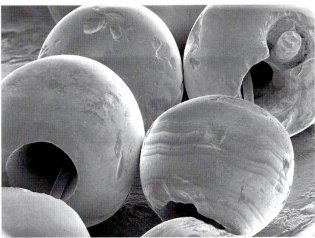

Figure 107 Carnelian and amethyst necklace; SEM detail of a few round carnelian beads in the necklace, showing the perfectly round drill hole in one bead, left, and also the abandoned partly drilled off-axis hole, right, with the central peg still in place showing that a hollow drill was used. Similar mistakes are found on other beads. Width (object detail): 9.8 mm

Figure 108 The rock crystal bead in transmitted light, showing the hole drilled from both sides, through the thin axis and meeting in the middle.

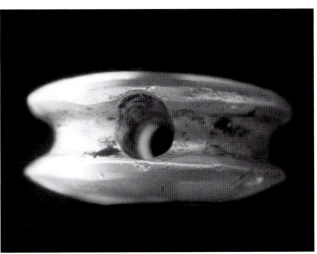

Figure 109 Edge view of the rock crystal bead showing the deep circumferential groove and the drilled central hole.

Figure 110 The gold cup, side view, showing the flat bottom, concave rim and embossed spiral groove decoration.

Figure 111 Gold cup, top view looking inside the vessel, showing the geometrical spiral pattern around the central embossed rosette. The three rivet holes to the side are pierced for attachment of a missing handle.

The Aigina Treasure: Catalogue and Technical Report

Figure 112 SEM detail of a thick block-twist wire with the characteristic twin opposing spiral grooves and solid core. This wire joins one of the monkeys to the hoop of a large gold earring. Width (object detail): 2.6 mm

Figure 113 SEM detail of strip-twist wire with characteristic hollow core (lower wire). This is looped through a block-twist wire with a solid core (upper wire). Width (object detail): 3 mm

Figure 114 SEM detail of chain links with excessive solder blobs joining the ends of the wire to close the links. Clearly each chain link has to have a soldered join. Most are neat but some have these solder blobs. The spiral grooves of the strip-twist wires are also seen. Width (object detail): 2.7 mm

Figure 115 Geological samples of the materials used to make the semi-precious stone beads in the Aigina Treasure. Clockwise: amethyst, lapis lazuli, carnelian, quartz (rock) crystal, green jasper.

Felten

List of monuments: **Z** Cisterns (MA), **1** So-called priests' houses (A-C), **2** Harbour wall (R), **3** South wall (R), **4** East wall (R), **5** North wall (R), **6** Acropolis wall (A–H), **7** Temple of Apollo (A), **8** Temple column, **9** Cistern (MA), **10** Altar (A), **11** Temple of Artemis (C), **12** Propylon (H?), **13, 14** Rectangular buildings (Naiskoi, H), **15** Round Building (Tholos, H), **16** Dining Hall (Thearion, A), **17** Small road (BA), **18** Circuit walls of the Inner Extension (BA), **19** Circuit walls of the Outer Extension (BA), **20** Warrior's grave (BA)

BA Bronze Age (3/2 millennia BC)
A   Archaic Age (7/6 centuries BC)
C   Classical Era (5/4 centuries BC)
H   Hellenistic Age (3/2 centuries BC)
R   Roman Period (1/5 centuries AD)
MA Middle Ages (6/10 centuries AD)

Prehistoric towns:
- Town II (EH II)
- Town III (EH II)
- Town IV (EH III)
- Town V (EH III)
- Town VI (EH III)
- Town VII (MH)
- Town VIII (MH)
- Town IX (MH)
- Town X (MH/LH)

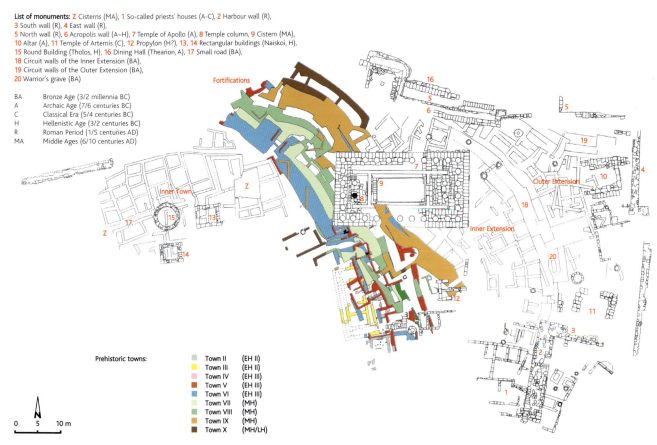

Figure 116 Aigina–Kolonna. Schematic plan and phases of the prehistoric fortifications. (Drawing C. Reinholdt)

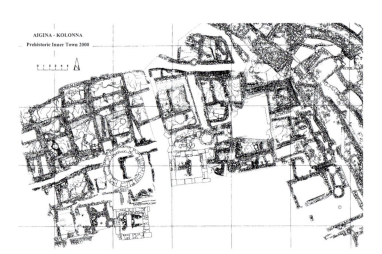

Figure 117 Plan of the prehistoric inner town, northern sector. (Drawing C. Reinholdt)

Figure 118 Final Neolithic jar with collar neck.

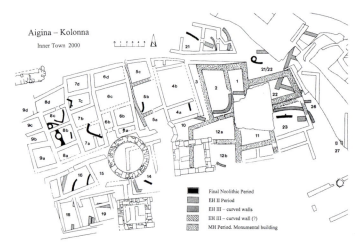

Figure 119 Schematic plan of the prehistoric inner town. (Drawing C. Reinholdt)

Figure 120 Final Neolithic wall with door pan under 'House 23'.

Figure 121 View of the MH inner town.

Figure 122 MH warrior's grave ('shaft grave') at the east side of the 'inner extension' fortification wall.

Figure 123 Final Neolithic male clay idol.

Figure 124 MH II cup from the 'monumental building'.

Figure 125 MH III/LH brown-slipped goblet from the 'outer extension'.

Figure 126 LH fortification wall of the 'outer extension'.

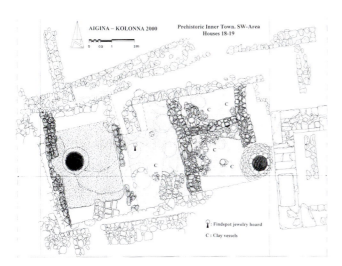

Figure 127 EH walls under 'House 19'. (Drawing C. Reinholdt)

Figure 128 EH III floor with vessels under 'House 19'.

Figure 129 EH III jug with dark-on-light decoration.

Figure 130 EH III red-slipped and polished jug.

Figure 131 Jewellery hoard, front view.

Figure 132 Jewellery hoard, back view.

Figure 133 Golden pin with loop terminal.

Figure 134 Golden disc pendant with soldered-wire decoration.

Figure 135 Gold band found at the Aigina Warrior Grave.

Figure 136 Pendant in the shape of a fish, from Knossos.

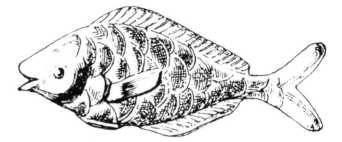

Figure 137 Egyptian pendant in the shape of a fish.

Figure 138 An Egyptian 18th Dynasty necklace consisting of duck-shaped beads.

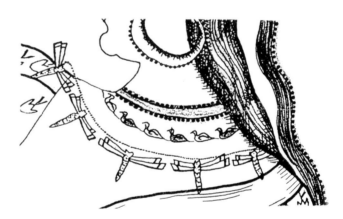

Figure 139 Necklace worn by the goddess from Thera/Akrotiri, Xeste 3.

Figure 140 A hair-pin from Mycenae, Shaft Grave III.

Figure 141 An example of papyrus flowers in Egyptian iconography.

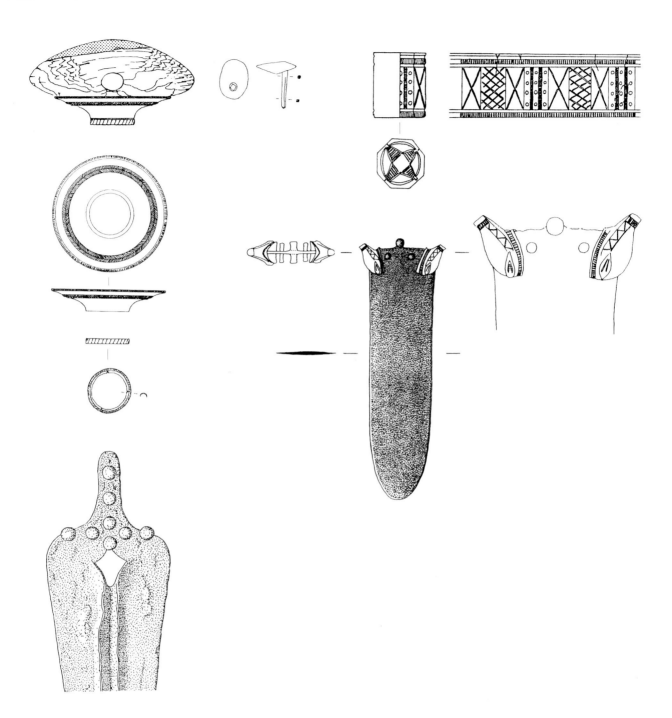

Figure 142 Gold sheet ornaments found in the Warrior Shaft Grave: a head band; a razor mounting in the shape of two animals; a hexagonal ornament; the mounting of a sword.

Figure 143 Gold ornament from the Shaft Graves at Mycenae. After Karo 1930, no. 696, pl. 64.

Figure 144 Gold ornament from the Shaft Graves at Mycenae. After Karo 1930, no. 698, pl. 65.

Figure 145 Gold band from Shaft Grave IV at Mycenae. After Karo 1930, nos 236–9, pl. 39.

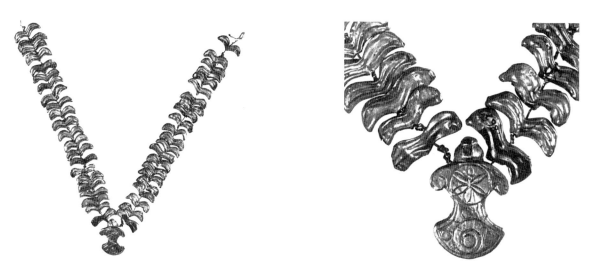

Figures 146 (left) and 147 (right) Gold necklace from Grave Omikron at Mycenae. After Mylonas 1972, pl. 181.

Figure 148 Gold band from Asine. After Dietz 1980, fig. 21.

Figure 149 Matt-painted polychrome jug from the Shaft Graves at Mycenae. After Karo 1930, no. 200, pl. 174.

Figure 150 Gold bracelet from Grave Alpha at Mycenae. After Mylonas 1972, pl. 21a.

Figure 151 Gold stemmed cup from the Shaft Graves at Mycenae. After Karo 1930, no. 656, pl. 129.

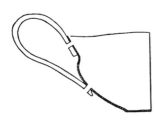

Figure 152 Gold cup from Peristeria. After Korres 1976, 498, fig. 8.

Figure 153 Gold beads in the EH Thyreatis treasure in Berlin. After Reinholdt 1993, 10, fig. 13.

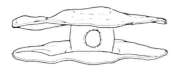
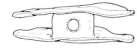
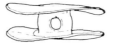

Figure 154 Reconstructed drawing of the impression on bullae from Acemhöyük (from Özgüç 1973, 25, fig. 4); diam. 2.5 cm.

Figure 155 Detail showing one of the sphinx heads on the impression of a cylinder seal in the Yale Babylonian Collection (Otto 1999, no. 59); haematite, height of seal 2.2 cm; 1800–1750 BC.

Figure 156 Seal impression on a fragmentary clay envelope from Tell Atchana (ancient Alalakh) between Antakya and Aleppo (Otto 1999, no. 57); height 1.75+ cm; 1800–1750 BC.

Figure 157 Sphinxes now in the Metropolitan Museum but originating at Acemhöyük; stained ivory with remains of gold leaf; scale not given; nineteenth–eighteenth century BC.

Figure 158 Sphinx on a red-burnished sherd from Karahöyük near Konya; scale not given; nineteenth–eighteenth century BC.

Figure 160 (above) Reconstructed drawing of the impression on bullae from Acemhöyük (from Özgüç 1973, 21, fig. 2); scale not given.

Figure 159 (left) Design on the impression of the cylinder seal of Matrunna, daughter of Aplahanda, king of Carchemish (N.B. the cuneiform inscription has not been drawn). From Minet el-Beidha on the north Syrian coast; Metropolitan Museum, New York; haematite, height 2.4 cm; 1800–1750 BC.

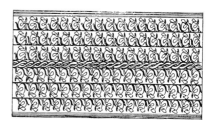

Figure 161 Reconstructed drawing of the impression on bullae from Acemhöyük (from Özgüç 1973, 22, fig. 3a–b); scale not given.

Figure 162 Impression of the cylinder seal of Iaush-Adu, king of Buzuran near Mari on the Middle Euphrates in Syria; Rosen Collection, New York; obsidian, height 2.4 cm.

Figure 163 Finger rings from the Royal Cemetery of Ur, southern Iraq; gold and lapis lazuli (BM ANE 121375–6, 121378–9); about 2600 BC.

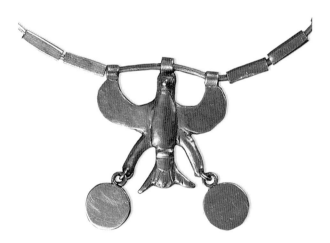

Figure 164 Detail of a necklace; British Museum (BM ANE 132116); gold; height of eagle 2.0 cm.

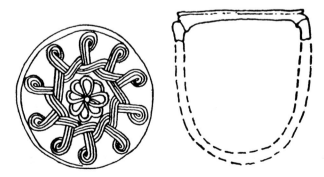

Figure 165 Seal ring from Boğazköy (from Boehmer and Güterbock 1987, no. 143 on p. 51 and pl. XIV); bronze, diam. 2.4 cm; 1650–1600 BC.

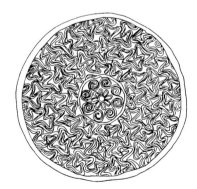

Figure 166 Design on a dish; Musée du Louvre, Paris (AO 21379); gold, diam. 19.7 cm.

Figure 167 Reverse of gold Mesopotamian pendant with bullman between human-headed bulls (Musée du Louvre, Paris).

Figure 168 Gold necklace with openwork pendant falcons (British Museum; ME 132116).

Figure 169 Gold ornament in the form of three Egyptian Geese, from Byblos. Dunand 1950, no. 17754.

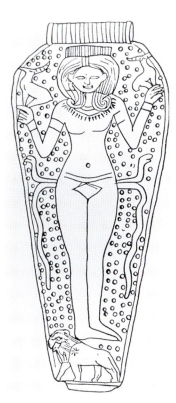

Figure 170 (left) Gold triangular pendant with nude female, from Minet el-Beidha (Musée du Louvre, Paris; AO 14714). (right) Drawing of this pendant from Schaeffer 1949, p. 36, fig. 10.

Figure 171 Gold triangular pendant with nude female, from the Uluburun shipwreck (Bodrum Museum of Underwater Archaeology, Turkey; 1.5.87 (KW 703).

Figure 172 Detail from the Boxer Rhyton. From Hagia Triada, steatite (Heraklion Archaeological Museum, Crete, 498).

Figure 173 Pectoral of Mereret, with pharoah slaying Asiatic enemy. From Dahshur, gold and semi-precious stones (Egyptian Museum, Cairo; CG 52003).

The Aigina Treasure | 105

Figure 174 Gold plaque with human head terminal, from Byblos. Dunand 1950, pl. 164:9306.

Figure 175 Drawing of a terracotta plaque with nude female. Albright 1939, p. 111:5.

Figure 176 Ivory nude female figure, from Megiddo (Oriental Institute Museum, Chicago; A 22257).

Figure 177 Limestone votive stele depicting the nude goddess Qudshu/Qadesh, from Deir el-Medina (Museo Egizio, Turin; 50066).

Figure 178 Drawing of a steatite triangular prism stamp seal, from Mallia, Crete. Demargne 1939, 122, fig. 1.

Figure 179 Modern impression of 'Cypro-Aegean' cylinder seal. From Enkomi, Cyprus, hematite (Cyprus Museum).

Figure 180 Bronze plaque with divinity and water birds, reported to come from near Cadiz (private collection).

Figure 181 Drawing of a terracotta plaque with nude female, from Alalakh. Badre 1980, pl. 20:48.

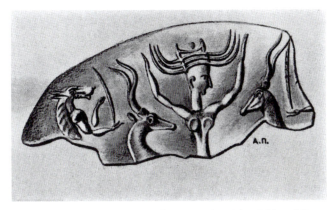

Figure 182 Drawing of a clay stamp seal impression, from Pylos. *CMS* I, no. 379.

Figure 183 Modern impression of Syrian cylinder seal. (The Pierpont Morgan Library, New York, cylinder seal no. 980).

Figure 184 Pectoral of Mereret. From Dahshur, gold and semi-precious stones (Egyptian Museum, Cairo; JE 30875).

Figure 185 Ivory plaque with incised griffin, attributed to Acemhöyük (Metropolitan Museum of Art, New York; 36,36.152.7).

Figure 186 Drawing of an onyx stamp seal, from Mycenae. *CMS* I, no. 81.

Figure 187 Ivory and silver Hathor plaque, from Byblos. Aruz 2008a, p. 55, cat. 26.

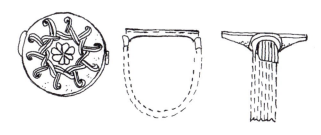

Figure 188 Drawing of a bronze finger ring (Ankara Museum of Anatolian Civilization, Boğazköy). Musche 1992, pl. 55, Fingerschmuck typ 2.

Figure 189 Drawings of clay stamp seal impressions (Konya Museum, Karahöyük). Alp 1968, p. 232, no. 235, and p. 185, no. 89.

Figure 190 Gold pendant from Tell el Dabʿa, F/1-p/17-tomb 14 (TD 7315, Cairo Museum, JdE 98553)

Figure 191 Back view of the Tell el Dabʿa pendant.

Figure 192 Silver pendant from the Petrie Museum of Egyptian Archaeology (UC 34342). Publication courtesy of the Petrie Museum and the British Museum.

Figure 193 Prism (from Sitea?), Giamalakis Collection. (A. Xénaki-Sakellariou, *Les Cachets Minoens de la Collection Giamalakis*, Études Crétoises 10, Paris, 1958, pl. IV, 111b).

Figure 194 Phaistos sealing. (*CMS* II, 5, Berlin, 1970, no. 318).

Figure 195 Phaistos sealing. (*CMS* II, 5, Berlin 1970, no. 317).

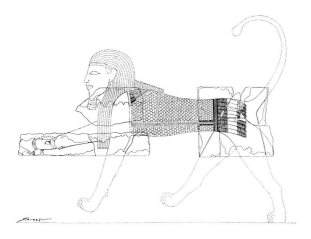

Figure 197 F/I-p/17-tomb 14, N–S section through tomb chamber. Reconstructed (not to scale).

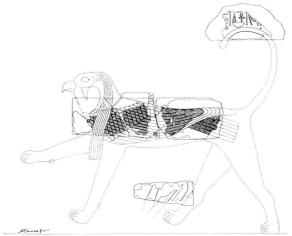

Figure 196 (left) Saqqara, causeway of pyramid complex of Pepi II, 6th Dynasty, reliefs showing winged sphinx (top) and griffin (bottom). Jequier, 1941, pl. 15.

Figure 198 Tell el-Dabʿa stratigraphy.

MB-PHASES	B.C.	EGYPT RELATIVE CHRONOLOGY	TELL EL - DABʿA					GENERAL PHASES
			TOWN CENTRE (Middle Kingdom) 'Ez. Rushdi	NEW CENTRE MB-Population	EASTERN TOWN	NORTHEASTERN TOWN	PALACE DISTRICT 'Ez. HELMI	
		Dyn.	R / I	F / I	A / I-IV	A / V	H / I-VI	
	1410							
LB I	1440	A II			TEMPLE OF SETH			
	1470	XVIII H T III	HIATUS			HIATUS	Pumice c	C / 2
	1500	T II T I					Paintings d	C / 3
	1530	A I AHMOSE	CONQUEST OF AVARIS				e / 1	D / 1
MB II C	1560		DENUDED		D / 2	D / 2	e / 2 - f	D / 2
	1590	XV HYKSOS		a / 2	D / 3	D / 3	g - h	D / 3
MB II B	1620		DENUDED a PITS		E / 1	E / 1		E / 1
	1650	KINGDOM OF AVARIS NEHESI		b / 1	E / 2	E / 2		E / 2
	1680			b / 2	E / 3			E / 3
MB II A-B	1710		DENUDED a STORAGE PITS	b / 3	F			F
	1740	XIII		EPIDEMIC c HIATUS	G / 1-3			G
	1770			d / 1	G / 4			G / 4
MB II A	1800	So A IV		d / 2 d / 2a d / 2b	H			H
	1830	A III	b / 1					
	1860	S III	b / 2					I
	1890	XII S II 5th year S III	c / 1-2 d	HIATUS				K
	1920	A II	e / 1-4			UNOCCUPIED		L
	1950	S I	f					M
?	1980	A I	?	e / 1				N
MB I	2000	XI		e / 2-3				N / 2-3
	2050	X	? HERACLEO-POLITAN FOUNDATION		EXPANSION OF THE SETTLEMENT →			

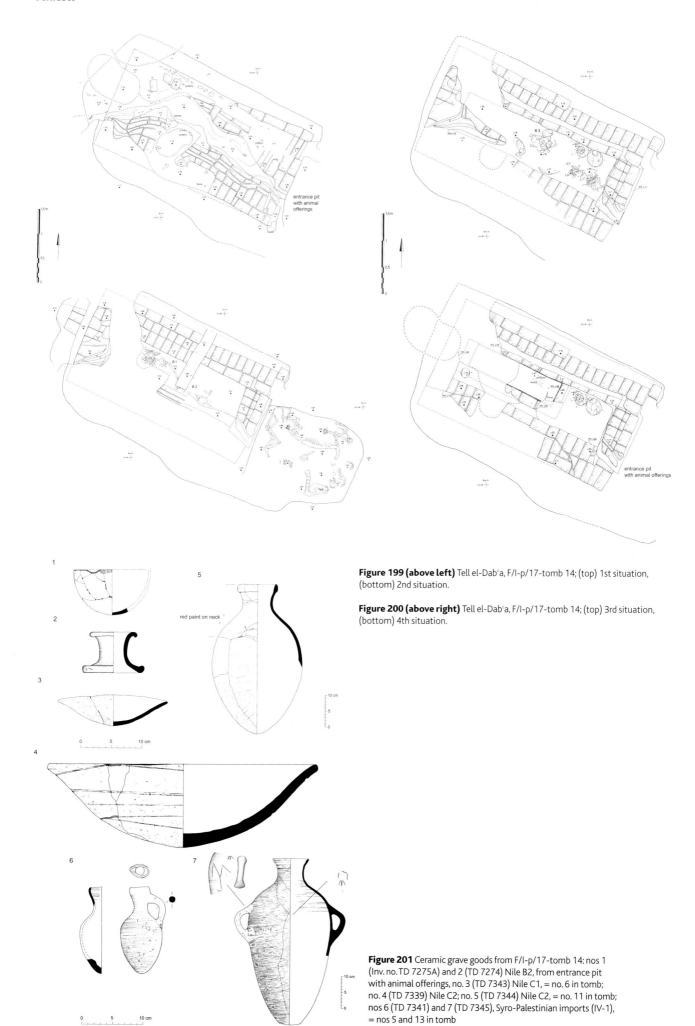

Figure 199 (above left) Tell el-Dabʿa, F/I-p/17-tomb 14; (top) 1st situation, (bottom) 2nd situation.

Figure 200 (above right) Tell el-Dabʿa, F/I-p/17-tomb 14; (top) 3rd situation, (bottom) 4th situation.

Figure 201 Ceramic grave goods from F/I-p/17-tomb 14: nos 1 (Inv. no. TD 7275A) and 2 (TD 7274) Nile B2, from entrance pit with animal offerings, no. 3 (TD 7343) Nile C1, = no. 6 in tomb; no. 4 (TD 7339) Nile C2; no. 5 (TD 7344) Nile C2, = no. 11 in tomb; nos 6 (TD 7341) and 7 (TD 7345), Syro-Palestinian imports (IV-1), = nos 5 and 13 in tomb

Figure 202 Spherical garnet beads (221) (TD 7316/10).

Figure 203 Spherical garnet beads (180) (TD 7316/10).

Figure 204 Barrel-shaped agate beads (31) (TD 7316/3 + 4).

Figure 205 Barrel and drop shaped agate beads (13) (TD 7316/1, 3 + 4).

Figure 206 Barrel-shaped agate beads (94) (TD 7316/5).

Figure 207 Agate beads, spherical and barrel shaped with ribbed thickened mid-section (11) (TD 7316/2 + 6).

Figure 208 Drop-, barrel- and double-conic-shaped electrum beads (30) (TD 7316/8 + 9).

Figure 209 Ribbed electrum beads (31) (TD 7316/7)

Figure 210 All beads assembled (TD 7316/1-10).

type		stone	metal
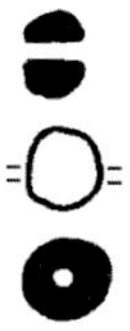	spheroid	agate, garnet	gold
	barrel shaped	agate	electrum
A 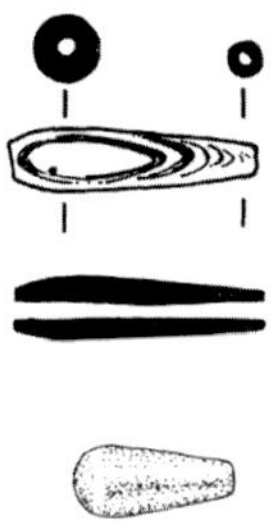 / B	drop shaped	agate (A)	electrum (B)
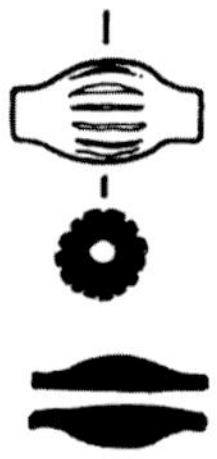	barrel shaped, with wide, ribbed mid section	agate	
	flattened, ribbed spheroid		electrum

Figure 211 Bead types from tomb p/17-no. 14.

Figure 212 Tell el-Dabʿa pendant with suggested reconstructed of suspension; scale 2:1.

Figure 213 Reef-knot bracelet, Egyptian, First Intermediate Period, 2130–1980 BC; from Sheikh Farag (tomb 5045); gold; Harvard University–Boston Museum of Fine Arts Expedition 24.1807. Photograph courtesy of the Museum of Fine Arts, Boston.

Figure 214 Scarab with reef knot, Egyptian, Middle Kingdom, Dynasty 12, c. 1800 BC; blue-glazed steatite. Private collection. Photograph courtesy of Yvonne Markowitz.

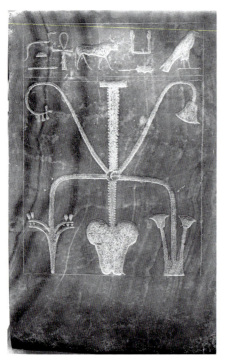

Figure 215 Back of a fragmentary statue of King Menkaure, Egyptian, Old Kingdom, Dynasty 4, reign of Menkaure, 2490–2472 BC; from the Valley Temple of Menkaure, Giza; travertine; Harvard University–Boston Museum of Fine Arts Expedition 09.202. Photograph courtesy of the Museum of Fine Arts, Boston.

Figure 216 The medallion of Dahshur, from the jewellery of Princess Khnumet.

Figure 217 Gold bird pendants, from the jewellery of Princess Khnumet.

Figure 218 View of the base of one of the cups in the Tod Treasure.

Figure 219 View of the base of one of the cups in the Tod Treasure.

Figure 220 The silver pendant from the Tod Treasure: bee/wasp side.

Figure 221 The silver pendant from the Tod Treasure: side with spiders.

Figure 222 View of the complete Tod Treasure (Musée du Louvre, Paris).

Bibliography

Akurgal, E., 1961, *Die Kunst der Hethiter*, Munich.

Albright, W., 1939, 'Astarte plaques and figurines from Tell Beit Mirsim', in *Mélanges Syriens offerts a Monsieur René Dussaud*, Bibliothèque Archéologique et Historique 30, Paris.

Aldred, C., 1965, *Egypt to the end of the Old Kingdom*, London.

Aldred, C., 1978, *Jewels of the Pharaohs*, London.

Alexiou, S., and P. Warren, 2004, *The Early Minoan Tombs of Lebena, Southern Crete*, Studies in Mediterranean Archaeology 30, Göteborg.

Alp, S., 1968, *Zylinder- und Stempelsiegel aus Karahöyük bei Konya*, Ankara.

Alram-Stern, E., ed., 1996, *Die ägäische Frühzeit, I. Serie Forschungsbericht 1975–1993: Das Neolithikum in Griechenland, mit Ausnahme von Kreta und Zypern*, 1, Vienna.

Alram-Stern, E., 1999, 'Kontinuität und Diskontinuität im Chalkolithikum und der beginnenden Frühbronzezeit Südgriechenlands', *Symposium Cernavoda 3, Boleráz. Ein vorgeschichtliches Phänomen zwischen dem Oberrhein und der Unteren Donau, Resumees*, Mangalia.

Andrews, C., 1981, *Catalogue of Egyptian Antiquities in the British Museum. 6, Jewellery 1: From the Earliest Times to the Seventeenth Dynasty*, London.

Andrews, C., 1990, *Ancient Egyptian Jewellery*, London.

Appelt, K., 1930, 'Lotosfrucht als Ornament', *Mitteilungen des Deutschen Instituts für Ägyptische Altertumskunde* 1.

Aravantinos, V.L., 1986, 'The EH II fortified building at Thebes', in R. Hägg and D. Konsola, eds, *Early Helladic Architecture and Urbanization*, Studies in Mediterranean Archaeology 76, Göteborg.

Arnold, Dieter, 1988, *The South Cemeteries of Lisht I: The Pyramid of Senwosret I*, Publications of the Metropolitan Museum of Art Egyptian Expedition 22, New York.

Arnold, Dieter, 1992, *The South Cemeteries of Lisht III: The Pyramid Complex of Senwosret I*, Publications of the Metropolitan Museum of Art Egyptian Expedition 25, New York.

Arnold, Dorothea, F. Arnold and S. Allen, 1995, 'Canaanite imports at Lisht, the Middle Kingdom capital of Egypt', *Egypt and the Levant* 5.

Aruz, J., 1993, 'Crete and Anatolia in the Middle Bronze Age: sealings from Phaistos and Karahöyük', in M. Mellink, E. Porada and T. Özgüç, eds, *Aspects of Art and Iconography: Anatolia and its Neighbors: Studies in Honour of Nimet Özgüç*, Ankara.

Aruz, J., 1995a, 'Imagery and interconnections', *Egypt and the Levant* 5.

Aruz, J., 1995b, 'Trade, power and cultural exchange: Hyksos Egypt and the eastern Mediterranean world 1800–1500 BC', *Egypt and the Levant* 5.

Aruz, J., 1997, '"Cypriot" and "Cypro-Aegean" seals', in A. Caubet, ed., *De Chypre à la Bactriane. Les sceaux du Proche-Orient ancien Actes du colloque international. Paris, 18 mars 1995*, Paris.

Aruz, J., ed., 2008a, *Beyond Babylon: Art, Trade and Diplomacy in the Second Millennium B.C.*, New York.

Aruz, J., 2008b, *Marks of Distinction. Seals and Cultural Exchange between the Aegean and the Orient (ca. 2600–1360 BC)*, CMS Beiheft 7.

Aston, B.G., J.A. Harrell and I. Shaw, 2000, 'Stone', in P.T. Nicholson and I. Shaw, eds, *Ancient Egyptian Materials and Technology*, Cambridge.

Aston, D., with M. Bietak, B. Bader, I. Forstner-Müller and R. Schiestl, 2004, *Tell el-Dabʿa XII: A Corpus of Late Middle Kingdom and Second Intermediate Period Pottery*, Untersuchungen der Zweigstelle Kairo des Österreichischen Archäologischen Instituts 23, Denkschriften der Gesamtakademie 28, Vienna.

Badre, L., 1980, *Les figurines anthropomorphes en terre cuite à l'âge du bronze en Syrie*, Paris.

Bagh, T., 2000, *The beginning of the Middle Bronze Age in Egypt and the Levant*, unpublished Ph.D. thesis, Copenhagen.

Baramki, D., 1973, 'A tomb of the Early and Middle Bronze Age at Byblos', *Bulletin du Musée de Beyrouth* 26.

Barnett, R., 1960, 'Ancient oriental goldwork', *British Museum Quarterly* 22, no. 1/2.

Barnett, R., 1982, *Ancient Ivories in the Middle East and Adjacent Countries*, Jerusalem.

Barrelet, M.T., 1958, 'Deux déesses Syro-Phéniciennes', *Syria* 35.

Barta, W., 1967–74, 'Der Greif als bildhafter Ausdruck einer altägyptischen Religionsvorstellung', *Jaarbericht van het Vooraziatisch-Egyptisch Genootschap 'Ex Oriente Lux'* 20–23.

Bass, G., C. Pulak, D. Collon and J. Weinstein, 1989, 'The Bronze Age Shipwreck at Ulu Burun: 1986 Campaign', *American Journal of Archaeology* 93.

Becatti, G., 1955, *Oriﬁcerie antiche dalle Minoiche all Babariche*, Rome.

Ben-Tor, D., 2007, *Scarabs, chronology and interconnections: Egypt and Palestine in the Second Intermediate Period*, Orbis Biblicus et Orientalis 27, Fribourg.

Benzi, M., 1997, 'The Late Early Bronze Age finds from Vathy Cave (Kalymnos) and their links with the northeast Aegean', in C. Doumas and V. La Rosa, eds, *Poliochni e l antica eta del bronzo nell'Egeo settentrionale*, Athens.

Bernabò-Brea, L., 1964, *Poliochni: Città preistorica nell'isola di Lemnos 1*, Rome.

Bernabò-Brea, L., 1976, *Poliochni: Città preistorica nell'isola di Lemnos 2*, Rome.

Bietak, M., 1975, *Tell el-Dabʿa II: Der Fundort im Rahmen einer archäologisch-geographischen Untersuchung über das ägyptische Ostdelta*, Vienna.

Bietak, M., 1984, 'Eine Palastanlage aus der Zeit des späten Mittleren Reichs und andere Forschungsergebnisse aus dem östlichen Nildelta (Tell el Dabʿa 1979–1984)', *Anzeiger der phil.-hist. Klasse der Österreichischen Akademie der Wissenschaften* 121.

Bietak, M., 1991a, 'Der Friedhof in einem Palastgarten aus der Zeit des späten mittleren Reiches und andere Grabungsergebnisse aus dem östlichen Nildelta (Tell el-Dabʿa 1984–1987)', *Egypt and the Levant* 2.

Bietak, M., 1991b, 'Egypt and Canaan during the Middle Bronze Age', *Bulletin of the American Schools of Oriental Research* 281.

Bietak, M., 1995, 'Connections between Egypt and the Minoan world: new results from Tell el-Dabʿa/Avaris', in W.V. Davies and L. Schofield, eds, *Egypt, the Aegean and the Levant: Interconnections in the Second Millennium BC*, London.

Bietak, M., 1996, *Avaris, the Capital of the Hyksos: Recent Excavations at Tell el-Dabʿa*, London.

Bietak, M., 1997, 'The Center of Hyksos Rule: Avaris (Tell el-Dabʿa)', in E. Oren, ed., *The Hyksos: New Historical and Archaeological Perspectives*, University Museum Symposium Series 8, University Museum Monograph 96, Philadelphia.

Bietak, M., and J. Dorner, 1994, 'Der Palastgartenfriedhof der frühen 13: Dynastie (Grabungsplatz F/I)', *Egypt and the Levant* 4.

Bietak, M., and I. Hein, eds, 1994, *Pharaonen und Fremde: Dynastien im Dunkel, Katalog der 194. Sonderausstellung des Historischen Museums der Stadt Wien*, Vienna.

Bietak, M., J. Dorner and P. Jánosi, 2001, 'Ausgrabungen in dem Palastbezirk von Avaris: Vorbericht Tell el-Dabʿa/ʿEzbet Helmi 1993–2000', *Egypt and the Levant* 11.

Bissing, F.-W. von, 1900–8, *Ein Thebanischer Grabfund aus dem Anfang des neuen Reichs*, Berlin.

Bisson de la Roque, F., G. Contenau and F. Chapouthier, 1953, *Le Trésor de Tôd*, Fouilles de l'Institut Français d'archéologie orientale du Caire 11, Cairo.

Blegen, C.W., 1950, *Troy*, 1, Princeton.

Blegen, C.W., et al., 1964, *Corinth XIII, The North Cemetery*, Athens.

BM Cat Bronzes: H.B. Walters, *Catalogue of Bronzes, Greek, Roman and Etruscan, in the Department of Greek and Roman Antiquities, British Museum*, London 1899.

BM Cat Finger Rings: F.H. Marshall, *Catalogue of the Finger Rings, Greek, Etruscan and Roman in the British Museum*, London 1907 (reprinted 1968).

BM Cat Jewellery: F.H. Marshall, *Catalogue of the Jewellery, Greek, Etruscan and Roman in the Departments of Antiquities, British Museum*, London 1911 (reprinted 1968).

BM Cat Sculpture: A.H. Smith, *A Catalogue of Sculpture in the Department of Greek and Roman Antiquities, British Museum*, vol. I, London 1892; vol. II, London 1900; vol. III, London 1904.

BM Cat Terracottas: R.A. Higgins, *Catalogue of the Terracottas in the British Museum*, vol. I, London 1954; vol. II, London 1959.

BM Cat Vases: E.J. Forsdyke, *Catalogue of the Greek and Etruscan Vases in the British Museum*, vol. I, part 1, London 1925.

Boehmer, R.M., and H.-G. Güterbock, 1987, *Glyptik aus dem Stadtgebiet von Boğazköy, Grabungskampagnen 1931–1939, 1952–1978*, Berlin.

Boehmer, R.M., and H. Hauptmann, eds, 1983, *Beiträge zur Altertumskunde Kleinasiens: Festschrift für Kurt Bittel, 1983*, Mainz.

Boessneck, J., and A. von den Driesch, 1992, *Tell el Dabʿa VII: Tiere und historische Umwelt im Nordost-Delta im 2. Jahrtausend v. Chr. anhand der Knochenfunde der Ausgrabungen 1975–1986*, Untersuchungen der Zweigstelle Kairo des Österreichischen Archäologischen Instituts 10, Denkschriften der Gesamtakademie 11, Vienna.

Borchardt, L., 1925, *Statuen und Statuetten von Königen und Privatleuten. 2: Catalogue Général des Antiquités Égyptiennes du Musée du Caire nos 381–653*, Berlin.

Bossert, E.M., 1967, 'Kastri auf Syros', *Archaiologikon Deltion* 22.

Bourriau, J., 1991, 'Patterns of change in burial customs during the Middle Kingdom', in S. Quirke, ed., *Middle Kingdom Studies*, New Malden.

Branigan, K., 1974, *Aegean Metalwork of the Early and Middle Bronze Age*, Oxford.

Branigan, K., 1981, 'Minoan colonialism', *Annual of the British School at Athens* 76.

Branigan, K., 1984, 'Minoan community colonies in the Aegean?', in R. Hägg and N. Marinatos, eds, *The Minoan Thalassocracy: Proceedings of the Third International Symposium at the Swedish Institute in Athens 1982*, Stockholm.

Broodbank, C., 2000, *An Island Archaeology of the Early Cyclades*, Cambridge.

Brunton, G., 1920, *Lahun 1: the Treasure*, British School of Archaeology in Egypt 27, London.

Buchholz, H.G., 1999, *Ugarit, Zypern und Ägäis: Kulturbeziehungen im zweiten Jahrtausend v. Chr.*, Alter Orient und Altes Testament 261, Münster.

Cadogan, G., 1983, 'Early and Middle Minoan chronology', *American Journal of Archaeology* 87.

Carter, H., and Earl of Carnarvon, 1912, *Five Years of Exploration at Thebes: a Record of Work Done 1907–1911*, London, New York, Toronto and Melbourne.

Carter, H., and A.C. Mace, 1923, *The Tomb of Tut-ankh-Amen*, London, New York, Toronto and Melbourne.

Caskey, J.L., 1966, 'Houses of the Fourth Settlement at Lerna', in *Charisterion eis A.K. Orlandon* 3, Athens.

Caskey, J.L., 1972, 'Investigations in Keos, Part II: A Conspectus of the Pottery', *Hesperia* 41.

Caubet, A., 1998, *Liban. l'autre rive*, exh. cat., Paris.

Chapman, R.J., R.C. Leake et al., 2000, 'The application of microchemical analysis of alluvial gold grains to the understanding of complex local and regional gold mineralization: a case study in the Irish and Scottish Caledonides', *Economic Geology* 95.

Chapman, R.J., R.C. Leake and M. Styles, 2002, 'Microchemical characterization of alluvial gold grains as an exploration tool', *Gold Bulletin* 35, 2.

Chéhab, M., 1939, 'Tombe Phénicienne de Sin el Fi', in *Mélanges Syriens offerts a Monsieur René Dussaud*, Bibliothèque Archéologique et Historique 30, Paris.

Cline, E., 1998, 'Rich beyond the dreams of Avaris: Tell el-Dabʿa and the Aegean world – a guide for the perplexed', *Annual of the British School at Athens* 93.

Cline, E., and D. Harris-Cline, eds, 1998, *The Aegean and the Orient in the Second Millennium: Proceedings of the 50th Anniversary Symposium, Cincinnati, 18–20 April 1997*, Aegaeum 18, Liège.

CMS: Corpus der Minoischen und Mykenischen Siegel.
I: A. Sakellariou, ed., *Die Minoischen und Mykenischen Siegel des Nationalmuseums in Athens*, 1964, repr. 1998.
II 1: N. Platon, ed., *Iraklion, Archäologisches Museum. Teil 1. Die Siegel der Vorpalastzeit*, 1969.
II 5: I. Pini, ed., *Iraklion, Archäologisches Museum. Teil 5. Die Siegelabdrücke von Phästos*, 1970.
V 1–2: I. Pini, ed., *Kleinere Griechische Sammlungen*, 1975.
X: J.H. Betts, ed., *Die Schweizer Sammlungen*, 1980.
Beiheft 7, see Aruz 2008.

Coggin Brown, J., and A.K. Dey, 1955, *India's Mineral Wealth: A Guide to the Occurrences and Economics of the Useful Minerals of India, Pakistan and Burma*, 3rd edn, Oxford.

Coldstream, J.N., and G.L. Huxley, 1972, *Kythera: excavations and studies*, London.

Collon, D., 1986a, *Catalogue of the Western Asiatic Seals in the British Museum, Cylinder Seals 3: Isin/Larsa and Old Babylonian Periods*, London.

Collon, D., 1986b, 'The green jasper cylinder seal workshop', in M.K. Buccellati et al., eds, *Papers in Honor of Edith Porada*, Malibu.

Collon, D., 1995, *Ancient Near Eastern Art*, London.

Collon, D., 1996, 'Mesopotamia and the Indus: the evidence of the seals', in J. Reade, ed., *The Indian Ocean in Antiquity*, London.

Collon, D., 2000, 'Implications of introducing a low Mesopotamian chronology', *British Association for Near Eastern Archaeology Newsletter* 13, July.

Collon, D., 2001, 'The green jasper seal workshop revisited', *Archaeology and History in Lebanon* 13.

Contenau, G., 1931, *Manuel d'archéologie orientale depuis les origines jusqu'a l'époque d'Alexandre* 2, Paris.

Cornelius, I., 1994, *The iconography of the Canaanite gods Reshef and Baʿal*, Orbis Biblicus et Orientalis 140, Fribourg.

Cosmopoulos, M.H., 1991, *The Early Bronze 2 in the Aegean*, Studies in Mediterranean Archaeology 98, Göteborg.

Craddock, P.T., 1995, *Early Metal Mining and Production*, Edinburgh.

Cresswell, E.J.J., 1921, *Sponges: their Nature, History, Modes of Fishing, Varieties, Cultivation etc.*, London, 2nd edn, 1930.

Crowley, J., 1989, *The Aegean and the East: an Investigation into the Transference of Artistic Motifs between the Aegean, Egypt and the Near East in the Bronze Age*, Jonsered.

Bibliography

Davis, E.N., 1977, *The Vapheio Cups and Aegean Gold and Silver Ware*, New York.

De Graeve, M.-C., 1981, *The ships of the Ancient Near East (c. 2000–500 BC)*, Orientalia Lovaniensia Analecta 7, Leuven.

De Morgan, J., 1895, *Fouilles à Dahchour. 1, 1894*, Vienna.

De Morgan, J., 1903, *Fouilles à Dahchour. 2, 1894–5*, Vienna.

Decamps de Mertzenfeld, C., 1954, *Inventaire commenté des ivoires phéniciens et apparentés découverts dans le Proche-Orient*, Paris.

Delaporte, L., 1923, *Musée du Louvre: Catalogue des cylindres orientaux. 2, Acquisitions*, Paris.

Demakopoulou, K., ed., 1990, *Troy, Mycenae, Tiryns, Orchomenos, Heinrich Schliemann: the 100th Anniversary of his Death*, exh. cat., Athens.

Demakopoulou, K., 1998, *Kosmemata tes hellenikes proistorias: Ho neolithikos thesauros*, Athens.

Demargne, P., 1939, 'Le maître des animaux sur une gemme Crétoise du MMI', in *Mélanges Syriens offerts a Monsieur René Dussaud*, Bibliothèque Archéologique et Historique 30, Paris.

Demargne, P., 1945, *Fouilles exécutées à Mallia: exploration des Nécropoles (1921–33) 1*, Études Crétoises 7, Paris.

Demargne, P., 1947, *La Crète dédalique*, Paris.

Demisch, H., 1977, *Die Sphinx: Geschichte ihrer Darstellung von den Anfängen bis zur Gegenwart*, Stuttgart.

Dessenne, A., 1957, *Le Sphinx: Étude iconographique. 1, Des origines a la fin du second millénaire*, Bibliothèque des Écoles Françaises d'Athènes et de Rome 186, Paris.

Detournay, B., J.-L. Poursat and F. Vandenabeele, 1980, *Fouilles exécutées à Mallia: le Quartier Mu*, Études Crétoises 26, Paris.

Dickinson, O.T.P.K., 1977, *The Origins of Mycenaean Civilisation*, Studies in Mediterranean Archaeology 49, Göteborg.

Dickinson, O.T.P.K., 1994, *The Aegean Bronze Age*, Cambridge.

Dietz, S., 1980, *Asine 2, Fascicule 2, The Middle Helladic Cemetery, the Middle Helladic and Early Mycenaean Deposits*, Stockholm.

Dietz, S., 1991, *The Argolid at the Transition to the Mycenaean Age: Studies in the Chronology and Cultural Development in the Shaft Grave Period*, Copenhagen.

Doumas, C., 1992, *The Wall-Paintings of Thera*, Athens.

Douzougli, A., 1998, *Aria Argolidos*, Athens.

Dugmore, J.M., and C.D. Des Forges, 1979, 'Stress-corrosion in gold alloys', *Gold Bulletin* 12, 4.

Dunand, M., 1939, *Fouilles de Byblos 1. 1926–1932*, Paris.

Dunand, M., 1950, *Fouilles de Byblos 2, 1933–1938*, Paris.

Dunham, D., 1967, *Second Cataract Forts 2: Uronarti, Shalfak, Mirgissa*, Boston.

Ebla, P.M., 1981, 'Osservazioni sui gioielli delle tombe principesche di Mardikh IIIB', *Studi Eblaiti* 4.

Effinger, M., 1996, *Minoischer Schmuck*, British Archaeological Reports International Series 646, Oxford.

Eigner, D., 1985, 'Der ägyptische Palast eines asiatischen Königs', *Jahreshefte des Österreichischen Archäologischen Instituts in Wien* 56.

Eigner, D., 1996, 'A palace of the early 13th dynasty at Tell el-Dabʿa', in M. Bietak, ed., *House and Palace in Ancient Egypt: International Symposium in Cairo, April 8 to 11, 1992*, Untersuchungen der Zweigstelle Kairo des Österreichischen Archäologischen Instituts 14, Denkschriften der Gesamtakademie 14, Vienna.

Eliopoulos, T., 1991, 'The earliest Minoan ritual hammer: notes on the emergence of a Cretan emblem', *Journal of Prehistoric Religion* 5.

Eluère, C., 1982, *Les Ors prehistoriques*, Paris.

Engelbach, R.E., 1915, *Riqqeh and Memphis VI*, British School of Archaeology in Egypt 25, London.

Engelbach, R.E., 1923, *Harageh*, British School of Archaeology in Egypt 28, London.

Englund, G., 1989, 'The treatment of opposites in temple thinking and Wisdom literature', in G. Englund, ed., *The Religion of the Ancient Egyptians: Cognitive Structure and Popular Expressions, Proceedings of Symposia in Uppsala and Bergen, 1987 and 1988*, Uppsala.

Evans, A.J., 1892–3, 'A Mykenaean treasure from Aegina', *Journal of Hellenic Studies* 13.

Evans, A.J., 1921, *The Palace of Minos at Knossos*, 1, London.

Evans, A.J., 1928, *The Palace of Minos at Knossos*, 2, London.

Evans, A.J., 1930, *The Palace of Minos at Knossos*, 3, London.

Evans, A.J., 1935, *The Palace of Minos at Knossos*, 4, London.

Felten, F., and S. Hiller, 1996, 'Ausgrabungen in der vorgeschichtlichen Innenstadt von Ägina-Kolonna', *Jahreshefte des Österreichischen Archäologischen Institutes in Wien* 65.

Feucht, E., 1971, *Pektorale Nichtköniglicher Personen*, Ägyptologische Abhandlungen 22, Wiesbaden.

Fitton, J.L., 1996, *The Discovery of the Greek Bronze Age*, Cambridge MA.

Fitton, J.L., 2002, *Minoans*, London.

Fitton, J.L., and S. Quirke, 1997, 'An Aegean origin for Egyptian spirals?', in J. Phillips, ed., *Ancient Egypt, the Aegean, and the Near East: Studies in Honour of Martha Rhoads Bell*, San Antonio.

Fitton, J.L., and S. Quirke, 1998, 'Northerners at Lahun: NAA of Minoan and related pottery in the British Museum', in S. Quirke, ed., *Lahun Studies*, Reigate.

Forsen, J., 1992, *The Twilight of the Early Helladics*, Studies in Mediterranean Archaeology pocket-book 116, Jonsered.

Frankfort, H., 1935–7, 'Notes on the Cretan griffin', *Annual of the British School of Archaeology at Athens* 37.

Frondel, C., 1962, *Dana's System of Mineralogy, III, Silicate Minerals*, 7th edn, New York and London.

Garstang, J., 1901, *El-Arabeh*, Egyptian Research Account 6, London.

Garstang, J., 1907, *The Burial Customs of Ancient Egypt, being a Report of Excavations made in the Necropolis of Beni-Hasan during 1902–3–4*, London.

Gates, C., 1989, 'Iconography at the crossroads: the Aegina Treasure', in R. Laffineur, ed., *Transition: le monde égéen du Bronze moyen au Bronze récent. Actes de la 2e Rencontre égéenne internationale de l'Université de Liège (18–20 April 1988)*, Aegaeum 3, Liège.

Gill, M., 1969, 'The Minoan "frame" on an Egyptian relief', *Kadmos* 8.

Goren, Y., and A. Cohen-Weinberger, 2004, 'Levantine–Egyptian interactions during the 12th to the 15th dynasties based on the petrography of the Canaanite pottery from Tell el-Dabʿa', *Egypt and the Levant* 14.

Grace, R., 1989, 'The use-wear analysis of drill bits from Kumartepe', *Anatolica* 16.

Graziado, G., 1988, 'The chronology of circle B at Mycenae: a new hypothesis', *American Journal of Archaeology* 92.

Graziado, G., 1991, 'The process of social stratification at Mycenae in the Shaft Grave Period: a comparative examination of the evidence', *American Journal of Archaeology* 95.

Guiges, P.E., 1937, 'Lébéa, Kafer-Garra, Qrayé: nécropoles de la région sidonienne', *Bulletin du Musée de Beyrouth* 1.

Gwinnett, A.J., and L. Gorelick, 1993, 'Beads, scarabs, and amulets: methods of manufacture in ancient Egypt', *Journal of the American Research Centre in Egypt* 30.

Hägg, R., and Y. Lindau, 1984, 'The Minoan "snake frame" reconsidered', *Opuscula Atheniensia* 15.

Hankey, V., 1991/2, 'From Chronos to chronology: Egyptian evidence for dating the Aegean Bronze Age', *Journal of the Ancient Chronology Forum* 5.

Harland, J.P., 1925, *Prehistoric Aigina*, Paris.

Harper, P.O., 1969, 'Dating a group of ivories from Anatolia', *Connoisseur* 172.

Harper, P.O., E. Klengel-Brandt, J. Aruz and K. Benzel, eds, 1995, *Assyrian Origins, Discoveries at Ashur on the Tigris: Antiquities in the Vorderasiatisches Museum, Berlin*, New York.

Hauptmann, A., T. Rehren and E. Pernicka, 1995, 'The composition of gold from the ancient mining district of Verespatak/Roflia Montan?, Romania', in G. Morteani and J.P. Northover, eds, *Prehistoric Gold in Europe*, Dordrecht.

Hayes, W.C., 1990, *The Scepter of Egypt: a Background to the Study of the Egyptian Antiquities in The Metropolitan Museum of Art*, New York.

Helck, W., 1995, *Die Beziehungen Ägyptens und Vorderasiens zur Ägäis bis ins 7. Jahrhundert v. Chr.*, Erträge der Forschungen 120, Darmstadt.

Herrmann, G., 1968, 'Lapis lazuli: the early phases of its trade', *Iraq* 30.

Higgins, R.A., 1957a, 'The Aegina Treasure reconsidered', *Annual of the British School at Athens* 52.

Higgins, R.A., 1957b, 'The Aegina Treasure reconsidered', *Bulletin of the Institute of Classical Studies* 4.

Higgins, R.A., 1961, *Greek and Roman Jewellery*, London.

Higgins, R.A., 1979, *The Aegina Treasure: an Archaeological Mystery*, London.

Higgins, R.A., 1980, *Greek and Roman Jewellery*, Berkeley and Los Angeles.

Higgins, R.A., 1987, 'A gold diadem from Aegina', *Journal of Hellenic Studies* 107.

Higgins, M.D., and R. Higgins, 1996, *A Geological Companion to Greece and the Aegean*, London.

Hiller, S., 1975, 'Mykenische Keramik', *Alt-Ägina* 4, 1.

Hiller, S., 1993, 'Minoan and Minoanizing pottery on Aegina', in C. and P. Zerner and J. Winder, eds, *Proceedings of the International Conference: Wace and Blegen: Pottery as Evidence for Trade in the Aegean Bronze Age 1939–89*, Athens.

Hood, S., 1978, *The Arts in Prehistoric Greece*, Harmondsworth.

Hopkins, C., 1962, 'The Aegina Treasure', *American Journal of Archaeology* 66.

Hornung, E., 1963, *Das Amduat. Die Schrift des verborgenen Raumes*, Ägyptische Abhandlungen 7, Wiesbaden.

Hornung, E., 1991, 'Egypt and Canaan during the Middle Bronze Age', *Bulletin of the American Schools of Oriental Research* 281.

Jánosi, P., 1994, 'Keminub – eine Gemahlin Amenemhet II?', in M. Bietak, J. Holaubek, H. Mukarovsky and H. Satzinger, eds, *Zwischen den beiden Ewigkeiten: Festschrift Gertrud Thausing*, Vienna.

Jean-Marie, M., 1999, *Tombes et nécropoles de Mari, Mission Archéologique de Mari 5*, Bibliothèque Archéologique et Historique 153, Beyrouth.

Jequier, G., 1941, *Le monument funéraire de Pépi II 3*, Cairo.

Kalicz, N., 1970, *Götter aus Ton: das Neolithikum und die Kupferzeit in Ungarn*, Budapest.

Kantor, H., 1947, *The Aegean and the Orient in the Second Millennium BC*, Archaeological Institute of America Monographs 1, Bloomington, Indiana.

Kaplony, P., 1981, *Die Rollsiegel des Alten Reichs*, Brussels.

Karo, G., 1930, *Die Schachtgräber von Mykenai*, Munich.

Kasimi-Sotou, M., 1980, 'Mesoelladikos Taphos pelmiste apo te Theba', *Archaiologikon Deltion* 35.

Keel, O., 1994a, 'Der Pharao als Sonnengott', in O. Keel, ed., *Studien zu den Stempelsiegeln aus Palästina/Israel, Band 4*, Orbis Biblicus et Orientalis 135, Göttingen.

Keel, O., 1994b, 'Stempelsiegel – das Problem palästinensischer Werkstätten', in O. Keel, ed., *Studien zu den Stempelsiegeln aus Palästina/Israel, Band 4*, Orbis Biblicus et Orientalis 135, Göttingen.

Keel, O., ed., 1994c, *Studien zu den Stempelsiegeln aus Palästina/Israel, Band 4*, Orbis Biblicus et Orientalis 135, Göttingen.

Keel, O., 1995, *Corpus der Stempelsiegel-Amulette aus Palästina/Israel: von den Anfängen bis zur Perserzeit, Einleitung*, Orbis Biblicus et Orientalis 10, Göttingen.

Keel, O., 1997, *Corpus der Stempelsiegel-Amulette aus Palästina/Israel: Katalog, Band I, von Tell Abu Farag bis ʿAtlit*, Orbis Biblicus et Orientalis 13, Göttingen.

Kemp, B.J., and R.S. Merrillees, 1980, *Minoan Pottery in Second Millennium Egypt*, Mainz.

Kenoyer, J.M., 1997, 'Trade and technology of the Indus Valley: new insights from Harappa, Pakistan', *World Archaeology* 29.

Keramopoullos, A.D., 1910, 'Mykenaikoi taphoi en Aigine kai en Thevais', *Archaiologiki Ephimeris*.

Kilian-Dirlmeier, I., 1984, *Die Nadeln der frühhelladischen bis archaischen Zeit von der Peloponnes*, Prähistorische Bronzefunde 13, 8, Stuttgart.

Kilian-Dirlmeier, I., 1986, 'Beobachtungen zu den Schachtgräbern von Mykenai und den Schmuckbeigaben mykenischer Männergräber', *Jahrbuch des Römisch-Germanischen Zentralmuseums Mainz* 33.

Kilian-Dirlmeier, I., 1997, 'Das Mittelbronzezeitliche Schachtgrab von Ägina', *Alt-Ägina* 4, 3.

Koch-Harnack, G., 1989, *Erotische Symbole: Lotosblüte und gemeinsamer Mantel auf antiken Vasen*, Berlin.

Konsola, D., 1986, 'Stages of urban transformation in the early Helladic architecture and urbanization', in R. Hägg and D. Konsola, eds, *Early Helladic Architecture and Urbanization*, Studies in Mediterranean Archaeology 76, Göteborg.

Kopetzky, K., 2000, 'Stratum b/3 of Tell el Dabʿa: the MB-corpus of the settlement layers', in *Proceedings of the 2nd International Congress of the Archaeology of Ancient Near East*, Copenhagen.

Korres, G.S., 1976, 'Anaskaphai en Peristeria pylou', *Praktika*.

Kouka, O., 1997, 'Organose kai chrese tou chorou ste Therme Lesbou kata ten Proïme Epoche tou Chalkou', in C. Doumas and V. La Rosa, eds, *E Poliochne kai e Proïme Epoche tou Chalkou sto Boreio Aigaio*, Athens.

Laffineur, R., 1988, *Réflexions sur le trésor de Tôd*, Aegaeum 2, Liège.

Laffineur, R., 1996, 'Polychrysos Mykene: toward a definition of Mycenaean goldwork', in A. Calinescu, ed., *Ancient Jewelry and Archaeology*, Bloomington, Indiana.

Laffineur, R., 1998, 'From West to East: the Aegean and Egypt in Early Late Bronze Age', in E. Cline and D. Harris-Cline, eds, *The Aegean and the Orient in the Second Millennium: Proceedings of the 50th Anniversary Symposium, Cincinnati, 18–20 April 1997*, Aegaeum 18, Liège.

Lamb, W., 1936, *Excavations at Thermi in Lesbos*, Cambridge.

Landström, B., 1970, *Ships of the Pharaohs*, Stockholm.

Lehrberger, G., 1995, 'The gold deposits of Europe', in G. Morteani and J.P. Northover, eds, *Prehistoric Gold in Europe*, Dordrecht.

Levi, D., 1957–8, 'L'Archivio di Cretule a Festòs', *Annuario della Scuola Archeologica di Atene e delle Missioni Italiane in Oriente* 35–6, nuova serie 19–20.

Lichtheim, M., 1973, *Ancient Egyptian Literature: a Book of Readings. Vol. 1, The Old and Middle Kingdoms*, Berkeley.

Lilyquist, C., 1994, 'The Dilbat hoard', *Metropolitan Museum Journal* 29.

Lilyquist, C., 1999, 'The use of ivories as interpreters of political history', *Bulletin of the American Schools of Oriental Research* 310.

Loud, G., 1939, *The Megiddo Ivories*, Oriental Institute Publications 52, Chicago.

Bibliography

Loud, G., 1948, *Megiddo II: Seasons of 1935–39*, Oriental Institute Publications 62, Chicago.

Lucas, A., and J.R. Harris, 1962, *Ancient Egyptian materials and industries*, 4th edn, London.

Lyman, T., ed., 1973, *Metals Handbook, 8, Metallography, Structures and Phase Diagrams*, 8th edn, Metals Park, Ohio.

MacGillivray, J., 1995, 'A Minoan cup at Tell el Dabᶜa', *Egypt and the Levant* 5.

McGovern, P., 1985, *Late Bronze Age Palestinian Pendants: Innovation in a Cosmopolitan Age*, Sheffield.

Makky, J., 1989, *The Tiszaszölös Treasure*, Budapest.

Manning, S., 1995, *The Absolute Chronology of the Aegean Early Bronze Age*, Sheffield.

Manti-Platonos, M., 1981, 'Teleourgikes sphyres kai rhopala sto Minoiko kosmo', *Archaiologiki Ephimeris*.

Maran, J., 1987, 'Die Silbergefässe von El-Tôd und die Schachtgraberzeit auf dem griechischen Festland', *Praehistorische Zeitschrift* 62 2.

Maran, J., 1998, *Kulturwandel auf dem griechischen Festland und den Kykladen im späten 3 Jahrtausend v. Chr.*, Bonn.

Maran, J., 2000, 'Das ägäische Chalkolithikum und das erste Silber in Europa', in *Studien zur Religion und Kultur Kleinasiens und des ägäischen Bereiches: Festschrift für Baki Öğün zum 75*, Asia Minor Studien 39, Bonn.

Marangou, L., ed., 1992, *Minoan and Greek Civilization from the Mitsotakis Collection*, Athens.

Marchetti, N., and L. Nigro, 1997, 'Cultic activities in the sacred area of Ishtar at Ebla during the Old Syrian Period: the Favissae F.5327 and F.5238', *Journal of Cuneiform Studies* 49.

Marinatos, N., 1984, *Art and Religion in Thera: Reconstructing a Bronze Age Society*, Athens.

Marinatos, S., and M. Hirmer, 1973, *Kreta, Thera und das mykenische Hellas*, Munich.

Markowitz, Y., 1995, 'Reef knot bracelet', in N. Thomas, ed., *The American Discovery of Ancient Egypt*, New York.

Matthews, R., W. Matthews and H. McDonald, 1994, 'Excavations at Tell Brak, 1994', *Iraq* 56.

Matthiae, P., 1981, 'Osservazioni sui gioielli delle tombe principesche di Mardikh IIIB', *Studi Eblaiti* 4.

Matthiae, P., 1984, *I tesori di Ebla*, Rome and Bari.

Matthiae, P., F. Pinnock and G. Sacandone Matthiae, eds, 1995, *Ebla – Alle origini della civiltà urbana*, exh. cat., Milan.

Maxwell-Hyslop, K., 1971, *Western Asiatic Jewellery c. 3000–612 BC*, London.

May, H., 1935, *Material Remains of the Megiddo Cult*, Chicago.

Meeks, N.D., 1988, 'A Greek gold necklace: a case of dual identity', in D. Williams, ed., *The Art of the Greek Goldsmith*, London.

Meeks, N.D., and M.S. Tite, 1980, 'The analysis of platinum-group element inclusions in gold antiquities', *Journal of Archaeological Science* 7.

Mellink, M., 1986, 'The Early Bronze Age in West Anatolia: Aegean and Asiatic correlations', in G. Cadogan, ed., *The End of the Early Bronze Age in the Aegean*, Cincinnati Classical Studies 6, Leiden.

Menu, M., 1994, 'Analyse du trésor de Tôd', *Bulletin de la Société Française de l'Egyptologie* 130, June.

Metropolitan Museum of Art, 1984, 'Ancient Near Eastern art', *The Metropolitan Museum of Art Bulletin*, spring.

Milojcic, V., 1961, *Die prähistorische Siedlung unter dem Heraion, Samos 1*, Bonn.

Mlinar, C., 2001, *Die Skarabäen von Tell el-Dabᶜa: Eine chronologische und typologische Untersuchung von Tell el-Dabᶜa aus der 13.–15. Dynastie*, unpublished PhD thesis, University of Vienna.

Mlinar, C., 2004, 'The scarab workshops of Tell el-Dabᶜa', in M. Bietak and E. Czerny, eds, *Scarabs of the Second Millennium BC from Egypt, Nubia, Crete and the Levant: Chronological and Historical Implications, Papers of a Symposium, Vienna, 10–13 January 2002*, Vienna.

Montero, I., and S. Rovira, 1991, 'El oro y sus aleaciones en la orfebrería prerromana', *Archivo Español de Arqueología* 64.

Montet, P., 1928, *Byblos et l'Egypte: Quatre Campagnes de Fouilles à Gebeil. 1921–24*, Paris.

Moorey, P.R.S., 1994, *Ancient Mesopotamian Materials and Industries: The Archaeological Evidence*, Oxford.

Moortgat, A., and U. Moortgat-Correns, 1974, 'Archäologische Bemerkungen zu einem Schatzfund in Vorsargonischen Palast in Mari', *Iraq* 36.

Morris, S., 1998, 'Daidalos and Kothar: the future of their relationship', in E. Cline and D. Harris-Cline, eds, *The Aegean and the Orient in the Second Millennium: Proceedings of the 50th Anniversary Symposium, Cincinnati, 18–20 April 1997*, Aegaeum 18, Liège.

Muhly, P., 1992, *A Minoan Chamber Tomb at Poros, Herakleion*, Athens.

Musche, B., 1992, *Vorderasiatischer Schmuck von den Anfängen bis zur Zeit der Achaemeniden*, Leiden and New York.

Mylonas, G.E., 1972, *Grave Circle B of Mycenae*, Athens (in Greek).

Mylonas, G.E., 1983, *Mycenae Rich in Gold*, Athens.

Negbi, O., 1961, 'On two bronze figurines with plumed helmets from the Louvre Collection', *Israel Exploration Journal* 11.

Negbi, O., 1970, *The Hoards of Goldwork from Tell el-Ajjul*, Studies in Mediterranean Archaeology 25, Göteborg.

Newberry, P.E., 1895, 'El Bershe I', *Archaeological Survey of Egypt* 3.

Niemeier, W.-D., 1995, *Aegina – first Aegean 'state' outside of Crete?*, Aegaeum 12, Liège.

Nordström, H.-Å., and J. Bourriau, 1993, 'Fascicle 2: Ceramic technology and fabrics', in J. Bourriau and D. Arnold, eds, *An Introduction to Ancient Egyptian Pottery*, Mainz.

Northover, J.P., 1995, 'Bronze Age gold in Britain', in G. Morteani and J.P. Northover, eds, *Prehistoric Gold in Europe*, Dordrecht.

O'Connor, D., 1997, 'The Hyksos period in Egypt', in E. Oren, ed., *The Hyksos: New Historical and Archaeological Perspectives*, University Museum Symposium Series 8, University Museum Monograph 96, Philadelphia.

Oddy, W.A., 1977, 'The production of gold wire in antiquity', *Gold Bulletin* 10, 3.

Ogden, J., 1977, 'Platinum group element inclusions in ancient gold artifacts', *Journal of the Historical Metallurgy Society* 11, 2.

Ogden, J., 1982, *Jewellery of the Ancient World*, London.

Ogden, J., 1983, 'Potentials and problems in the scientific study of ancient gold artefacts', in P.A. England and L. Van Zelst, eds, *Application of Science in the Examination of Works of Art: Proceedings of the Seminar, September 7–9, 1983*, Boston.

Orthmann, W., ed., 1975, *Der alte Orient*, Propyläen Kunstgeschichte 14, Berlin.

Ory, J., 1938, 'Excavations at Ras el ᶜAin. 2', *Quarterly of the Department of Antiquities in Palestine* 6.

Otten, H., H. Ertem, E. Akurgal and A. Süel, eds, 1992, *Hittite and other Anatolian and Near Eastern studies in honour of Sedat Alp*, Ankara.

Otto, A., 2000, *Die Entstehung und Entwicklung der Klassisch-Syrischen Glyptik*, Untersuchungen zur Assyriologie und Vorderasiatischen Archäologie 8, Berlin and New York.

Özgüç, N., 1965, *The Anatolian Group of Cylinder Seal Impressions from Kültepe*, Ankara.

Özgüç, N., 1966, 'Excavations at Acemhöyük', *Anatolia* 10.

Özgüç, N., 1968, *Seals and Seal Impressions of Level IB from Kültepe*, Ankara.

Özgüç, N., 1971, 'A stamp seal from Nioğade region and four seal impressions found in Acemhöyük', *Anatolia* 15.

Özgüç, N., 1980, 'Seal impressions from Acemhöyük', in E. Porada, ed., *Ancient Art in Seals*, Princeton.

Özgüç, N., 1983, 'The sealings from Acemhöyük in the Metropolitan Museum of Art, New York', in *Beiträge zur Altertumskunde Kleinasiens. Festschrift für Kurt Bittel*, Mainz.

Özgüç, N., 1991, 'The composite creatures in Anatolian art during the period of Assyrian trading colonies', in M. Mori, ed., *Near Eastern Studies Dedicated to HIH Prince Takahito Mikasa on the Occasion of his Seventy-Fifth Birthday* (Bulletin of the Middle Eastern Culture Center in Japan 5), Wiesbaden.

Özten, A., 1988, 'Acemhöyük tas kapları', *Belleten* 52/203.

Parrot, A., 1958, 'Acquisitions et inédits du Musée du Louvre', *Syria* 35.

Parrot, A., 1964, 'Antiquités et inédits du Musée du Louvre, 20: assiettes mycéniennes', *Syria* 41.

Pelon, O., 1983, 'L'épée à l'acrobate et la chronologie Maliote', *Bulletin de Corréspondance Hellenique* 107.

Perea, A., and S. Rovira, 1995, 'The gold from Arrabalde', in G. Morteani and J.P. Northover, eds, *Prehistoric Gold in Europe*, Dordrecht.

Petrie, W.M.F., 1900, *Dendereh*, Memoirs of the Egypt Exploration Fund 17, London.

Petrie, W.M.F., 1914, 'The treasure of Lahun', *Ancient Egypt* 3.

Petrie, W.M.F., 1927, *Objects of Daily Use: the Petrie Egyptian collection and excavations*, British School of Archaeology in Egypt 42, London.

Philip, G., 1989, *Metal Weapons of the Early and Middle Bronze Ages in Syria–Palestine*, British Archaeological Reports International Series 526(1), Oxford.

Philip, G., 1995, 'Tell el-Dabʿa metalwork: patterns and purpose', in W.V. Davies and L. Schofield, eds, *Egypt, the Aegean and the Levant: Interconnections in the Second Millennium BC*, London.

Picard, O., and J.P. Sodini, eds, 1971, *Bijoux et petits objets*, Collection Hélène Stathatos 4, Athens.

Pierpont, G. de, 1987, 'Réflexions sur la destination des edifices de Chrysolakkos', in R. Laffineur, ed., *Thanatos: Les Coutumes funeraires en Egee a l'âge du Bronze*, Liège.

Pierrat, G., 1994, 'A propos de la date et de l'origine du trésor de Tôd', *Bulletin de la Société Française de l'Egyptologie* 130, June.

Pini, I., 1990, 'Eine Fruhkretische Siegelwerkstatt?', in *Pepragmena of the 6th Cretological Congress*, Herakleion.

Pini, I., 2000, 'Eleven early Cretan scarabs', in A. Karetsou, ed., *Kriti–Aigyptos: Politismikoi desmoi trion chilietion*, Athens.

Platon, N., 1971, *Zakros: the Discovery of a Lost Palace of Ancient Crete*, New York.

Platt, E., 1976, 'Triangular jewelry plaques', *Bulletin of the American Schools of Oriental Research* 221.

Plesters, J., 1993, 'Ultramarine blue, natural and artificial', in A. Roy, ed., *Artists' Pigments: A Handbook of their History and Characteristics*, Washington.

Porada, E., 1942, 'The warrior with plumed helmet', *Berytus* 7.

Porada, E., 1948, *Corpus of Ancient Near Eastern Seals in North American Collections. Vol. 1, The Collection of the Pierpont Morgan Library*, Washington.

Porada, E., 1976, 'New galleries at the British Museum', *Archaeology* 29.

Porada, E., 1982, 'Remarks on the Tôd Treasure in Egypt', in *Societies and Languages of the Ancient Near East: Studies in honour of I.M. Diakonoff*, Warminster.

Porada, E., 1984, 'The Cylinder Seal from Tell-el Dabʿa', *American Journal of Archaeology* 88.

Potts, D., 2003, 'Tell Abraq', in J. Aruz with R. Wallenfels, eds, *Art of the First Cities: The Third Millennium BC from the Mediterranean to the Indus*, New York.

Poursat, J.C., 1973, 'Le sphinx minoen: un nouveau document', in *Antichità cretesi: Studi in onore di Doro Levi*, Cronache di Archeologia 12, Catania.

Primas, M., 1995, 'Gold and silver during the 3rd mill. cal. BC', in G. Morteani and J.P. Northover, eds, *Prehistoric Gold in Europe*, Dordrecht.

Protonotariou-Deilaki, E., 1990, 'Burial customs and funerary rites in the prehistoric Argolid', in *Celebrations of Death and Divinity in the Bronze Age Argolid: Proceedings of the Sixth International Symposium at the Swedish Institute at Athens, 11–13 June 1988*, Athens.

Pulak, C., 1997, 'The Uluburun Shipwreck', in S. Swiny, R.L. Hohlfelder and H.W. Swiny, eds, *Res Maritimae: Cyprus and the Eastern Mediterranean from Prehistory to Late Antiquity*, American Schools of Oriental Research Archaeological Reports 4, Atlanta.

Quibell, J.E., 1908, *Catalogue Général des Antiquités Égyptiennes du Musée du Caire, Nos 51001–191, Tomb of Yuaa and Thuiu*, Cairo.

Quirke, S., 1991, 'Royal power in the 13th dynasty', in S. Quirke, ed., *Middle Kingdom Studies*, New Malden.

Ramage, A., and P.T. Craddock, 2000, *King Croesus' Gold: Excavations at Sardis and the History of Gold Refining*, London.

Rapson, W.S., and T. Groenewald, 1978, *Gold Usage*, London.

Raub, C.J., 1995, 'The metallurgy of gold and silver in prehistoric times', in G. Morteani and J.P. Northover, eds, *Prehistoric Gold in Europe*, Dordrecht.

Reade, J., 1979, *Early Etched Beads and the Indus–Mesopotamia Trade*, British Museum Occasional Paper 2, London.

Rehak, P., 1996, 'Aegean breechcloths, kilts, and the Keftiu paintings', *American Journal of Archaeology* 100.

Reinholdt, C., 1992, 'Ein minoischer Steinhammer in Ägina', *Archäologisches Instituts Korrespondenzblatt* 22.

Reinholdt, C., 1993a, 'Der Thyreatis-Hortfund in Berlin: Untersuchungen zum vormykenischen Edelmetallschmuck in Griechenland', *Jahrbuch des Deutschen Archäologischen Instituts* 108.

Reinholdt, C., 1993b, 'Entwicklung und Typologie mittelbronzezeitlicher Lanzenspitzen mit Schäftungsschuh in Griechenland', *Mitteilungen der Berliner Gesellschaft für Anthropologie, Ethnologie und Urgeschichte* 14.

Reinholdt, C., 2003, 'The Early Bronze Age Jewelry Hoard from Kolonna, Aigina', in J. Aruz with R. Wallenfels, eds, *Art of the First Cities: The Third Millennium BC from the Mediterranean to the Indus*, New York.

Reinholdt, C., 2004, 'Der Frühbronzezeitliche Schmuck-Hortfund von Kap Kolonna/Ägina', in Alram-Stern, E., ed., *Die ägäische Frühzeit, 2. Serie Forschungsbericht 1975–2000. 2. Band teil 2: Die Frühbronzezeit in Griechenland mit Ausnahme von Kreta*, Vienna.

Renfrew, C., 1972, *The Emergence of Civilization: the Cyclades and the Aegean in the third Millennium BC*, London.

Rudolph, W., 1995, *A Golden Legacy: Ancient Jewelry from Burton Y. Berry Collection at the Indiana University Art Museum*, Bloomington, Indiana.

Bibliography

Russell, P., 1999, 'Aegean peoples', in K.A. Bard, ed., *Encyclopedia of the Archaeology of Ancient Egypt*, London and New York.

Rutter, J.B., 1993, 'Review of Aegean prehistory 2: the prepalatial Bronze Age of the southern and central Greek mainland', *American Journal of Archaeology* 97.

Rutter, J.B., 1995, *The Pottery of Lerna IV*, Princeton.

Rutter, J.B., 2001, 'Review of Aegean prehistory 2: the prepalatial Bronze Age of the southern and central Greek mainland', in T. Cullen, ed., *Aegean Prehistory: a Review*, American Journal of Archaeology Supplement I, Boston.

Ryholt, K.S.B., 1997, *The Political Situation in Egypt during the Second Intermediate Period c. 1800–1550 BC*, Carsten Niebuhr Institute Publications 20, Copenhagen.

Sabatino, M., M. Eugenia and A. Semmler, 1988, *I Fenici*, Milan.

Sahrage, D., 1988, *Fischfang und Fischkult im Alten Ägypten*, Mainz.

Saidah, R., 1993–4, 'Beirut in the Bronze Age: the Kharji Tombs', *Berytus* 41.

Saleh, M., and H. Sourouzian, 1986, *Die Hauptwerke im Ägyptischen Museum Kairo*, Mainz.

Sax, M., J. McNabb and N.D. Meeks, 1998, 'Methods of engraving cylinder seals: experimental confirmation', *Archaeometry* 40.

Schaeffer, C., 1949, *Ugaritica* 2, Paris.

Schiestl, R., 2000, 'Eine archäologische Notiz: Eine neue Parallele zum Anhänger aus Tell el-Dabᶜa aus dem Petrie Museum, University College London', *Egypt and the Levant* 10.

Schiestl, R., 2003, *Die Palastnekropole von Tell el-Dabᶜa: Die Gräber des Areals F/I der Straten d/2 und d/1*, unpublished PhD thesis, University of Vienna, in preparation for print.

Schliemann, H., 1881, *Ilios. Stadt und Land der Trojaner: Forschungen und Entdeckungen in der Troas und besonders auf der Baustelle von Troja*, Leipzig.

Schmitz, B., 1994, 'Ein neuer Beleg für den Gott Sched: Amulett Hildesheim Pelizäus Museum 5922', in B. Bryan and D. Lorton, eds, *Essays in Egyptology in Honor of H. Goedicke*, San Antonio.

Seeher, J., 2000, 'Die bronzezeitliche Nekropole von Demircihüyük-Sariket', *Istanbuler Forschungen* 44.

Semantoni-Bournia, E., 2003, 'O "Thisavros tes Aiginas". Neo fos sto misterio tis lathraias exagogos tou', in E. Konsolaki-Giannopoulou, ed., *Argosaronikos*, Athens.

Shaw, J.W., 1987, 'The early Helladic II corridor house: development and form', *American Journal of Archaeology* 91.

Shaw, J.W., 1990, 'The early Helladic II corridor house: problems and possibilities', *Bulletin de Corréspondance Hellenique* Suppl. 19.

Siebenmorgen, H., ed., 2000, *Im Labyrinth des Minos. Kreta, die erste europäische Hochkultur*, exh. cat., Munich.

Sinos, S., 1971, *Die vorklassischen Hausformen in der Ägäis*, Mainz am Rhein.

Smith, W.S., 1965, *Interconnections in the Ancient Near East: a Study of the Relationships between the Arts of Egypt, the Aegean, and Western Asia*, New Haven and London.

Spartz, E., 1962, *Das Wappenbild des Herrn und der Herrin der Tiere in der Minoisch-Mykenischen und Frühgriechischen Kunst*, Munich.

Spurr, S., N. Reeves and S. Quirke, 1999, *Egyptian Art at Eton College: Selections from the Myers Museum*, Windsor and New York.

Staïs, V., 1895, 'Proistorikoi synoikismoi en Attike kai Aigine', *Archaiologiki Ephimeris*.

Stevenson-Smith, W., 1981, *Art and Architecture in Ancient Egypt*, New Haven.

Stocks, D.A., 1989, 'Ancient factory mass-production techniques: indications of large-scale stone bead manufacture during the Egyptian New Kingdom Period', *Antiquity* 63.

Szafranski, Z., 1998, 'Seriation and aperture index 2 of the beer bottles from Tell el-Dabᶜa', *Egypt and the Levant* 7.

Taracha, P., 1993, 'Weapons in the shaft graves of Mycenae: aspects of the relative chronology of circle A and B burials', *Archeologia* 43.

Teissier, B., 1996, *Egyptian iconography on Syro-Palestinian seals of the Middle Bronze Age*, Orbus Biblicus et Orientalis 11, Fribourg.

Terrace, E.L.B., and H.G. Fischer, 1970, *Treasures of the Cairo Museum*, London.

Themelis, P., 1984, 'Early Helladic monumental architecture', *Archäologische Mitteilungen* 99.

Tolstikov, V.P., 1996, *Der Schatz aus Troia*, exh. cat., Stuttgart.

Tolstikov, V., and M. Treister, 1996, *The Gold of Troy: Searching for Homer's Fabled City*, New York.

Tsountas, C., and J.I. Manatt, 1897, *The Mycenaean Age*, repr. 1969, Chicago.

Tufnell, O., 1983, 'Some gold bird ornaments: falcon or wryneck?', *Anatolian Studies* 33.

Tylecote, R.F., 1987, *The Early History of Metallurgy in Europe*, London.

Untracht, O., 1982, *Jewellery Concepts and Technology*, London.

Vandenabeele, F., 1992, *Malia*, Athens.

Walberg, G., 1991a, 'A gold pendant from Tell el-Dabᶜa', *Egypt and the Levant* 2.

Walberg, G., 1991b, 'The finds at Tell el-Dabᶜa and middle Minoan chronology', *Egypt and the Levant* 2.

Walberg, G., 1998, 'The date and origin of the Kamares cup from Tell el-Dabᶜa', *Egypt and the Levant* 8.

Walker, C.B.F., 1995, 'Mesopotamian chronology', in D. Collon, *Ancient Near Eastern Art*, London.

Walter, H., 1981, 'Anaskaphe sto lopho Kolona, Aigina', *Athens Annals of Archaeology* 14.

Walter, H., 1983, *Die Leute im alten Ägina*, Stuttgart.

Walter, H., and F. Felten, 1981, 'Die vorgeschichtliche Stadt', *Alt-Ägina* 3.

Walter, H., and H.J. Weisshaar, 1993, 'Alt-Ägina: die prähistorische Innenstadt westlich des Apollontempels', *Archäologischer Anzeiger* heft 3.

Walters, H.B., 1897, 'On some black-figured vases recently acquired by the British Museum', *Journal of Hellenic Studies* 17.

Walters, H.B., 1898, 'On some antiquities of the Mycenaean Age recently acquired by the British Museum', *Journal of Hellenic Studies* 18.

Wapnish, P., 1997, 'Middle Bronze equid burials at Tell Jemmeh and a reexamination of a purportedly "Hyksos" practice', in E. Oren, ed., *The Hyksos: New Historical and Archaeological Perspectives*, University Museum Symposium Series 8, University Museum Monograph 96, Philadelphia.

Warren, P., 1995, 'Minoan Crete and Pharaonic Egypt', in W.V. Davies and L. Schofield, eds, *Egypt, the Aegean and the Levant: Interconnections in the Second Millennium BC*, London.

Warren, P., and V. Hankey, 1989, *Aegean Bronze Age Chronology*, Bristol.

Webster, R., and P.G. Read, 1994, *Gems: Their Sources, Descriptions and Identification*, 5th edn, Oxford.

Wegner, J., 1998, 'Excavations at the town of Enduring-are-the-Places-of-Khakaure-Maa-Kheru-in-Abydos: a preliminary report on the 1994 and 1997 seasons', *Journal of the American Research Center in Egypt* 35.

Weisshaar, H.J., 1994, 'Keramik des Südwest: Ägäischen Chalkolitikums von Ägina', in C. Dobiat, ed., *Festschrift für Herrmann Frey zum 65*, Marburger Studien zur Vor- und Frühgeschichte 16, Marburg.

Welter, G., 1937, 'Aiginetische Keramik', *Archäologischer Anzeiger* 52.

Welter, G., 1938a, *Aigina*, Berlin.

Welter, G., 1938b, 'Aegenitica XIII–XXIV', *Archäologischer Anzeiger* 53.

Welter, G., 1962, *Aigina*, Athens.

Wiencke, M.W., 1989, 'Change in the Early Helladic II', *American Journal of Archaeology* 93.

Wiese, A., 1990, *Zum Bild des Königs auf ägyptischen Siegelamuletten*, Orbus Biblicus et Orientalis 96, Fribourg.

Wiese, A., 2001, *Antikenmuseum Basel und Sammlung Ludwig: die Ägyptische Abteilung*, Antike Welt Sonderband 32, Mainz.

Wilkinson, A., 1971, *Ancient Egyptian Jewellery*, London.

Wilkinson, C.K., and M. Hill, 1983, *Egyptian Wall Paintings: the Metropolitan Museum of Art's Collection of Facsimiles*, New York.

Williams, B., 1977, 'The date of Senebtisi at Lisht and the chronology of major groups and deposits of the Middle Kingdom', *Serapis* 3.

Williams, D., and J. Ogden, 1994, *Greek Gold: Jewellery of the Classical World*, London.

Winlock, H.E., 1920, 'Notes on the jewels from Lahun', *Ancient Egypt* E.3.

Winlock, H.E., 1934, *The Treasure of El-Lahun*, Publications of the Metropolitan Museum of Art 4, New York.

Wohlmayr, W., 1989, 'Ägina–Kolonna: die schachtgräberzeitliche Siedlung', in R. Laffineur, ed., *Transition: le monde égéen du Bronze moyen au Bronze récent. Actes de la 2e Rencontre égéenne internationale de l'Université de Liège (18–20 April 1988)*, Aegaeum 3, Liège.

Wohlmayr, W., 2000, 'Schachtgräberzeitliche Keramik aus Ägina', in F. Blakolmer, ed., *Österreichische Forschungen zur ägäischen Bronzezeit 1998*, Vienna.

Woolley, C.L., 1934, *Ur Excavations II: the Royal Cemetery*, London.

Xénaki-Sakellariou, A., 1958, *Les cachets minoens de la collection Giamalakis*, Études Crétoises 10, Paris.

Yadin, Y., *et al.*, 1960, *Hazor* 2, Jerusalem.

Younger, J., and P. Rehak, 1998, 'International styles in ivory carving in the Bronze Age', in E. Cline and D. Harris-Cline, eds, *The Aegean and the Orient in the Second Millennium: Proceedings of the 50th Anniversary Symposium, Cincinnati, 18–20 April 1997*, Aegaeum 18, Liège.

Yule, P., 1985, appendix to P. Astrom, 'The Middle Minoan chronology again', in *Pepragmena of the 5th Cretological Conference*, A1, Herakleion.

Zunker, A., 1988, *Untersuchungen zur Aiakidensage auf Aegina*, St Ottilien.

Index

References to figure numbers are in italics. The Aigina Treasure is not included as a group, but is listed by its individual components.

Acemhöyük, 43, 49
  bullae from, 43–4, 45, 62, *154*, *160*, *161*
  cylinder seal attributed to, 49
  ivory attributed to, 49, *185*
  ivories from, 41, 43–4, 47, 62, *157*
  seal impressions from, 41, 49, *189*
  stamp cylinder from, 44, *161*
  stamp seal from, 44, *160*
  vessels from, 43
acorn-shaped beads, *see* necklaces, gold and green jasper beads
'Admonitions of Ipuwer', 59
agate beads from Tell el-Dabʿa, 55
Aghia Marina, 9
Ahhotep,
  Ahmose axe from the tomb of, 52
  gold lions from the tomb of, 37
  pectoral of, 53
Aiakos, king of Aigina, 32
Aigina (island of), 7, 8, 9–10, 11–15, 30, 32, 61–2, 65, *1*
Aigina–Kolonna (town), 7, 9–10, 11–12, 15, 30, 32–5, 65, *2*, *9*, *10*, *116*, *117*, *119*, *121*
  Town V, 9, 33, 35
  Town VI, 9, 33
  Town VII, 9, 33
  Town VIII, 9, 33
  Town IX, 9, 15, 33, 34
  Town X, 9
Akovitika, 33
Alaca Hüyük,
  seal ring from, 44
  sphinxes at, 44
Alalakh, *see* Tell Atchana
Alishar Höyük, 49
Alones, 9
Amenemhat II, 60, 63, 64
  pyramid complex of, 53, 60, 65
amethyst, 27, 44–5, 63, *115*
  See also necklaces (Aigina Treasure)
Ammenemes II, 45
Amorites, 44
Anat-Asherah (goddess), 48
Anatolia, 41, 43–5, 46–50, 49
  pendant with sun goddess from, 46
  necklace with pendant birds from, 44, 46–7, *164*, *168*
  possible origin of Tod Treasure, 64
  ring design from, 49
  See also specific sites
andjty crown, 52
Aphaia (goddess),
  cult of, 10
  temple of (Aigina), 9, 10
Aplahanda of Carchemish, King, 43, 44
Apollo, temple of (Aigina), 9, 11, 15, 32, *2*, *9*
Ashmolean Museum, Oxford, 14, 15
Asine,
  gold band from, *148*
  gold rings from, 41
Astarte (goddess), 47
atef crown, 40–41, 48, 52
Avaris, *see* Tell el-Dabʿa

Bahrein,
  seals from, 43
Balkans, 37, 38
bands, gold (Aigina Treasure), 10, 15, 16, 21, 30, 37, 38, 41, 62, 66
  See also diadems
bead, single rock crystal (Aigina Treasure), 24, 29, 30, 41, 42, 44, 63, 64, *101*, *108–109*
  See also necklaces (Aigina Treasure)
bee motif, 46, 52, 62, 64
Beirut,
  vessels from Kharji Tomb 1, 55
Bietak, Manfred, 54
birds,
  in the Aigina Treasure, 18–21, 28–9, 40, 42, 44, 60, 65
  in the jewellery of Princess Khnumet, 52, 60, 65
  in jewellery from Chrysolakkos, 40, 62, 65
  See also owls, water birds
Boğazköy (Hattusas), 43, 44, 49
  seal ring from, 44, *165*
Bokhara, SS, 13
Boston Museum of Fine Arts, 59
bracelet, gold (Aigina Treasure), 15, 21, 30, 41, *71*
British Museum, 7, 9, 11–15, 61
Brown, Edward, 12
Brown, Eliza, 12, 13, 15
Brown, George (first), 12, 13, 15
Brown, George (second), 11–15, *6*
Brown, George (third), 12, 13, 15
Brown, George (fourth), 12, 13
Brunton, Guy, 55
Burushhanda, 43
Buzuran,
  obsidian seal from, 44, *162*
Byblos, 44, 64
  beads from a tomb at, 55
  dagger sheath from, 52
  gold ornament with water birds from, 47, 48, *169*
  ivory and silver plaque from, 49, *187*
  pectorals from, 49
  seal perhaps made at, 44
  sheet gold plaque from, 47, *174*
  vessels from a tomb at, 55

Canaanite jewellery, 47–50
carnelian, 26–7, 28, 44, 62, 63, *115*
  See also chain ornament, earrings, necklaces (Aigina Treasure)
chain ornament, gold and carnelian with twin owls (Aigina Treasure), 19, 21, 28, 30, 42, *48*, *53*, *61*
chains, loop-in-loop, 25, 59
champlevé enamelling, 59
Chrysolakkos, 12, 40, 62
  gold bee pendant, 46, 52, 62
  gold bird, 62, 64, 65
  gold flower pin, 62
clasp, tongue-in-groove, 59
cloisonné enamelling, 51, 59
coinage, 9
cow motif, 60
Cresswell Bros, 11–15, *6*
Cresswell, Ernest, 12–14
Cresswell, Frederick, 11–15, 62, *6*, *7*
Crete, 37, 41, 61, 64
  trade with Aigina, 33
  as possible place of origin of the Aigina Treasure, 40
  as 'peer polity' of Aigina, 65
  contact with Egypt, 61, 64
  Minoan scarabs from, 61
  connections with the Tod Treasure, 63
  See also Minoan *and specific sites*

Index

cup, gold (Aigina Treasure), 15, 24, 29, 30, 36, 40, 41, 44, 45, 63, 64, *110–111*
Cyclades, trade with Aigina, 33

Dahshur,
  jewellery of Princess Khnumet from, 53, 60, 61, 62, 65
    gold bird pendants, 52, 60, 65, *217*
    'Medallion of Dahshur', 60, 65, *216*
  jewellery of Princess Mereret from,
    pectorals, 47, 49, 51–2, 55, 62, *173*, *184*
Deir el-Medina,
  votive stele from, 47, *177*
diadems, gold (Aigina Treasure), 10, 15, 16, 21, 29, 30, 62, *66–70*
  See also bands
discs, 54 gold (Aigina Treasure), 16, 21, 28, 29, 30, 40, 41, 44, 45, 46, 49, 62, *63–65*
discs, pendant,
  in the Aigina Treasure, 18–20, 28–30, 40, 44, 47, 62
  in the new Early Bronze Age treasure, 35, *134*
  on an Anatolian necklace, 44, 46–7, *164*, *168*
dogs, 49, 62
  in the Aigina Treasure, 18–19, 41, 49, 52,
  on the Tell el-Dabʿa gold pendant, 41, 49, 52
doll, gold, 12
donkey burials, 54–5
Drakopoulou, Avra, 14–15
dress ornaments (Aigina Treasure), *see* discs
drilling (Aigina Treasure), 26–9
duck motif, 36, *138*, *139*
  See also birds

Early Bronze Age treasure (Aigina), 9, 10, 35, 38, 62, 63, 65, *131*, *132*
  gold bracelet, 35
  gold pins, 35, *133*
  necklaces, 35
  silver bracelet, 35
earrings(?) (Aigina Treasure), 16, 18–19, 28–30, 41, 42, 44, 45, 46, 62, *18–29*, *31–34*, *37*, *39–40*, *112–113*
Egypt, 51–2, 59–60, 64
  connections with the Aegean, 61, 64, 65
  contact with Crete, 61, 64
  iconography, 36, 40–41, 47–49, 51–3, 59–60
  jewellery, 36, 44, 55, 9–60, *137*, *138*
  royal thrones, 59, *215*
  techniques of jewellery making in, 51, 59
  See also specific sites
Elba, 44, 45
  beads from, 44
  amethyst knob from, 44
  cloisonné finger ring from, 44
  gold disc from, 45
Emmanuel, Michel D., 12–15, 6
Emmanuel, Michel G., 12, 13, 15
Enkomi,
  cylinder seal found at, 48, *179*
Evans, Sir Arthur, 11, 14, 47, 53, 61

falcons, 41, 46–7, 49, 59, 60
  on an unprovenanced ornament (British Museum), 53
feldspar, in the Tod Treasure, 63
figurines,
  marble, 9
  shell, 9, *4*, *5*
  terracotta, 9, 10, 32, *123*
filigree, 20, 42, 46
'find-spot' (Aigina Treasure), 7, 11–15, 25, 30, 61, *10*
finger rings (Aigina Treasure), 29, 41–2, 44, 63
  sheet gold with cross-hatch decoration, 23, *85*
  reef knot with inlaid lapis lazuli, 22, 30, 59, *85*, *88–91*
  double-axe or shield with inlaid lapis lazuli, 22–3, 30, *85*, *92–93*
  meander-pattern with inlaid lapis lazuli, 22, 30, *86*, *94–95*
  fluted-pattern with inlaid lapis lazuli, 23, 30, *87*, *96–98*
fish motif, 36, *136*, *137*
fortification walls (Aigina–Kolonna), 9, 32–4, *116*, *120*, *126*

gazelles, 48
Gebel el-Arak,
  knife handle from, 48
geese, *see* water birds
glyptic,
  Egyptian, 61
  Minoan, 41, 48
  Syrian, 41, 52
goldwork (Aigina Treasure), 25–30, 62, 63
  analysis, 17, 25–7, 31
  Egyptian, 36
  Minoan, 36, 63
Gournia,
  kantharos from, 64
granulation, 46–7, 59, 60
griffins, 49, 51–2, 62, *185*

Hagia Triada,
  Boxer rhyton from, 47, *172*
Harageh, cemetery, 55
  Minoan pottery from, 61
Harland, J.P., 11, 13
Harvard University, 59
Hathor wigs, 47–9
Hattusas, *see* Boğazköy
helmets, conical, 9, 32
Higgins, Reynold, 7, 11, 12, 13, 14, 15, 20, 36, 37, 38, 43, 44, 46, 49, 53, 61, 62, 65
hoops, gold (Aigina Treasure), *see* rings
Horus (god), 59

Ibbi-Sin, king of Ur, 44
Iberian peninsula,
  bronze plaque probably from (near Cadiz?), 48, *180*
Iliad, 32

jasper, green, 23, 27, 44, 45, 63, *115*
  See also necklaces, gold and green jasper beads

Kafr Ammar, 51
Kafr Tarkhan, 51
Kanesh, *see* Kültepe
Kapodistrias, 9
Karahöyük, 44, 49
  image of a nude goddess from, 47
  seal impressions from, 41, 49, *189*
  sherd with sphinx from, 44, *158*
Karantina, 15
Kastri, 33
Keramopoullos, A.D., 11–14
Khaniale Tekke,
  ajouré pendant from, 42
Khnumet, princess, jewellery of, 53, 60, 61, 62, 65
  gold bird pendants, 52, 60, 65, *217*
  'Medallion of Dahshur', 60, 65, *216*
Kilindra, 10
Knossos,
  pendant in the shape of a fish from, 36, *136*
  silver cup from the Palace at, 36, 40
Kolonna, *see* Aigina–Kolonna
Kültepe (Kanesh), 43, 49
Kythera,
  jewellery from, 40, 41

Index

Lahun,
    Minoan pottery from, 61
    Sithathoryunet, princess, tomb of, 55
        beads from, 37, 55
lapis lazuli, 22–3, 27, 44, 63, *81*, *115*
    in the Tod Treasure, 45
    See also finger rings, necklaces (Aigina Treasure)
Larsa,
    jewellery hoard from, 46
laser Raman microscopy, 17
Lazarides, 10
Lebanon,
    gold dishes, ?found in, 45, *166*
Lebea,
    vessels from Tomb I, 55
Lenda, tholos tombs,
    pottery from, 61
Lerna, 33
Levantine iconography, 40–41, 46–9, 52–3
lions, 37, 44, 46–7, 52, 64
    See also lion's head ornament (Aigina Treasure)
lion's head ornament (Aigina Treasure), 19, 20, 28, 29, 30, 37, 42, 62, *48–52, 54–60, 62*
Lisht,
    Middle Kingdom relief from, 53
    pyramid of Amenemhat I, 63
lotus flowers, 40, 47–8, 52–3, 59

Mallia, 62, 64
    leopard stone axe from, 37, 41, 49
    Near Eastern influence at, 41
    seal from, 48, *178*
    See also Chrysolakkos, Quartier Mu
Mari,
    Investiture wall painting, 47
    thunderbird pendant from, 46
'Master of Animals' pendant (Aigina Treasure), 14, 18, 28, 29, 30, 40–41, 46–50, 51–3, 62, *11–17*
Megiddo,
    ivories from, 47, *176*
    vessels from, 55
melon-shaped beads, see necklaces, gold and green jasper beads
Mereret, princess,
    pectorals of, 47, 49, 51–2, 55, 62, *173*, *184*
Meroe, 59
Mesopotamia, 44, 46, 63
    pendant with bullman from, 46, *167*
metal refining, 59
Minet el-Beidha,
    cylinder seal from, 44, *159*
    gold triangular pendant with nude female from, 47–8, *170*
Minoan
    colony on Aigina, 10, 36–7, 62, 65
    communal tombs, 37
    goldwork, 36, 40
    iconography, 36, 40–41, 47, 52
    techniques of jewellery making, 37, 40
    See also Crete
'Mistress of Animals', 47, 48
Mitsotakis Collection, Athens, 40
Mochlos,
    clay vessel in the shape of a goddess from, 40
Mohenjo-Daro,
    circular seal excavated at, 43
monkeys, 44
    in the Aigina Treasure, 18–19, 44, 62
monster heads, 43
Mont (god), 63
monumental houses (Aigina–Kolonna), 9, 33–4
    monumental building (Town IX), 34
    White House, 9, 33
Mostagedda,
    bracelet from, 59

Mount Oros, see Oros
Murray, A.S., 11, 14
Mycenae,
    stamp seal from, 49, *186*
    Shaft Graves, 62–3, 64
        gold band from, 41, 62, *145*
        gold bracelet from, 41, *150*
        gold hair pin from, 36, 41, 52, 53, *140*
        gold lions from, 37
        gold ornaments from, 41, *143*, *144*
        gold stemmed cup from, 36, 41, *151*
        polychrome jug from, 41, *149*
        palm-leaf gold bead necklace from, 41, 63, *146*, *147*
        pendant with goddess framed by lotuses, 48
        sword with animal heads from, 37

Near Eastern
    iconography, 40–41, 44, 46–50, 52–3
    jewellery, 46
necklaces (Aigina Treasure), 14, 16
    carnelian and amethyst beads, 24, 28–30, 42, 44, 63, *30*, *101*, *103*, *106–107*
    carnelian, lapis lazuli and gold beads, 22, 28, 29, 30, 40, 44, 63, *79–80, 82–84*, *101*
    double-arc-shaped gold beads (43), 22, 28, 29, 30, 40, 41, 63, *72–73*, *75*
    double-arc-shaped gold beads (52), 22, 28, 29, 30, 40, 41, 63, *72–73*, *76*
    gold beads, 23, 24, 28, 29, 30, 42, *72*, *74*, *77–78*
    gold and green jasper beads, 23–4, 28, 29, 30, 42, 44, 46, *101–102*, *104–105*
Nimrud,
    ivories from, 47
nude females, 47

openwork, 40, 46, 62
optical binocular microscopy, 17
Oros, Mount (Aigina), 9, 10
Osiris (god), 41
owls, two half (Aigina Treasure), 16, 19, 28, 30, *35–36*, *38*, *48*
    See also birds and chain ornament (Aigina Treasure)
Özgüç, Nimet, 43
Özgüç, Tahsin, 43

Palace of Minos, see Knossos
palm-leaf beads, see necklaces, double-arc-shaped beads
papyrus flowers, 36, *140*, *141*
pectoral ornament with profile heads (Aigina Treasure), 14, 16, 19–20, 28, 29, 30, 40, 41, 43, 46, 49, 53, 62, *41–47*
Peleus, 32
Pepi II, pyramid complex of, 52, *196*
Peristeria,
    gold cup from, 41, *152*
    necklaces from, 41
    silver kantharoi from, 64
Petrie Museum,
    silver pendant in, 49, 51–6, 62, *192*
Petrie, W.M.F., 51, 53, 55
pharaohs, 47
Phaistos,
    sealings from, 52, *194*, *195*
plaques, gold (Aigina Treasure), see discs
Poliochni, 33
Poros,
    finger ring from, 41
Pylos,
    sealing from, 48, *182*

Quartier Mu,
    terracotta lids from, 41
    terracotta relief from, 40
    vase with sphinx from, 41, 52
quartz, see amethyst, rock crystal
Qudshu/Qadesh (goddess), 47–8

Index

Ras el-ᶜAin, *see* Tel Aphek
reef-knot motif, 22, 59–60, 63
Reisner, George Andrew, 59
rings, five plain gold (Aigina Treasure), 15, 23, 30, 41, *99–100*
　See also finger rings
Riqqeh, tombs at, 55
rock crystal, 9, 27, 35, 63, *115*
　See also bead (Aigina Treasure)
rosette decoration, 21, 24, 41, 44, 45, 63
roundels (Aigina Treasure), *see* discs

Saqqara, pyramid complex of Pepi II, 52, *196*
scanning electron microscopy (SEM), 17
scarabs, 43, 44, 56, 59, 60, 61, 63, 64, *214*
scorpion motif, 64
sea trade, 9, 32, 61
seed-shaped beads, *see* necklaces, gold beads
Senwosret III, 51–2, 62
Seth (god), 59
shaft grave (Aigina), *see* warrior shaft grave
Shamshi-Adad I, 43
Sheikh Farag,
　bracelet from, 59, *213*
shroud ornaments, *see* bands *and* discs
silver in the Tod Treasure, 63–4
Sinclair, Margaret, 11, 15
Sin el Fil,
　vessels from a tomb at, 55
Sitea,
　sphinx prism probably from, 52, *193*
Sithathoryunet, princess, tomb of, 55
　beads from, 37, 55
Smith, A.H., 15
snakes, 48, 62, 64
　in the Aigina Treasure, 18–19
soldering, 25–6
spacer beads, 24, 44
sphinxes, 40, 41, 43–4, 47, 49, 52, *155, 157, 158*
spider motif, 64
spirals, 21, 24, 29, 41, 45, 52, 61
sponge-fishing, 12–13
Staïs, Valerios, 11, 13
Stathatos Collection, Athens,
　gold cup, 41
stress corrosion cracking, 25, 29
strips, gold (Aigina Treasure), *see* bands, gold (Aigina Treasure)
Syria, 41, 45, 46, 49
　cylinder seal from, *183*
　See also specific sites

Telamon, 32
Tel Aphek (Ras el-ᶜAin),
　vessels from, 55
Tell Asmar,
　thunderbird pendant from, 46
Tell Atchana (Alalakh),
　seal impression from, 43, *156*
　plaque from, 48, *181*
Tell Brak,
　lion pendant from, 46
　thunderbird pendant from, 46
Tell el-ᶜAjjul,
　earrings from, 47
Tell el-Dabᶜa (Avaris), 41, 53–6
　'palace necropolis' of, 54–6, *197, 199, 200*
　　beads from, 55, *202–210, 211*
　　excavations at, 54–6
　　gold pendant from, 41–2, 48–50, 51–6, 60, 62, *190, 191, 212*
　　pottery from, 54–6, *201*
　　weapons from, 54–6
　ᶜEzbet Helmi frescoes at, 50, 53, 60, 61
terracotta plaques with nude female, 47, *175, 181*

Thebes, 33
Thera, Akrotiri,
　necklace with duck-shaped beads from, 36, *139*
Thermi, 33
thrones, Egyptian, 59, *215*
thunderbird, 46
Thyreatis Treasure,
　gold beads, 41, *153*
Tod Treasure, 36, 42, 45, 61, 63–5, *222*
　beads, 63, 64
　cylindrical container, 64
　lapis lazuli, 45
　lion, 64
　silver bowls, 45, 63–4
　silver cups, 63, *218, 219*
　silver pendant, 64, *220, 221*
'Troy Treasure(s)', 42
turtle, emblem of Aigina, 9, *3*

Ugarit, 47
Uluburun shipwreck,
　gold triangular pendant with nude female from, 47, *171*
Ur, 44
　Royal Cemetery at,
　　beads from, 44–5
　　finger rings from, 44, *163*
　　gold bands, 62
　　pendants from, 46
uraeus motif, 41, 48

Vapheio, seal from, 48

Walter, Hans, 15
warrior shaft grave (Aigina), 10, 15, 34, 35, 36–8, 62, 65, *122*
　boar's tusk helmet, 10, 15
　bronze daggers, 15
　bronze spear-head, 15
　bronze sword with gold and ivory hilt, 10, 15, 37, *142*
　gold band, 10, 15, 36, 37, 38, *135, 142*
　gold hexagonal ornament, 37, *142*
　knife/razor with gold animal-head fittings, 10, 15, 37, *142*
　obsidian arrow-heads, 15
　pottery, 10, 15, 34, 36, 37, 38
wasp motif, 64
water birds, 18, 47–8
wealth on Aigina, 9–10, 30, 33–5, 37, 65
weaponry, 15, 36–8, 41, 54–6
Welter, Gabriel, 10, 12, 13, 15, 33, 34, 37
Windmill Hill (Aigina), 12, 13, 14, 15, 33, 34, *9*
Windmill Ridge (Aigina), 10, 11, 15
wire, technology, 25, 28

Xeflouda, 9
x-ray diffraction analysis (XRD), 17
x-ray microanalysis (EDX), 17

'Zakro Treasure', 42
Zeus Hellianos, sanctuary of (Aigina), 9